Francis William Newman

Phase of Faith

Or Passages from the History of my Creed

Francis William Newman

Phase of Faith

Or Passages from the History of my Creed

ISBN/EAN: 9783337338435

Printed in Europe, USA, Canada, Australia, Japan

Cover: Foto ©Thomas Meinert / pixelio.de

More available books at **www.hansebooks.com**

PHASES OF FAITH;

OR,

PASSAGES FROM THE HISTORY

OF

MY CREED.

BY FRANCIS W. NEWMAN.

NEW EDITION,

WITH REPLY TO PROFESSOR HENRY ROGERS, AUTHOR OF "THE ECLIPSE OF FAITH."

LONDON:
TRÜBNER & CO., LUDGATE HILL.
1881.

CONTENTS.

CHAP.		PAGE
I.	My Youthful Creed	1
II.	Strivings after a more primitive Christianity	16
III.	Calvinism abandoned	41
IV.	The Religion of the Letter renounced	65
V.	Faith at Second Hand found to be vain	88
VI.	History discovered to be no part of Religion	124
VII.	On the Moral Perfection of Jesus	139
VIII.	On Bigotry and Progress	164
IX.	Reply to the "Defence of the Eclipse of Faith"	178
	Appendix I.	210
	Appendix II.	213

PREFACE TO FIRST EDITION.

THIS is perhaps an egotistical book ; egotistical certainly in its form, yet not in its purport and essence.

Personal reasons the writer cannot wholly disown, for desiring to explain himself to more than a few, who on religious grounds are unjustly alienated from him. If by any motive of curiosity or lingering remembrances they may be led to read his straightforward account, he trusts to be able to show them that he has had *no choice* but to adopt the intellectual conclusions which offend them ;—that the difference between them and him turns on questions of Learning, History, Criticism and Abstract Thought ;—and that to make *their* results (if indeed they have ever deeply and honestly investigated the matter) the tests of *his* spiritual state, is to employ unjust weights and a false balance, which are an abomination to the Lord. To defraud one's neighbour of any tithe of mint and cummin, would seem to them a sin : is it less to withhold affection, trust and free intercourse, and build up unpassable barriers of coldness and alarm, against one whose sole offence is to differ from them intellectually ?

But the argument before the writer is something immensely greater than a personal one. So it happens, that to vindicate himself is to establish a mighty truth ; a truth which can in no other way so well enter the heart, as when it comes embodied in an individual case. If he can show, that to have shrunk from his successive convictions *would* have been "infidelity" to God and Truth and Righteousness ; but that he has been "faithful" to the highest and most urgent duty;—it will be made clear that Belief is one thing and Faith another; that to believe is intellectual, nay possibly "earthly, devilish;" and that to set up any fixed creed as a test of spiritual character is a most unjust, oppressive and mischievous superstition. The historical form has been deliberately selected, as easier and more interesting to the reader; but it must not be imagined that the author has given his mental history in general, much less an autobiography. The progress of his *creed* is his sole subject; and other topics are introduced either to illustrate this or as digressions suggested by it.

March 22*nd*, 1850.

PREFACE TO SIXTH EDITION.

I HAD long thought that the elaborate reply made for me in the "Prospective Review" (1854) to Mr. Henry Rogers's Defence of the "Eclipse of Faith," superseded anything more from my pen. But in the course of six years a review is forgotten and buried away, while Mr. Rogers is circulating the ninth edition of his misrepresentations.

As my publisher announces to me the opportunity, I at length consent to reply myself to the Defence, cancelling what was previously my last chapter, written against the "Eclipse."

All that follows p. 175 in this edition is new.

June, 1860.

PHASES OF FAITH.

CHAPTER I.

MY YOUTHFUL CREED.

I FIRST began to read religious books at school, and especially the Bible, when I was eleven years old; and almost immediately commenced a habit of secret prayer. But it was not until I was fourteen that I gained any definite idea of a " scheme of doctrine," or could have been called a " converted person" by one of the Evangelical School. My religion then certainly exerted a great general influence over my conduct; for I soon underwent various persecution from my schoolfellows on account of it: the worst kind consisted in their deliberate attempts to corrupt me. An Evangelical clergyman at the school gained my affections, and from him I imbibed more and more distinctly the full creed which distinguishes that body of men; a body whose bright side I shall ever appreciate, in spite of my present perception that they have a dark side also. I well remember, that one day when I said to this friend of mine, that I could not understand how the doctrine of Election was reconcilable to God's Justice, but supposed that I should know this in due time, if I waited and believed His word;—he replied with emphatic commendation, that this was the spirit which God always blessed. Such was the beginning and foundation of my faith,—an unhesitating unconditional acceptance of whatever was found in the Bible. While I am far from saying that my *whole* moral conduct was subjugated by my creed, I must insist that it was no mere fancy resting in my intellect: it was really operative on my temper, tastes, pursuits and conduct.

When I was sixteen, in 1821, I was "confirmed" by Dr. Howley, then Bishop of London, and endeavoured to take on myself with greater decision and more conscientious consistency the whole yoke of Christ. Every thing in the Service was solemn to me, except the bishop: he seemed to me a *made-up* man and a mere pageant. I also remember that when I was examined by the clergyman for confirmation, it troubled me much that he only put questions which tested my *memory* concerning the Catechism and other formulas, instead of trying to find out whether I had any actual faith in that about which I was to be called to profess faith: I was not then aware that his sole duty was to try my *knowledge*. But I already felt keenly the chasm that separated the High from the Low Church; and that it was impossible for me to sympathize with those who imagined that Forms could command the Spirit.

Yet so entirely was I enslaved to one Form,—that of observing the Sunday, or, as I had learned falsely to call it, the Sabbath,—that I fell into painful and injurious conflict with a superior kinsman, by refusing to obey his orders on the Sunday. He attempted to deal with me by mere authority, not by instruction; and to yield my conscience to authority would have been to yield up all spiritual life. I erred, but I was faithful to God.

When I was rather more than seventeen, I subscribed the 39 Articles at Oxford in order to be admitted to the University. Subscription was "no bondage," but pleasure; for I well knew and loved the Articles, and looked on them as a great bulwark of the truth; a bulwark, however, not by being imposed, but by the spiritual and classical beauty which to me shone in them. But it was certain to me before I went to Oxford, and manifest in my first acquaintance with it, that very few academicians could be said to believe them. Of the young men, not one in five seemed to have any religious convictions at all: the elder residents seldom or never showed sympathy with the doctrines that pervade that formula. I felt from my first day there, that the system of compulsory subscription was hollow, false, and wholly evil.

Oxford is a pleasant place for making friends,—friends of all sorts that young men wish. One who is above envy and scorns servility,—who can praise and delight in all the good qualities of his equals in age, and does not desire to set himself above them, or to vie with his superiors in rank,—may have more than enough of friends, for pleasure and for profit. So certainly had I; yet no one of my equals gained any ascendancy over me, nor perhaps could I have looked up to any for advice. In some the intellect, in others the religious qualities, were as yet insufficiently developed: in part also I wanted discrimination, and did not well pick out the profounder minds of my acquaintance. However, on my very first residence in College, I received a useful lesson from another freshman,—a grave and thoughtful person, older (I imagine) than most youths in their first term. Some readers may be amused, as well as surprized, when I name the delicate question on which I got into discussion with my fellow freshman. I had learned from Evangelical books, that there is a *twofold* imputation to every saint,—not of the "sufferings" only, but also of the "righteousness" of Christ. They alleged that, while the sufferings of Jesus are a compensation for the guilt of the believer and make him innocent, yet this suffices not to give him a title to heavenly glory; for which he must over and above be invested in active righteousness, by all Christ's good works being made over to him. My new friend contested the latter part of the doctrine. Admitting fully that guilt is atoned for by the sufferings of the Saviour, he yet maintained, there was no farther imputation of Christ's active service as if it had been our service. After a rather sharp controversy, I was sent back to study the matter for myself, especially in the third and fourth chapters of the Epistle to the Romans; and some weeks after, freely avowed to him that I was convinced. Such was my first effort at independent thought against the teaching of my spiritual fathers, and I suppose it had much value for me. This friend might probably have been of service to me, though he was rather cold and lawyerlike; but he was abruptly withdrawn from Oxford to be employed in active life.

I first received a temporary discomfort about the 39 Articles from an irreligious young man, who had been my schoolfellow; who one day attacked the article which asserts that Christ carried "his flesh and bones" with him into heaven. I was not moved by the physical absurdity which this youth mercilessly derided; and I repelled his objections as an impiety. But I afterwards remembered the text, "*Flesh* and *blood* shall not inherit the kingdom of God;" and it seemed to me as if the compilers had really gone a little too far. If I had immediately then been called on to subscribe, I suppose it would have somewhat discomposed me; but as time went on, I forgot this small point, which was swallowed up by others more important. Yet I believe that henceforth a greater disposition to criticize the Articles grew upon me.

The first novel opinion of any great importance that I actually embraced, so as to give roughness to my course, was that which many then called the Oriel heresy about Sunday. Oriel College at this time contained many active and several original minds; and it was rumoured that one of the Fellows rejoiced in seeing his parishioners play at cricket on Sunday: I do not know whether that was true, but so it was said. Another of them preached an excellent sermon before the University, clearly showing that Sunday had nothing to do with the Sabbath, nor the Sabbath with us, and inculcating on its own ground a wise and devout use of the Sunday hours. The evidently pious and sincere tone of this discourse impressed me, and I felt that I had no right to reject as profane and undeserving of examination the doctrine which it enforced. Accordingly I entered into a thorough searching of the Scripture without bias, and was amazed to find how baseless was the tenet for which in fact I had endured a sort of martyrdom. This, I believe, had a great effect in showing me how little right we have at any time to count on our opinions as final truth, however necessary they may just then be felt to our spiritual life. I was also scandalized to find how little candour or discernment some Evangelical friends, with whom I communicated, displayed in discussing the subject.

In fact, this opened to me a large sphere of new thought. In the investigation, I had learned, more distinctly than before, that the preceptive code of the Law was an essentially imperfect and temporary system, given "for the hardness of men's hearts." I was thus prepared to enter into the Lectures on Prophecy, by another Oriel Fellow,—Mr. Davison,—in which he traces the successive improvements and developments of religious doctrine, from the patriarchal system onward. I in consequence enjoyed with new zest the epistles of St. Paul, which I read as with fresh eyes; and now understood somewhat better his whole doctrine of "the Spirit," the coming of which had brought the church out of her childish into a mature condition, and by establishing a higher law had abolished that of the letter. Into this view I entered with so eager an interest, that I felt no bondage of the letter in Paul's own words: his wisdom was too much above me to allow free criticism of his weak points. At the same time, the systematic use of the Old Testament by the Puritans, as if it were "the rule of life" to Christians, I saw to be a glaring mistake, intensely opposed to the Pauline doctrine. This discovery, moreover, soon became important to me, as furnishing a ready evasion of objections against the meagre or puerile views of the Pentateuch; for without very minute inquiry how far I must go to make the defence adequate, I gave a general reply, that the New Testament *confessed* the imperfections of the older dispensation. I still presumed the Old to have been perfect for its own objects and in its own place; and had not defined to myself how far it was correct or absurd, to imagine morality to change with time and circumstances.

Before long, ground was broken in my mind on a still more critical question, by another Fellow of a College; who maintained that nothing but unbelief could arise out of the attempt to understand *in what way* and *by what moral right* the blood of Christ atoned for sins. He said, that he bowed before the doctrine as one of "Revelation," and accepted it reverentially by an act of faith; but that he certainly felt unable to understand *why* the sacrifice of Christ, any more than the Mosaic sacrifices, should compensate for the punishment of our sins. Could carnal reason discern that human or divine blood, any more than that of beasts, had efficacy to make the sinner as it were sinless? It appeared to him a necessarily inscrutable mystery, into which we ought not to look.—The matter being thus forced on my attention, I certainly saw that to establish the abstract moral *right* and *justice* of vicarious punishment was not easy, and that to make out the fact of any "compensation" —(*i. e.* that Jesus really endured on the cross a true equivalent for the eternal sufferings due to the whole human race,)—was harder still. Nevertheless I had difficulty in adopting the conclusions of this gentleman; FIRST, because, in a passage of the Epistle to the Hebrews, the sacred writer, in arguing— "*For* it is impossible that the blood of bulls and goats can take away sins," &c., &c. ... .—seems to expect his readers to see an inherent impropriety in the sacrifices of the Law, and an inherent moral fitness in the sacrifice of Christ. SECONDLY: I had always been accustomed to hear that it was by seeing the moral fitness of the doctrine of the Atonement, that converts to Christianity were chiefly made: so said the Moravians among the Greenlanders, so Brainerd among the North American Indians, so English missionaries among the negroes at Sierra Leone:—and I could not at all renounce this idea. Indeed I seemed to myself to see this fitness most emphatically; and as for the *forensic* difficulties, I passed them over with a certain conscious reverence. I was not as yet ripe for deeper inquiry: yet I, about this time, decidedly modified my boyish creed on the subject, on which more will be said below.

Of more immediate practical importance to me was the controversy concerning Infant Baptism. For several years together I had been more or less conversant with the arguments adduced for the practice; and at this time I read Wall's defence of it, which was the book specially recommended at Oxford. The perusal brought to a head the doubts which had at an earlier period flitted over my mind. Wall's historical attempt to trace Infant Baptism up to the apostles seemed to me a clear failure:* and if he failed, then who was likely to succeed? The arguments from Scripture had never recommended themselves to me. Even allowing that they might confirm, they certainly could not suggest and establish the practice. It now appeared that there was no basis at all; indeed, several of the arguments struck me as cutting the other way. "Suffer little children to come unto me," was urged as decisive: but it occurred to me that the disciples would not have scolded the little children away, if they had ever been accustomed to baptize them. Wall also, if I remember aright, declares that the children of proselytes were baptized by the Jews; and deduces, that unless the contrary were stated, we must assume that also Christ's disciples baptized children: but I reflected that the baptism *of John* was one of "repentance," and therefore could not have been administered to infants; which (if precedent is to guide us) afforded the truer presumption concerning *Christian* baptism. Prepossessions being thus overthrown, when I read the apostolic epistles with a view to this special question, the proof so multiplied against the Church doctrine, that I did not see what was left to be said for it. I talked much and freely of this, as of most other topics, with equals in age, who took interest in religious questions; but the more the matters were discussed, the more decidedly impossible it seemed to maintain that the popular Church views were apostolic.

* It was not until many years later that I became aware, that unbiassed ecclesiastical historians, as Neander and others, while approving of the practice of Infant Baptism, freely concede that it is not apostolic. Let this fact be my defence against critics, who snarl at me for having dared, at that age, to come to *any* conclusion on such a subject. But, in fact, the subscriptions compel young men to it.

Here also, as before, the Evangelical clergy whom I consulted were found by me a broken reed. The clerical friend whom I had known at school wrote kindly to me, but quite declined attempting to solve my doubts; and in other quarters I soon saw that no fresh light was to be got. One person there was at Oxford, who might have seemed my natural adviser: his name, character, and religious peculiarities have been so made public property, that I need not shrink to name him:—I mean my elder brother, the Rev. John Henry Newman. As a warm-hearted and generous brother, who exercised towards me paternal cares, I esteemed him and felt a deep gratitude; as a man of various culture and peculiar genius, I admired and was proud of him; but my doctrinal religion impeded my loving him as much as he deserved, and even justified my feeling some distrust of him. He never showed any strong attraction towards those whom I regarded as spiritual persons: on the contrary, I thought him stiff and cold towards them. Moreover, soon after his ordination, he had startled and distressed me by adopting the doctrine of Baptismal Regeneration; and in rapid succession worked out views which I regarded as full-blown "Popery." I speak of the years 1823-6: it is strange to think that twenty years more had to pass before he learnt the place to which his doctrines belonged.

In the earliest period of my Oxford residence I fell into uneasy collision with him concerning Episcopal powers. I had on one occasion dropt something disrespectful against bishops or a bishop,—something which, if it had been said about a clergyman, would have passed unnoticed: but my brother checked and reproved me,—as I thought, very uninstructively—for "wanting reverence towards Bishops." I knew not then, and I know not now, why Bishops, *as such*, should be more reverenced than common clergymen; or Clergymen, *as such*, more than common men. In the World I expected pomp and vain show and formality and counterfeits: but of the Church, as Christ's own kingdom, I demanded reality and could not digest legal fictions. I saw round me what sort of young men were preparing to be clergymen: I knew the attractions of family "livings" and fellowships, and of a respectable position and undefinable hopes of preferment. I farther knew, that when youths had become clergymen through a great variety of mixed motives, bishops were selected out of these clergy on avowedly political grounds; it therefore amazed me how a man of good sense should be able to set up a duty of religious veneration towards bishops. I was willing to honour a Lord Bishop as a peer of Parliament; but his office was to me no guarantee of spiritual eminence.—To find my brother thus stop my mouth, was a puzzle; and impeded all free speech towards him. In fact, I very soon left off the attempt at intimate religious intercourse with him, or asking counsel as of one who could sympathize. We talked, indeed, a great deal on the surface of religious matters; and on some questions I was overpowered and received a temporary bias from his superior knowledge; but as time went on, and my own intellect ripened, I distinctly felt that his arguments were too fine-drawn and subtle, often elaborately missing the moral points and the main points, to rest on some ecclesiastical fiction; and his conclusions were to me so marvellous and painful, that I constantly thought I had mistaken him. In short, he was my senior by a very few years: nor was there any elder resident at Oxford, accessible to me, who united all the qualities which I wanted in an adviser. Nothing was left for me but to cast myself on Him who is named the Father of Lights, and resolve to follow the light which He might give, however opposed to my own prejudices, and however I might be condemned by men. This solemn engagement I made in early youth, and neither the frowns nor the grief of my brethren can make me ashamed of it in my manhood.

Among the religious authors whom I read familiarly was the Rev. T. Scott, of Aston Sandford, a rather dull, very unoriginal, half-educated, but honest, worthy, sensible, strongminded man, whose works were then much in vogue among the Evangelicals. One day my attention was arrested by a sentence in his defence of the doctrine of the Trinity. He complained that Anti-Trinitarians unjustly charged Trinitarians with self-contradiction. "If indeed we said" (argued he) "that God is three *in the same sense* as that in which He is one, that would be self-refuting; but we hold Him to be *three in one sense, and one in another.*" It crossed my mind very forcibly, that, if that was all, the Athanasian Creed had gratuitously invented an enigma. I exchanged thoughts on this with an undergraduate friend, and got no fresh light: in fact, I feared to be profane, if I attempted to understand the subject. Yet it came distinctly home to me, that, whatever the depth of the mystery, if we lay down anything about it *at all*, we ought to understand our own words; and I presently augured that Tillotson had been right in "wishing our Church well rid" of the Athanasian Creed; which seemed a mere offensive blurting out of intellectual difficulties. I had, however, no doubts, even of a passing kind, for years to come, concerning the substantial truth and certainty of the ecclesiastical Trinity.

When the period arrived for taking my Bachelor's degree it was requisite again to sign the 39 Articles, and I now found myself embarrassed by the question of Infant Baptism. One of the articles contains the following words, "The baptism of young children is in any wise to be retained, as most agreeable to the institution of Christ." I was unable to conceal from myself that I did not believe this sentence; and I was on the point of refusing to take my degree. I overcame my scruples by considering, 1. That concerning this doctrine I had no active *dis*-belief, on which I would take any practical step, as I felt myself too young to make any counterdeclaration: 2. That it had no possible practical meaning to me, since I could not be called on to baptize, nor to give a child for baptism. Thus I persuaded myself. Yet I had not an easy conscience, nor can I now defend my compromise; for I believe that my repugnance to Infant Baptism was really intense, and my conviction that it is unapostolic as strong then as now. The topic of my "youth" was irrelevant; for, if I was not too young to subscribe, I was not too young to refuse subscription. The argument that the article was "unpractical" to me, goes to prove, that if I were ordered by a despot to qualify myself for a place in the Church by solemnly renouncing the first book of Euclid as false, I might do so without any loss of moral dignity. Altogether, this humiliating affair showed me what a trap for the conscience these subscriptions are: how comfortably they are passed while the intellect is torpid or immature, or where the conscience is callous, but how they undermine truthfulness in the active thinker, and torture the sensitiveness of the tenderminded. As long as they are maintained, in Church or University, these institutions exert a positive influence to deprave or eject those who ought to be their most useful and honoured members.

It was already breaking upon me, that I could not fulfil the dreams of my boyhood as a minister in the Church of England. For, supposing that with increased knowledge I might arrive at the conclusion that Infant Baptism was a fore-arranged "development,"—not indeed practised in the *first* generation, but expedient, justifiable, and intended for the *second*, and probably then sanctioned by one still living apostle,—even so, I foresaw the still greater difficulty of Baptismal Regeneration behind. For any one to avow that Regeneration took place in Baptism, seemed to me little short of a confession that he had never himself experienced what Regeneration is. If I *could* then have been convinced that the apostles taught no other regeneration, I almost think that even their authority would have snapt under the strain: but this is idle theory; for it was as clear as daylight to me that they held a totally different doctrine, and that the High Church and Popish fancy is a superstitious perversion, based upon carnal inability to understand a strong spiritual metaphor. On the other hand, my brother's arguments that the Baptismal Service of the Church taught "spiritual regeneration" during the ordinance, were short, simple, and overwhelming. To imagine a *twofold* "spiritual regeneration" was evidently a hypothesis to serve a turn, nor in any of the Church formulas was such an idea broached. Nor could I hope for relief by searching through the Homilies or by drawing deductions from the Articles: for if I there elicited a truer doctrine, it would never show the Baptismal Service not to teach the Popish tenet; it would merely prove the Church-system to contain contradictions, and not to deserve that absolute declaration of its truth, which is demanded of Church ministers. With little hope of advantage, I yet felt it a duty to consult many of the Evangelical clergymen whom I knew, and to ask how *they* reconciled the Baptismal Service to their consciences. I found (if I remember) three separate theories among them,—all evidently mere shifts invented to avoid the disagreeable necessity of resigning their functions. Not one of these good people seemed to have the most remote idea that it was their duty to investigate the meaning of the formulary with the same unbiassed simplicity as if it belonged to the Gallican Church. They did not seek to know what it was written to mean, nor what sense it must carry to every simpleminded hearer; but they solely asked, how they could manage to assign to it a sense not wholly irreconcilable with their own doctrines and preaching. This was too obviously hollow. The last gentleman whom I consulted, was the rector of a parish, who from week to week baptized children with the prescribed formula: but to my amazement, he told me that *he* did not like the Service, and did not approve of Infant Baptism; to both of which things he submitted, solely because, as an inferior minister of the Church, it was his duty to obey established authority! The case was desperate. But I may here add, that this clergyman, within a few years from that time, redeemed his freedom and his conscience by the painful ordeal of abandoning his position and his flock, against the remonstrances of his wife, to the annoyance of his friends, and with a young family about him.

Let no reader accept the preceding paragraph as my testimony that the Evangelical clergy are less simpleminded and less honourable in their subscriptions than the High Church. I do not say, and I do not believe this. *All* who subscribe, labour under a common difficulty, in having to give an absolute assent to formulas that were made by a compromise and are not homogeneous in character. To the High Churchman, the *Articles* are a difficulty; to the Low Churchman, various parts of the *Liturgy*. All have to do violence to some portion of the system; and considering at how early an age they are entrapped into subscription, they all deserve our sincere sympathy and very ample allowance, as long as they are pleading for the rights of conscience: only when they become overbearing, dictatorial, proud of their chains, and desirous of ejecting others, does it seem right to press them with the topic of inconsistency. There is, besides, in the ministry of the Established Church a sprinkling of original minds, who cannot be included in either of the two great divisions; and from these *à priori* one might have hoped much good to the Church. But such persons no sooner speak out, than the two hostile parties hush their strife, in order the more effectually to overwhelm with just and unjust imputations those who dare to utter truth that has not yet been consecrated by Act of Parliament or by Church Councils. Among those who have subscribed, to attack others is easy, to defend oneself most arduous. Recrimination is the only powerful weapon; and noble minds are ashamed to use this. No hope, therefore, shows itself of Reform from within.—For myself, I feel that nothing saved me from the infinite distresses which I should have encountered, had I become a minister of the Episcopal Church, but the very unusual prematureness of my religious development.

Besides the great subject of Baptismal Regeneration, the entire Episcopal theory and practice offended me. How little favourably I was impressed, when a boy, by the lawn sleeves, wig, artificial voice and manner of the Bishop of London, I have already said: but in six years more, reading and observation had intensely confirmed my first auguries. It was clear beyond denial, that for a century after the death of Edward VI. the bishops were the tools of court-bigotry, and often owed their highest promotions to base subservience. After the Revolution, the Episcopal order (on a rough and general view) might be described as a body of supine persons, known to the public only as a dead weight against all change that was distasteful to the Government. In the last century and a half, the nation was often afflicted with sensual royalty, bloody wars, venal statesmen, corrupt constituencies, bribery and violence at elections, flagitious drunkenness pervading all ranks, and insinuating itself into Colleges and Rectories. The prisons of the country had been in a most disgraceful state; the fairs and waits were scenes of rude debauchery, and the theatres were—still, in this nineteenth century—whispered to be haunts of the most debasing immorality. I could not learn that any bishop had ever taken the lead in denouncing these iniquities: nor that when any man or class of men rose to denounce them, the Episcopal Order failed to throw itself into the breach to defend corruption by at least passive resistance. Neither Howard, Wesley and Whitfield, nor yet Clarkson, Wilberforce, or Romilly, could boast of the episcopal bench as an ally against inhuman or immoral practices. Our oppressions in India, and our sanction to the most cruel superstitions of the natives, led to no outcry from the Bishops. Under their patronage the two old Societies of the Church had gone to sleep until aroused by the Church Missionary and Bible Societies, which were opposed by the Bishops. Their policy seemed to be, to do nothing, until somebody else was likely to do it; upon which they at last joined the movement in order to damp its energy, and get some credit from it. Now what were Bishops for, but to be the originators and energetic organs of all pious and good works? and what were they in the House of Lords for, if not to set a higher tone of purity, justice, and truth? and if they never did this, but weighed down those who attempted it, was not that a condemnation (not, perhaps, of all possible Episcopacy, but) of Episcopacy as it exists in England? If such a thing as a moral argument *for* Christianity was admitted as valid, surely the above was a moral argument *against* English Prelacy.

It was, moreover, evident at a glance, that this system of ours neither was, nor could have been, apostolic: for as long as the civil power was hostile to the Church, *a Lord bishop nominated by the civil ruler* was an impossibility: and this it is, which determines the moral and spiritual character of the English institution, not indeed exclusively, but preeminently.

I still feel amazement at the only defence which (as far as I know) the pretended followers of Antiquity make for the nomination of bishops by the Crown. In the third and fourth centuries, it is well known that every new bishop was elected by the universal suffrage of the laity of the church; and it is to these centuries that the High Episcopalians love to appeal, because they can quote thence out of Cyprian* and others in favour of Episcopal authority. When I alleged the dissimilarity in the mode of election, as fatal to this argument in the mouth of an English High Churchman, I was told that "the Crown now *represents* the Laity!" Such a fiction may be satisfactory to a pettifogging lawyer, but as the basis of a spiritual system is indeed supremely contemptible.

With these considerations on my mind,—while quite aware that some of the bishops were good and valuable men,—I could not help feeling that it would be a perfect misery to me to have to address one of them taken at random as my " Right Reverend Father in God," which seemed like a foul hypocrisy; and when I remembered who had said, " Call no man Father on earth; for one is your Father, who is in heaven:"—words, which not merely in the letter, but still more distinctly in the spirit, forbid the state of feeling which suggested this episcopal appellation,—it did appear to me, as if " Prelacy" had been rightly coupled by the Scotch Puritans with " Popery" as antichristian.

Connected inseparably with this, was the form of Ordination, which, the more I thought of it, seemed the more offensively and outrageously Popish, and quite opposed to the Article on the same subject. In the Article I read, that we were to regard such to be legitimate ministers of the word, as had been duly appointed to this work *by those who have public authority for the same.* It was evident to me that this very

* I remember reading about that time a sentence in one of his Epistles, in which this same Cyprian, the earliest mouthpiece of "proud prelacy," claims for the *populace* supreme right of deposing an unworthy bishop. I quote the words from memory, and do not know the reference. " Plebs summam habet potestatem episcopos seu dignos eligendi seu indignos detrudendi "

wide phrase was adapted and intended to comprehend the "public authorities" of all the Reformed Churches, and could never have been selected by one who wished to narrow the idea of a legitimate minister to Episcopalian Orders; besides that we know Lutheran and Calvinistic ministers to have been actually admitted in the early times of the Reformed English Church, by the force of that very Article. To this, the only genuine Protestant view of a Church, I gave my most cordial adherence: but when I turned to the Ordination Service, I found the Bishop there, by his authoritative voice, absolutely to bestow on the candidate for Priesthood the power to forgive or retain sins!—"Receive ye the Holy Ghost! Whose sins ye forgive, they are forgiven: whose sins ye retain, they are retained." If the Bishop really had this power, he of course had it only *as* Bishop, that is, by his consecration; thus it was formally transmitted. To allow this, vested in all the Romish bishops a spiritual power of the highest order, and denied the legitimate priesthood in nearly all the Continental Protestant Churches;—a doctrine irreconcilable with the article just referred to and intrinsically to me incredible. That an unspiritual—and it may be, a wicked—man, who can have no pure insight into devout and penitent hearts, and no communion with the Source of holy discernment, could never receive by an outward form the divine power to forgive or retain sins, or the power of bestowing this power, was to me then, as now, as clear and certain as any possible first axiom. Yet if the Bishop had not this power, how profane was the pretension! Thus again I came into rude collision with English Prelacy.

The year after taking my degree, I made myself fully master of Paley's acute and original treatise, the "Horæ Paulinæ," and realized the whole life of Paul as never before. This book greatly enlarged my mind as to the resources of historical criticism. Previously, my sole idea of criticism was that of the direct discernment of style; but I now began to understand what powerful argument rose out of combinations: and the very complete establishment which this work gives to the narrative concerning Paul in the latter half of the "Acts," appeared to me to reflect critical honour* on the whole New

---

* A critic absurdly complains that I do not account for this. Account for what? I still hold the authenticity of nearly all the Pauline epistles, and that the Pauline Acts are compiled from some valuable source, from chap. xiii. onward; but it was gratuitous to infer that this could accredit the four gospels.

Testament. In the epistles of this great apostle, notwithstanding their argumentative difficulties, I found a moral reality and a depth of wisdom perpetually growing upon me with acquaintance: in contrast to which I was conscious that I made no progress in understanding the four gospels. Their first impression had been their strongest: and their difficulties remained as fixed blocks in my way. Was this possibly because Paul is a reasoner, (I asked)? hence, with the cultivation of my understanding, I have entered more easily into the heart of his views:—while Christ enunciates divine truth dogmatically; consequently insight is needed to understand him? On the contrary, however, it seemed to me, that the doctrinal difficulties of the gospels depend chiefly either on obscure metaphor or on apparent incoherence: and I timidly asked a friend, whether the *dislocation* of the discourses of Christ by the narrators may not be one reason why they are often obscure: for on comparing Luke with Matthew, it appears that we cannot deny occasional dislocation. If at this period a German divinity professor had been lecturing at Oxford, or German books had been accessible to me, it might have saved me long peregrinations of body and mind.

About this time I had also begun to think that the old writers called *Fathers* deserved but a small fraction of the reverence which is awarded to them. I had been strongly urged to read Chrysostom's work on the Priesthood, by one who regarded it as a suitable preparation for Holy Orders; and I did read it. But I not only thought it inflated, and without moral depth, but what was far worse, I encountered in it an elaborate defence of falsehood in the cause of the Church, and generally of deceit in any good cause.* I rose from the treatise in disgust, and for the first time sympathized with Gibbon; and augured that if he had spoken with moral indignation, instead of pompous sarcasm, against the frauds of the ancient "Fathers," his blows would have fallen far more heavily on Christianity itself.

* He argues from the Bible, that a victory gained by deceit is more to be esteemed than one obtained by force; and that, provided the end aimed at be good, we ought not to call it *deceit*, but a sort of *admirable management*. A learned friend informs me that in his 45th Homily on Genesis, this father, in his zeal to vindicate Scriptural characters at any cost, goes further still in immorality. My friend adds, "It is really frightful to reflect to what guidance the moral sentiment of mankind was committed for many ages: Chrysostom is usually considered one of the best of the fathers."

I also, with much effort and no profit, read the Apostolic Fathers. Of these, Clement alone seemed to me respectable, and even he to write only what I could myself have written, with Paul and Peter to serve as a model. But for Barnabas and Hermas I felt a contempt so profound, that I could hardly believe them genuine. On the whole, this reading greatly exalted my sense of the unapproachable greatness* of the New Testament. The moral chasm between it and the very earliest Christian writers seemed to me so vast, as only to be accounted for by the doctrine in which all spiritual men (as I thought) unhesitatingly agreed,—that the New Testament was dictated by the immediate action of the Holy Spirit. The infatuation of those, who, after this, rested on *the Councils*, was to me unintelligible. Thus the Bible in its simplicity became only the more all-ruling to my judgment, because I could find no Articles, no Church Decrees, and no apostolic individual, whose rule over my understanding or conscience I could bear. Such may be conveniently regarded as the first period of my Creed.

CHAPTER II.

STRIVINGS AFTER A MORE PRIMITIVE CHRISTIANITY.

My second period is characterized, partly by the great ascendancy exercised over me by one powerful mind and still more powerful will, partly by the vehement effort which throughout its duration urged me to long after the establishment of Christian Fellowship in a purely Biblical Church as the first great want of Christendom and of the world.

I was already uneasy in the sense that I could not enter the ministry of the Church of England, and knew not what course

---

* I thought that the latter part of this book would sufficiently show how and why I now need to modify this sentiment. I *now* see the doctrine of the Atonement, especially as expounded in the Epistle of the Hebrews, to deserve no honour. I see false interpretations of the Old Testament to be dogmatically proposed in the New. I see the moral teaching concerning Patriotism, Property, Slavery, Marriage, Science, and indirectly Fine Art, to be essentially defective, and the threats against unbelief to be a pernicious immorality. See also p. 80. Why will critics use my frankly-stated juvenile opinions as a stone to pelt me with ?

of life to choose. I longed to become a missionary for Christ among the heathen,—a notion I had often fostered while reading the lives of missionaries: but again, I saw not how that was to be effected. After taking my degree, I became a Fellow of Balliol College; and the next year I accepted an invitation to Ireland, and there became private tutor for fifteen months in the house of one now deceased, whose name I would gladly mention for honour and affection;—but I withhold my pen. While he repaid me munificently for my services, he behaved towards me as a father, or indeed as an elder brother, and instantly made me feel as a member of his family. His great talents, high professional standing, nobleness of heart and unfeigned piety, would have made him a most valuable counsellor to me: but he was too gentle, too unassuming, too modest; he looked to be taught by his juniors, and sat at the feet of one whom I proceed to describe.

This was a young relative of his,—a most remarkable man, —who rapidly gained an immense sway over me. I shall henceforth call him "the Irish clergyman." His "bodily presence" was indeed "weak!" A fallen cheek, a bloodshot eye, crippled limbs resting on crutches, a seldom shaven beard, a shabby suit of clothes and a generally neglected person, drew at first pity, with wonder to see such a figure in a drawing-room. It was currently reported that a person in Limerick offered him a halfpenny, mistaking him for a beggar; and if not true, the story was yet well invented. This young man had taken high honours in Dublin University and had studied for the bar, where under the auspices of his eminent kinsman he had excellent prospects; but his conscience would not allow him to take a brief, lest he should be selling his talents to defeat justice. With keen logical powers, he had warm sympathies, solid judgment of character, thoughtful tenderness, and total self-abandonment. He before long took Holy Orders, and became an indefatigable curate in the mountains of Wicklow. Every evening he sallied forth to teach in the cabins, and roving far and wide over mountain and amid bogs, was seldom home before midnight. By such exertions his strength was undermined, and he so suffered in his limbs that not lameness only, but yet more serious results were feared. He did not fast on purpose, but his long walks through wild country and indigent people inflicted on him much severe deprivation: moreover, as he ate whatever food offered itself,—food unpalatable and often indigestible to him, his whole frame might have vied in emaciation with a monk of La Trappe.

Such a phenomenon intensely excited the poor Romanists, who looked on him as a genuine "saint" of the ancient breed. The stamp of heaven seemed to them clear in a frame so wasted by austerity, so superior to worldly pomp, and so partaking in all their indigence. That a dozen such men would have done more to convert all Ireland to Protestantism, than the whole apparatus of the Church Establishment, was ere long my conviction; though I was at first offended by his apparent affectation of a mean exterior. But I soon understood, that in no other way could he gain equal access to the lower and lowest orders, and that he was moved not by asceticism, nor by ostentation, but by a self-abandonment fruitful of consequences. He had practically given up all reading except that of the Bible; and no small part of his movement towards me soon took the form of dissuasion from all other voluntary study.

In fact, I had myself more and more concentrated my religious reading on this one book: still, I could not help feeling the value of a cultivated mind. Against this, my new eccentric friend, (himself having enjoyed no mean advantages of cultivation,) directed his keenest attacks. I remember once saying to him, in defence of worldly station,—" To desire to be rich is unchristian and absurd; but if I were the father of children, I should wish to be rich enough to secure them a good education." He replied: "If I had children, I would as soon see them break stones on the road, as do any thing else, if only I could secure to them the Gospel and the grace of God." I was unable to say Amen, but I admired his unflinching consistency;—for now, as always, all he said was based on texts aptly quoted and logically enforced. He more and more made me ashamed of Political Economy and Moral Philosophy, and all Science; all of which ought to be "counted dross for the excellency of the knowledge of Christ Jesus our Lord." For the first time in my life I saw a man earnestly turning into reality the principles which others confessed with their lips only. That the words of the New Testament contained the highest truth accessible to man,—truth not to be taken from nor added to,—all good men (as I thought) confessed: never before had I seen a man so resolved that no word of it should be a dead letter to him. I once said: "But do you really think that *no* part of the New Testament may have been temporary in its object? for instance, what should we have lost, if St. Paul had never written the verse, 'The cloak which I have left at Troas, bring with thee, and the books, but especially the parchments.'" He answered with the greatest promptitude: "*I* should certainly have lost something; for that is exactly the verse which alone saved me from selling my little library. No! every word, depend upon it, is from the Spirit, and is for eternal service."

A political question was just then exceedingly agitating Ireland, in which nearly everybody took a great interest;— it was, the propriety of admitting Romanist members of Parliament. Those who were favourable to the measure, generally advocated it by trying to undervalue the chasm that separates Romish from Protestant doctrine. By such arguments they exceedingly exasperated the real Protestants, and, in common with all around me, I totally repudiated that ground of comprehension. But I could not understand why a broader, more generous and every way safer argument was not dwelt on; viz. the unearthliness of the claims of Christianity. When Paul was preaching the kingdom of God in the Roman empire, if a malicious enemy had declared to a Roman proconsul that the Christians were conspiring to eject all Pagans out of the senate and out of the public administration; who can doubt what Paul would have replied?—The kingdom of God is not of this world: it is within the heart, and consists in righteousness, peace and joy in the Holy Ghost. These are our "honours" from God: we ask not the honours of empire and title. Our King is in heaven; and will in time return to bring to an end these earthly kingdoms: but until then, we claim no superiority over you on earth. As the riches of this world, so the powers of this world belong to another king: we dare not try to appropriate them in the name of our heavenly King; nay, we should hold it as great a sin to clutch empire for our churches, as to clutch wealth: God forbid that we covet either!—But what then if the enemy had had foresight to reply, O proconsul, this Paul talks finely, and perhaps sincerely: but if so, yet cheat not yourself to think that his followers will tie themselves to his mild equity and disinterestedness. Now indeed they are weak: now they profess unworldliness and unambition: they wish only to be recognised as peaceable subjects, as citizens and as equals: but if once they grow strong enough, they will discover that their spears and swords are the symbol of their Lord's return from heaven; that he now at length commissions them to eject you, as vile infidels, from all seats of power,—to slay you with the sword, if you dare to offer sacrifice to the immortal gods,—to degrade you so, that you shall only not enter the senate, or the privy council of the prince, or the judgment seat, but not even the jury-box, or a municipal corporation, or the pettiest edileship of Italy; nay, you shall not be lieutenants of armies, or tribunes, or anything above the lowest centurion. You shall become a plebeian class,—cheap bodies to be exposed in battle or to toil in the field, and pay rent to the lordly Christian. Such shall be the fate of *you*, the worshippers of Quirinus and of Jupiter Best and Greatest, if you neglect to crush and extirpate, during the weakness of its infancy, this ambitious and unscrupulous portent of a religion. —Oh, how would Paul have groaned in spirit, at accusations such as these, hateful to his soul, aspersing to his churches, but impossible to refute! Either Paul's doctrine was a fond dream, (felt I,) or it is certain, that he would have protested with all the force of his heart against the principle that Christians *as such* have any claim to earthly power and place; or that they could, when they gained a numerical majority, without sin enact laws to punish, stigmatize, exclude, or otherwise treat with political inferiority the Pagan remnant. To uphold such exclusion, is to lay the axe to the root of the spiritual Church, to stultify the apostolic preaching, and at this moment justify Mohammedans in persecuting Christians. For the Sultan might fairly say,—"I give Christians the choice of exile or death: I will not allow that sect to grow up here; for it has fully warned me, that it will proscribe my religion in my own land, as soon as it has power."

On such grounds I looked with amazement and sorrow at spiritual Christians who desired to exclude the Romanists from full equality; and I was happy to enjoy as to this the passive assent of the Irish clergyman; who, though "Orange" in his connexions, and opposed to *all* political action, yet only so much the more deprecated what he called "political Protestantism."

In spite of the strong revulsion which I felt against some of the peculiarities of this remarkable man, I for the first time in my life found myself under the dominion of a superior. When I remember, how even those bowed down before him, who had been to him in the place of parents,—accomplished and experienced minds,—I cease to wonder in the retrospect, that he riveted me in such a bondage. Henceforth I began to ask: what will *he* say to this and that? In *his* reply I always expected to find a higher portion of God's Spirit, than in any I could frame for myself. In order to learn divine truth, it became to me a surer process to consult him, than to search for myself and wait upon God: and gradually, (as I afterwards discerned,) my religious thought had merged into the mere process of developing fearlessly into results all his principles, without any deeper examining of my foundations. Indeed, but for a few weaknesses which warned me that he might err, I could have accepted him as an apostle commissioned to reveal the mind of God.

In his after-course (which I may not indicate) this gentleman has every where displayed a wonderful power of bending other minds to his own, and even stamping upon them the tones of his voice and all sorts of slavish imitation. Over the general results of his action I have long deeply mourned, as blunting his natural tenderness and sacrificing his wisdom to the Letter, dwarfing men's understandings, contracting their hearts, crushing their moral sensibilities, and setting those at variance who ought to love: yet oh! how specious was it in the beginning! he *only* wanted men "to submit their understandings *to God*," that is, to the Bible, that is, to his interpretation! From seeing his action and influence I have learnt, that if it be dangerous to a young man (as it assuredly is) to have *no* superior mind to which he may look up with confiding reverence, it may be even more dangerous to think that he has found such a mind: for he who is most logically consistent, though to a one-sided theory, and most ready to sacrifice self to that theory, seems to ardent youth the most assuredly trustworthy guide. Such was Ignatius Loyola in his day.

My study of the New Testament at this time had made it impossible for me to overlook that the apostles held it to be a duty of all disciples to expect a near and sudden destruction of the earth by fire, and constantly to be expecting *the return of the Lord from heaven*. It was easy to reply, that "experience disproved" this expectation; but to this an answer was ready provided in Peter's 2nd Epistle, which forewarns us that we shall be taunted by the unbelieving with this objection, but bids us, *nevertheless*, continue to look out for the speedy fulfilment of this great event. In short, the case stood thus:—If it was not *too soon* 1800 years ago to stand in daily expectation of it, it is not too soon now: to say that it is *too late*, is not merely to impute error to the apostles, on a matter which they made of first-rate moral importance, but is to say, that those whom Peter calls " ungodly scoffers, walking after their own lusts"— were right, and he was wrong, on the very point for which he thus vituperated them.

The importance of this doctrine is, that *it totally forbids all working for earthly objects distant in time:* and here the Irish clergyman threw into the same scale the entire weight of his character. For instance; if a youth had a natural aptitude for mathematics, and he asked, ought he to give himself to the study, in hope that he might diffuse a serviceable knowledge of it, or possibly even enlarge the boundaries of the science? my friend would have replied, that such a purpose was very proper, if entertained by a worldly man. Let the dead bury their dead; and let the world study the things of the world: they know no better, and they are of use to the Church, who may borrow and use the jewels of the Egyptians. But such studies cannot be eagerly followed by the Christian, except when he yields to unbelief. In fact, what would it avail even to become a second La Place after thirty years' study, if in five and thirty years the Lord descended from heaven, snatched up all his saints to meet him, and burned to ashes all the works of the earth? Then all the mathematician's work would have perished, and he would grieve over his unwisdom, in laying up store which could not stand the fire of the Lord. Clearly; if we are bound to act *as though* the end of all earthly concerns may come, " at cockcrowing or at midday," then to work for distant earthly objects is the part of a fool or of an unbeliever.

I found a wonderful dulness in many persons on this important subject. Wholly careless to ask what was the true apostolic doctrine, they insisted that " Death is to us *practically* the coming of the Lord," and were amazed at my seeing so much emphasis in the other view. This comes of the abominable selfishness preached as religion. If I were to labour at some useful work for ten years,—say, at clearing forest land, laying out a farm, and building a house,—and were then to die, I should leave my work to my successors, and it would not be lost. Some men work for higher, some for lower, earthly ends; ("in a great house there are many vessels, &c.;") but all the results are valuable, if there is a chance of transmitting them to those who follow us. But if all is to be very shortly burnt up, it is then folly to exert ourselves for such objects. To the dead man, (it is said,) the cases are but one. This is to the purpose, if self absorbs all our heart; away from the purpose, if we are to work for unselfish ends.

Nothing can be clearer, than that the New Testament is entirely pervaded by the doctrine,—sometimes explicitly stated, sometimes unceremoniously assumed,—that earthly things are very speedily to come to an end, and *therefore* are not worthy of our high affections and deep interest. Hence, when thoroughly imbued with this persuasion, I looked with mournful pity on a great mind wasting its energies on any distant aim of this earth. For a statesman to talk about providing for future generations, sounded to me as a melancholy avowal of unbelief. To devote good talents to write history or investigate nature, was simple waste: for at the Lord's coming, history and science would no longer be learned by these feeble appliances of ours. Thus an inevitable deduction from the doctrine of the apostles, was, that "we must work for speedy results only." Vitæ summa brevis spem nos vetat inchoare longam. I *then* accepted the doctrine, in profound obedience to the absolutely infallible system of precepts. I *now* see that the falsity and mischief of the doctrine is one of the very many disproofs of the assumed, but unverified infallibility. However, the hold which the apostolic belief then took of me, subjected my conscience to the exhortations of the Irish clergyman, whenever he inculcated that the highest Christian must necessarily decline the pursuit of science, knowledge, art, history,—except so far as any of these things might be made useful tools for immediate spiritual results.

Under the stimulus to my imagination given by this gentleman's character, the desire, which from a boy I had more or less nourished, of becoming a teacher of Christianity *to the heathen*, took stronger and stronger hold of me. I saw that I was shut out from the ministry of the Church of England, and knew not how to seek connexion with Dissenters. I had met one eminent Quaker, but was offended by the violent and obviously false interpretations by which he tried to get rid of the two Sacraments; and I thought there was affectation involved in the forms which the doctrine of the Spirit took with him. Besides, I had not been prepossessed by those Dissenters whom I had heard speak at the Bible Society. I remember that one of them talked in pompous measured tones of voice, and with much stereotyped phraseology, about "the Bible only, the religion of Protestants:" altogether, it did not seem to me that there was at all so much of nature and simple truth in them as in Church clergymen. I also had a vague, but strong idea, that all Dissenting churches assumed some special, narrow, and sectarian basis. The question indeed arose: "Was I *at liberty* to preach to the heathen without ordination?" but I with extreme ease answered in the affirmative. To teach a Church, of course needs the sanction of the church: no man can assume pastoral rights without assent from other parties: but to speak to those without, is obviously a natural right, with which the Church can have nothing to do. And herewith all the precedents of the New Testament so obviously agreed, that I had not a moment's disquiet on this head.

At the same time, when asked by one to whom I communicated my feelings, "whether I felt that I had *a call* to preach to the heathen," I replied: I had not the least consciousness of it, and knew not what was meant by such language. All that I knew was, that I was willing and anxious to do anything in my power either to teach, or to help others in teaching, if only I could find out the way. That after eighteen hundred years no farther progress should have been made towards the universal spread of Christianity, appeared a scandalous reproach on Christendom. Is it not, perhaps, because those who are in Church office cannot go, and the mass of the laity think it no business of theirs? If a persecution fell on England, and thousands were driven into exile, and, like those who were scattered in Stephen's persecution, "went everywhere preaching the word,"—might not this be the conversion of the world, as indeed that began the conversion of the Gentiles? But the laity leave all to the clergy, and the clergy have more than enough to do.

About this time I heard of another remarkable man, whose name was already before the public,—Mr. Groves,—who had written a tract called Christian Devotedness, on the duty of devoting all worldly property for the cause of Christ, and utterly renouncing the attempt to amass money. In pursuance of this, he was going to Persia as a teacher of Christianity. I read his tract, and was inflamed with the greatest admiration; judging immediately that this was the man whom I should rejoice to aid or serve. For a scheme of this nature alone appeared to combine with the views which I had been gradually consolidating concerning the practical relation of a Christian Church to Christian Evidences. On this very important subject it is requisite to speak in detail.

The Christian Evidences are an essential part of the course of religious study prescribed at Oxford, and they had engaged from an early period a large share of my attention. Each treatise on the subject, taken by itself, appeared to me to have great argumentative force; but when I tried to grasp them all together in a higher act of thought, I was sensible of a certain confusion, and inability to reconcile their fundamental assumptions. *One* either formally stated, or virtually assumed, that the deepest basis of all religious knowledge was the testimony of sense to some fact, which is ascertained to be miraculous when examined by the light of Physics or Physiology: and that we must, at least in a great degree, distrust and abandon our moral convictions or auguries, at the bidding of sensible miracle. *Another* treatise assumed that men's moral feelings and beliefs are, on the whole, the most trustworthy thing to be found; and starting from them as from a known and ascertained foundation, proceeded to glorify Christianity because of its expanding, strengthening, and beautifying all that we know by conscience to be morally right. That the former argument, if ever so valid, was still too learned and scholastic, not for the vulgar only, but for every man in his times of moral trial, I felt instinctively persuaded: yet my intellect could not wholly dispense with it, and my belief in the depravity of the moral understanding of men inclined me to go some way in defending it. To endeavour to combine the two arguments by saying that they were adapted to different states of mind, was plausible; yet it conceded, that neither of the two went to the bottom of human thought, or showed what were the real *fixed points* of man's knowledge; without knowing which, we are in perpetual danger of mere *argumentum ad hominem*, or, in fact, arguing in a circle;—as to prove miracles from doctrine, and doctrine from miracles. I however conceived that the most logical minds among Christians would contend that there was another solution; which, in 1827, I committed to paper in nearly the following words:

"May it not be doubted whether Leland sees the real circumstance that makes a revelation necessary?

"No revelation is needed to inform us,—of the invisible power and deity of God; that we are bound to worship Him; that we are capable of sinning against Him and liable to his just judgment; nay, that we have sinned, and that we find in nature marks of his displeasure against sin; and yet, that He is merciful. St. Paul and our Lord show us that these things are knowable by reason. The ignorance of the heathens is *judicial blindness*, to punish their obstinate rejection of the true God.

"But a revelation *is* needed to convey a SPECIAL message, such as this: that God has provided an Atonement for our sins, has deputed his own Son to become Head of the redeemed human family, and intends to raise those who believe in Him to a future and eternal life of bliss. These are external truths, (for 'who can believe, unless one be sent to preach them?') and are not knowable by any reasonings drawn from nature. They transcend natural analogies and moral or spiritual experience. To reveal them, a specific communication must be accorded to us: and on this the necessity for miracle turns."

Thus, in my view, at that time, the materials of the Bible were in theory divisible into two portions: concerning the *one*, (which I called Natural Religion,) it not only was not presumptuous, but it was absolutely essential, to form an independent judgment; for this was the real basis of all faith: concerning the *other*, (which I called Revealed Religion,) our business was, not to criticize the message, but to examine the credentials* of the messenger; and,—after the most unbiassed possible examination of these,—then, if they proved sound, to receive his communication reverently and unquestioningly.

Such was the theory with which I came from Oxford to Ireland; but I was hindered from working out its legitimate results by the overpowering influence of the Irish clergyman; who, while pressing the authority of every letter of the Scrip-

---

* Very unintelligent criticism of my words induces me to add, that "the *credentials* of Revelation," as distinguished from "the *contents* of Revelation," are here intended. Whether such a distinction can be preserved is quite another question. The view here exhibited is essentially that of Paley, and was in my day the prevalent one at Oxford. I do not think that the present Archbishop of Canterbury will disown it, any more than Lloyd, and Burton, and Hampden,—bishops and Regius Professors of Divinity.

ture with an unshrinking vehemence that I never saw surpassed, yet, with a common inconsistency, showed more than indifference towards learned historical and critical evidence on the side of Christianity; and indeed, unmercifully exposed erudition to scorn, both by caustic reasoning, and by irrefragable quotation of texts. I constantly had occasion to admire the power with which he laid hold of the moral side of every controversy; whether he was reasoning against Romanism, against the High Church, against learned religion or philosophic scepticism: and in this matter his practical axiom was, that the advocate of truth had to address himself to the *conscience* of the other party, and if possible, make him feel that there was a moral and spiritual superiority against him. Such doctrine, when joined with an inculcation of man's *natural blindness and total depravity*, was anything but clearing to my intellectual perceptions: in fact, I believe that for some years I did not recover from the dimness and confusion which he spread over them. But in my entire inability to explain away the texts which spoke with scorn of worldly wisdom, philosophy, and learning, on the one hand; and the obvious certainty, on the other, that no historical evidence for miracle was possible except by the aid of learning; I for the time abandoned this side of Christian Evidence,—not as invalid, but as too unwieldy a weapon for use,—and looked to direct moral evidence alone. And now rose the question, How could such moral evidence become appreciable to heathens and Mohammedans?

I felt distinctly enough, that mere talk could bring no conviction, and would be interpreted by the actions and character of the speaker. While nations called Christian are only known to heathens as great conquerors, powerful avengers, sharp traders,—often lax in morals, and apparently without religion,—the fine theories of a Christian teacher would be as vain to convert a Mohammedan or Hindoo to Christianity, as the soundness of Seneca's moral treatises to convert me to Roman Paganism. Christendom has to earn a new reputation before Christian precepts will be thought to stand in any essential or close relation with the mystical doctrines of Christianity. I could see no other way to this, but by an entire church being formed of new elements on a heathen soil:— a church, in which by no means all should be preachers, but all should be willing to do for all whatever occasion required. Such a church had I read of among the Moravians in Greenland and in South Africa. I imagined a little colony, so animated by primitive faith, love, and disinterestedness, that the collective moral influence of all might interpret and enforce the words of the few who preached. Only in this way did it appear to me that preaching to the heathen could be attended with success. In fact, whatever success had been attained, seemed to come only after many years, when the natives had gained experience in the characters of the Christian family around them.

When I had returned to Oxford, I induced the Irish clergyman to visit the University, and introduced him to many of my equals in age, and juniors. Most striking was it to see how instantaneously he assumed the place of universal father-confessor, as if he had been a known and long-trusted friend. His insight into character, and tenderness pervading his austerity, so opened young men's hearts, that day after day there was no end of secret closetings with him. I began to see the prospect of so considerable a movement of mind, as might lead many in the same direction as myself; and *if* it was by a collective Church that Mohammedans were to be taught, the only way was for each separately to be led to the same place by the same spiritual influence. As Groves was a magnet to draw me, so might I draw others. In no other way could a pure and efficient Church be formed. If we waited, as with worldly policy, to make up a complete colony before leaving England, we should fail of getting the right men: we should pack them together by a mechanical process, instead of leaving them to be united by vital affinities. Thus actuated, and other circumstances conducing, in September 1830, with some Irish friends, I set out to join Mr. Groves at Bagdad. What I might do there, I knew not. I did not go as a minister of religion, and I everywhere pointedly disowned the assumption of this character, even down to the colour of my dress. But I thought I knew many ways in which I might be of service, and I was prepared to act according to circumstances.

Perhaps the strain of practical life must in any case, before long, have broken the chain by which the Irish clergyman unintentionally held me; but all possible influence from him was now cut off by separation. The dear companions of my travels no more aimed to guide my thoughts, than I theirs:

neither ambition nor suspicion found place in our hearts; and my mind was thus able again without disturbance to develop its own tendencies.

I had become distinctly aware, that the modern Churches in general by no means hold the truth as conceived of by the apostles. In the matter of the Sabbath and of the Mosaic Law, of Infant Baptism, of Episcopacy, of the doctrine of the Lord's return, I had successively found the prevalent Protestantism to be unapostolic. Hence arose in me a conscious and continuous effort to read the New Testament with fresh eyes and without bias, and so to take up the real doctrines of the heavenly and everlasting Gospel.

In studying the narrative of John I was strongly impressed by the fact, that the glory and greatness of the Son of God is constantly ascribed to the will and pleasure of the Father. I had been accustomed to hear this explained of his *mediatorial* greatness only, but this now looked to me like a make-shift, and to want the simplicity of truth—an impression which grew deeper with closer examination. The emphatic declaration of Christ, " My Father is greater than I," especially arrested my attention. Could I really expound this as meaning, " My Father, the Supreme God, is greater than I am, *if you look solely to my human nature?*" Such a truism can scarcely have deserved such emphasis. Did the disciples need to be taught that God was greater than man? Surely, on the contrary, the Saviour must have meant to say: *Divine as I am*, yet my heavenly Father is greater than I, *even when you take cognizance of my divine nature.*" I did not then know, that my comment was exactly that of the most orthodox Fathers; I rather thought they were against me, but for them I did not care much. I reverenced the doctrine of the Trinity as something vital to the soul; but felt that to love the Fathers or the Athanasian Creed more than the Gospel of John would be a supremely miserable superstition. However, that Creed states that there is no inequality between the Three Persons: in John it became increasingly clear to me that the divine Son is unequal to the Father. To say that " the Son of God" meant " Jesus as man," was a preposterous evasion: for there is no higher title for the Second Person of the Trinity than this very one—Son of God. Now, in the 5th chapter, when the Jews accused Jesus " of making himself equal to God," by calling himself Son of God, Jesus even hastens to protest against the inference as a misrepresentation

—beginning with: "The Son can do nothing of himself:" and proceeds elaborately to ascribe all his greatness to the Father's will. In fact, the Son is emphatically "he who is sent," and the Father is "he who sent him:" and all would feel the deep impropriety of trying to exchange these phrases. The Son who is sent,—sent, not *after* he was humbled to become man, but *in order to* be so humbled,—was NOT EQUAL TO, but LESS THAN, the Father who sent him. To this I found the whole Gospel of John to bear witness; and with this conviction, the truth and honour of the Athanasian Creed fell to the ground. One of its main tenets was proved false; and yet it dared to utter anathemas on all who rejected it!

I afterwards remembered my old thought, that we must surely understand *our own words*, when we venture to speak at all about divine mysteries. Having gained boldness to gaze steadily on the topic, I at length saw that the compiler of the Athanasian Creed did *not* understand his own words. If any one speaks of *three men*, all that he means is, "three objects of thought, of whom each separately may be called Man." So also, all that could possibly be meant by *three gods*, is, "three objects of thought, of whom each separately may be called God." To avow the last statement, as the Creed does, and yet repudiate Three Gods, is to object to the phrase, yet confess to the only meaning which the phrase can convey. Thus the Creed really teaches polytheism, but saves orthodoxy by forbidding any one to call it by its true name. Or to put the matter otherwise: it teaches three Divine Persons, and denies three Gods; and leaves us to guess what else is a Divine Person but a God, or a God but a Divine Person. Who, then, can deny that this intolerant creed is a malignant riddle?

That there is nothing in the Scripture about Trinity in Unity and Unity in Trinity I had long observed; and the total absence of such phraseology had left on me a general persuasion that the Church had systematized too much. But in my study of John I was now arrested by a text, which showed me how exceedingly far from a *Tri-unity* was the Trinity of that Gospel,—if trinity it be. Namely, in his last prayer, Jesus addresses to his Father the words: "This is life eternal, that they may know *Thee, the only True God*, and Jesus Christ, whom thou hast sent." I became amazed, as I considered these words more and more attentively, and without prejudice; and I began to understand how prejudice, when embalmed with reverence, blinds the mind. Why had I never before seen what is here so plain, that the *One God* of Jesus was not a Trinity, but was *the First Person* of the ecclesiastical Trinity?

But on a fuller search, I found this to be Paul's doctrine also: for in 1 Corinth. viii., when discussing the subject of Polytheism, he says that "though there be to the heathen many that are called Gods, yet to us there is but *One God*, the Father, *of* whom are all things; and *One Lord*, Jesus Christ, *by* whom are all things." Thus he defines Monotheism to consist in holding the person of the Father to be the One God; although this, if any, should have been the place for a "Trinity in Unity."

But did I proceed to deny the Divinity of the Son? By no means: I conceived of him as in the highest and fullest sense divine, short of being Father and not Son. I now believed that by the phrase "only begotten Son," John, and indeed Christ himself, meant to teach us that there was an impassable chasm between him and all creatures, in that he had a true, though a derived divine nature; as indeed the Nicene Creed puts the contrast, he was "begotten, not made." Thus all Divine glory dwells in the Son, but it is *because* the Father has willed it. A year or more afterward, when I had again the means of access to books, and consulted that very common Oxford book, "Pearson on the Creed," (for which I had felt so great a distaste that I never before read it)—I found this to be the undoubted doctrine of the great Nicene and Post Nicene Fathers, who laid much emphasis on two statements, which with the modern Church are idle and dead—viz. that "the Son was *begotten* of his Father *before all worlds*," and that "the Holy Spirit *proceedeth from* the Father and the Son." In the view of the old Church, the Father alone was the Fountain of Deity,—(and *therefore* fitly called, The One God,—and, the Only True God,)—while the Deity of the other two persons was real, yet derived and subordinate. Moreover, I found in Gregory Nazianzen and others, that to confess this derivation of the Son and Spirit and the underivedness of the Father alone, was in their view quite essential to save Monotheism; the *One* God being the underived Father.

Although in my own mind all doubt as to the doctrine of John and Paul on the main question seemed to be quite cleared away from the time that I dwelt on their explanation of Monotheism, this in no respect agitated me, or even engaged me in any farther search. There was nothing to force me into controversy, or make this one point of truth unduly preponderant. I concealed none of my thoughts from my companions; and concerning them I will only say, that whether they did or did not feel acquiescence, they behaved towards me with all the affection and all the equality which I would have wished myself to maintain, had the case been inverted. I was, however, sometimes uneasy, when the thought crossed my mind,—" What if we, like Henry Martyn, were charged with Polytheism by Mohammedans, and were forced to defend ourselves by explaining in detail our doctrine of the Trinity? *Perhaps* no two of us would explain it alike, and this would expose Christian doctrine to contempt." Then farther it came across me: How very remarkable it is, that the Jews, those strict Monotheists, never seem to have attacked the apostles for polytheism! It would have been so plausible an imputation, one that the instinct of party would so readily suggest, if there had been any external form of doctrine to countenance it. Surely it is transparent that the Apostles did not teach as Dr. Waterland. I had always felt a great repugnance to the argumentations concerning the *Personality* of the Holy Spirit; no doubt from an inward sense, however dimly confessed, that they were all words without meaning. For the disputant who maintains this dogma, tells us in the very next breath that *Person* has not in this connexion its common signification; so that he is elaborately enforcing upon us we know not what. That the Spirit of God meant in the New Testament *God in the heart*, had long been to me a sufficient explanation: and who by logic or metaphysics will carry us beyond this?

While we were at Aleppo, I one day got into religious discourse with a Mohammedan carpenter, which left on me a lasting impression. Among other matters, I was peculiarly desirous of disabusing him of the current notion of his people, that our gospels are spurious narratives of late date. I found great difficulty of expression; but the man listened to me with much attention, and I was encouraged to exert myself. He waited patiently till I had done, and then spoke to the following effect: "I will tell you, sir, how the case stands. God has given to you English a great many good gifts. You make fine ships, and sharp penknives, and good cloth and cottons; and you have rich nobles and brave soldiers; and you write and print many learned books: (dictionaries and grammars:) all this is of God. But there is one thing that God has withheld from you, and has revealed to us; and that is, the knowledge of the true religion, by which one may be saved." When he thus ignored my argument, (which was probably quite unintelligible to him,) and delivered his simple protest, I was silenced, and at the same time amused. But the more I thought it over, the more instruction I saw in the case. His position towards me was exactly that of a humble Christian towards an unbelieving philosopher; nay, that of the early Apostles or Jewish prophets towards the proud, cultivated, worldly wise and powerful heathen. This not only showed the vanity of any argument to him, except one purely addressed to his moral and spiritual faculties; but it also indicated to me that Ignorance has its spiritual self-sufficiency as well as Erudition; and that if there is a Pride of Reason, so is there a Pride of Unreason. But though this rested in my memory, it was long before I worked out all the results of that thought.

Another matter brought me some disquiet. An Englishman of rather low tastes who came to Aleppo at this time, called upon us; and as he was civilly received, repeated his visit more than once. Being unencumbered with fastidiousness, this person before long made various rude attacks on the truth and authority of the Christian religion, and drew me on to defend it. What I had heard of the moral life of the speaker made me feel that his was not the mind to have insight into divine truth; and I desired to divert the argument from external topics, and bring it to a point in which there might be a chance of touching his conscience. But I found this to be impossible. He returned actively to the assault against Christianity, and I could not bear to hear him vent historical falsehoods and misrepresentations damaging to the Christian cause, without contradicting them. He was a half-educated man, and I easily confuted him to my own entire satisfaction: but he was not either abashed or convinced; and at length withdrew as one victorious.—On reflecting over this, I felt painfully, that if a Moslem had been present and had understood all that had been said, he would have remained in total uncertainty which of the two disputants was in the right: for the controversy had turned on points wholly remote from the sphere of his knowledge or thought.

Yet to have declined the battle would have seemed like conscious weakness on my part. Thus the historical side of my religion, though essential to it, and though resting on valid evidence, (as I unhesitatingly believed,) exposed me to attacks in which I might incur virtual defeat or disgrace, but in which, from the nature of the case, I could never win an available victory. This was to me very disagreeable, yet I saw not my way out of the entanglement.

Two years after I left England, a hope was conceived that more friends might be induced to join us; and I returned home from Bagdad with the commission to bring this about, if there were suitable persons disposed for it. On my return, and while yet in quarantine on the coast of England, I received an uncomfortable letter from a most intimate spiritual friend, to the effect, that painful reports had been every where spread abroad against my soundness in the faith. The channel by which they had come was indicated to me; but my friend expressed a firm hope, that when I had explained myself, it would all prove to be nothing.

Now began a time of deep and critical trial to me and to my Creed; a time hard to speak of to the public; yet without a pretty full notice of it, the rest of the account would be quite unintelligible.

The Tractarian movement was just commencing in 1833. My brother was taking a position, in which he was bound to show that he could sacrifice private love to ecclesiastical dogma; and upon learning that I had spoken at some small meetings of religious people, (which he interpreted, I believe, to be an assuming of the Priest's office,) he separated himself entirely from my private friendship and acquaintance. To the public this may have some interest, as indicating the disturbing excitement which animated that cause: but my reason for naming the fact here is solely to exhibit the practical positions into which I myself was thrown. In my brother's conduct there was not a shade of unkindness, and I have not a thought of complaining of it. My distress was naturally great, until I had fully ascertained from him that I had given no personal offence. But the mischief of it went deeper. It practically cut me off from other members of my family, who were living in his house, and whose state of feeling towards me, through separation and my own agitations of mind, I for some time totally mistook.

I had, however, myself slighted relationship in comparison

with Christian brotherhood;—*sectarian* brotherhood, some
may call it;—I perhaps had none but myself to blame: but
in the far more painful occurrences which were to succeed one
another for many months together, I was blameless. Each
successive friend who asked explanations of my alleged heresy,
was satisfied,—or at least left me with that impression,—after
hearing me: not one who met me face to face had a word to
reply to the plain Scriptures which I quoted. Yet when I
was gone away, one after another was turned against me by
somebody else whom I had not yet met or did not know: for
in every theological conclave which deliberates on joint action,
the most bigoted seems always to prevail.

I will trust my pen to only one specimen of details. The
Irish clergyman was not able to meet me. He wrote a very
desultory letter of grave alarm and inquiry, stating that he
had heard that I was endeavouring to sound the divine nature
by the miserable plummet of human philosophy,—with much
beside that I felt to be mere commonplace which every body
might address to every body who differed from him. I however
replied in the frankest, most cordial and trusting tone,
assuring him that I was infinitely far from imagining that I
could "by searching understand God;" on the contrary, concerning
his higher mysteries, I felt I knew absolutely nothing
but what he revealed to me in his word; but in studying this
word, I found John and Paul to declare the Father, and not
the Trinity, to be the One God. Referring him to John xvii. 3,
1 Corinth. viii. 5, 6, I fondly believed that one so "subject
to the word" and so resolutely renouncing man's authority *in
order that* he might serve God, would immediately see as I
saw. But I assured him, in all the depth of affection, that I
felt how much fuller insight he had than I into all divine
truth; and not he only, but others to whom I alluded; and
that if I was in error, I only desired to be taught more truly;
and either with him, or at his feet, to learn of God. He
replied, to my amazement and distress, in a letter of much
tenderness, but which was to the effect,—that if I allowed the
Spirit of God to be with him rather than with me, it was
wonderful that I set my single judgment against the mind of
the Spirit and of the whole Church of God; and that as for
admitting into Christian communion one who held my doctrine,
it had this absurdity, that while I was in such a state of
belief, it was my duty to anathematize *them* as idolaters.—
Severe as was the shock given me by this letter, I wrote again

most lovingly, humbly, and imploringly: for I still adored him, and could have given him my right hand or my right eye,—anything but my conscience. I showed him that if it was a matter of action, I would submit; for I unfeignedly believed that he had more of the Spirit of God than I: but over my secret convictions I had no power. I was shut up to obey and believe God rather than man, and from the nature of the case, the profoundest respect for my brother's judgment could not in itself alter mine. As to the whole *Church* being against me, I did not know what that meant: I was willing to accept the Nicene Creed, and this I thought ought to be a sufficient defensive argument against the Church. His answer was decisive;—he was exceedingly surprized at my recurring to mere ecclesiastical creeds, as though they could have the slightest weight; and he must insist on my acknowledging, that, in the two texts quoted, the word Father meant the Trinity, if I desired to be in any way recognized as holding the truth.

The Father meant the Trinity!! For the first time I perceived, that so vehement a champion of the sufficiency of the Scripture, so staunch an opposer of Creeds and Churches, was wedded to an extra-Scriptural creed of his own, by which he tested the spiritual state of his brethren. I was in despair, and like a man thunderstruck. I had nothing more to say. Two more letters from the same hand I saw, the latter of which was, to threaten some new acquaintances who were kind to me, (persons wholly unknown to him,) that if they did not desist from sheltering me and break off intercourse, they should, as far as his influence went, themselves everywhere be cut off from Christian communion and recognition. This will suffice to indicate the sort of social persecution, through which, after a succession of struggles, I found myself separated from persons whom I had trustingly admired, and on whom I had most counted for union: with whom I fondly believed myself bound up for eternity; of whom some were my previously intimate friends, while for others, even on slight acquaintance, I would have performed menial offices and thought myself honoured; whom I still looked upon as the blessed and excellent of the earth, and the special favourites of heaven; whose company (though oftentimes they were considerably my inferiors either in rank or in knowledge and cultivation) I would have chosen in preference to that of nobles; whom I loved solely because I thought them to love

God, and of whom I asked nothing, but that they would admit me as the meanest and most frail of disciples. My heart was ready to break: I wished for a woman's soul, that I might weep in floods. Oh, Dogma! Dogma! how dost thou trample under foot love, truth, conscience, justice! Was ever a Moloch worse than thou? Burn me at the stake; then Christ will receive me, and saints beyond the grave will love me, though the saints here know me not. But now I am alone in the world: I can trust no one. The new acquaintances who barely tolerate me, and old friends whom reports have not reached, (if such there be,) may turn against me with animosity to-morrow, as those have done from whom I could least have imagined it. Where is union? where is the Church, which was to convert the heathen?

This was not my only reason, yet it was soon a sufficient and at last an overwhelming reason, against returning to the East. The pertinacity of the attacks made on me, and on all who dared to hold by me in a certain connexion, showed that I could no longer be anything but a thorn in the side of my friends abroad; nay, I was unable to predict how they themselves might change towards me. The idea of a Christian Church propagating Christianity while divided against itself was ridiculous. Never indeed had I had the most remote idea, that my dear friends there had been united to me by agreement in intellectual propositions; nor could I yet believe it. I remembered a saying of the noble-hearted Groves: "Talk of loving me while I agree with them! Give me men that will love me when I differ from them and contradict them: those will be the men to build up a true Church." I asked myself,—was I then possibly different from all? With me,—and, as I had thought, with all my spiritual friends,—intellectual dogma was not the test of spirituality. A hundred times over had I heard the Irish clergyman emphatically enunciate the contrary. Nothing was clearer in his preaching, talking, and writing, than that salvation was a present real experienced fact; a saving of the soul from the dominion of baser desires, and an inward union of it in love and homage to Christ, who, as the centre of all perfection, glory, and beauty, was the revelation of God to the heart. He who was thus saved, could not help knowing that he was reconciled, pardoned, beloved; and therefore he rejoiced in God his Saviour: indeed, to imagine joy without this personal assurance and direct knowledge, was quite preposterous. But on the other hand, the soul thus spiritually minded has a keen sense of like qualities in others. It cannot but discern when another is tender in conscience, disinterested, forbearing, scornful of untruth and baseness, and esteeming nothing so much as the fruits of the Spirit: accordingly, John did not hesitate to say: "*We know* that we have passed from death unto life, *because* we love the brethren." Our doctrine certainly had been, that the Church was the assembly of the saved, gathered by the vital attractions of God's Spirit; that in it no one was Lord or Teacher, but one was our Teacher, even Christ: that as long as we had no earthly bribes to tempt men to join us, there was not much cause to fear false brethren; for if we were heavenly minded, and these were earthly, they would soon dislike and shun us. Why should we need to sit in judgment and excommunicate them, except in the case of publicly scandalous conduct?

It is true, that I fully believed certain intellectual convictions to be essential to genuine spirituality: for instance, if I had heard that a person unknown to me did not believe in the Atonement of Christ, I should have inferred that he had no spiritual life. But if the person had come under my direct knowledge, my *theory* was, on no account to reject him on a question of Creed, but in any case to receive all those whom Christ had received, all on whom the Spirit of God had come down, just as the Church at Jerusalem did in regard to admitting the Gentiles, Acts xi. 18. Nevertheless, was not this perhaps a theory pleasant to talk of, but too good for practice? I could not tell; for it had never been so severely tried. I remembered, however, that when I had thought it right to be baptized as an adult, (regarding my baptism as an infant to have been a mischievous fraud,) the sole confession of faith which I made, or would endure, at a time when my "orthodoxy" was unimpeached, was:* "I believe that Jesus Christ is the Son of God:" to deny which, and claim to be acknowledged as within the pale of the Christian Church, seemed to be an absurdity. On the whole, therefore, it did not appear to me that this Church-theory had been hollow-hearted with *me* nor unscriptural, nor in any way unpractical; but that *others* were still infected with the leaven of creeds and formal tests, with which they reproached the old Church.

Were there, then, no other hearts than mine, aching under miserable bigotry, and refreshed only when they tasted in others the true fruits of the Spirit,—"love, joy, peace, long-

* Borrowed from Acts viii. 37.

suffering, gentleness, goodness, fidelity, meekness, self-control?"—To imagine this was to suppose myself a man supernaturally favoured, an angel upon earth. I knew there must be thousands in this very point more true-hearted than I: nay, such still might some be, whose names I went over with myself: but I had no heart for more experiments. When such a man as he, the only mortal to whom I had looked up as to an apostle, had unhesitatingly, unrelentingly, and without one mark that his conscience was not on his side, flung away all his own precepts, his own theories, his own magnificent rebukes of Formalism and human Authority, and had made *himself* the slave and *me* the victim of these old and ever-living tyrants,—whom henceforth could I trust? The resolution then rose in me, to love all good men from a distance, but never again to count on permanent friendship with any one who was not himself cast out as a heretic.

Nor, in fact, did the storm of distress which these events inflicted on me, subside, until I willingly received the task of withstanding it, as God's trial whether I was faithful. As soon as I gained strength to say, "O my Lord, I will bear not this only, *but more also*,* for thy sake, for conscience, and for truth,"—my sorrows vanished, until the next blow and the next inevitable pang. At last my heart had died within me; the bitterness of death was past; I was satisfied to be hated by the saints, and to reckon that those who had not yet turned against me would not bear me much longer.—Then I conceived the belief, that if we may not make a heaven on earth for ourselves out of the love of saints, it is in order that we may find a truer heaven in God's love.

The question about this time much vexed me, what to do about receiving the Holy Supper of the Lord, the great emblem of brotherhood, communion, and church connexion. At one time I argued with myself, that it became an unmeaning form, when not partaken of in mutual love; that I could never again have free intercourse of heart with any one;—why then use the rite of communion, where there is no communion? But, on the other hand, I thought it a mode of confessing Christ, and that permanently to disuse it was an unfaithfulness. In the Church of England I could have been easy as far as the communion formulary was concerned; but

---

* Virgil (Æneid vi.) gives the Stoical side of the same thought:
Tu ne cede malis, *sed contra audentior ito.*

to the entire system I had contracted an incurable repugnance, as worldly, hypocritical, and an evil counterfeit. I desired, therefore, to creep into some obscure congregation, and there wait till my mind had ripened as to the right path in circumstances so perplexing. I will only briefly say, that I at last settled among some who had previously been total strangers to me. To their good will and simple kindness I feel myself indebted: peace be to them! Thus I gained time, and repose of mind, which I greatly needed.

From the day that I had mentally decided on total inaction as to all ecclesiastical questions, I count the termination of my Second Period. My ideal of a spiritual Church had blown up in the most sudden and heartbreaking way; overpowering me with shame, when the violence of sorrow was past. There was no change whatever in my own judgment, yet a total change of action was inevitable: that I was on the eve of a great transition of mind I did not at all suspect. Hitherto my reverence for the authority of the whole and indivisible *Bible* was overruling and complete. I never really had dared to criticize it; I did not even exact from it self-consistency. If two passages appeared to be opposed, and I could not evade the difficulty by the doctrine of Development and Progress, I inferred that there was *some* mode of conciliation unknown to me; and that perhaps the depth of truth in divine things could ill be stated in our imperfect language. But from the man who dared to interpose *a human comment* on the Scripture, I most rigidly demanded a clear, single, self-consistent sense. If he did not know what he meant, why did he not hold his peace? If he did know, why did he so speak as to puzzle us? It was for this uniform refusal to allow of self-contradiction, that it was more than once sadly predicted of me at Oxford that I should become "a Socinian;" yet I did not apply this logical measure to any compositions but those which were avowedly "uninspired" and human.

As to moral criticism, my mind was practically prostrate before the Bible. By the end of this period I had persuaded myself that morality so changes with the commands of God, that we can scarcely attach any idea of *immutability* to it. I am, moreover, ashamed to tell any one how I spoke and acted against my own common sense under this influence, and when I was thought a fool, prayed that I might think it an honour to become a fool for Christ's sake. Against no doctrine did I dare to bring moral objections, except that of "Reprobation." To Election, to Preventing Grace, to the Fall and Original Sin of man, to the Atonement, to Eternal Punishment, I reverently submitted my understanding; though as to the last, new inquiries had just at this crisis been opening on me. Reprobation, indeed, I always repudiated with great vigour, of which I shall presently speak. That was the full amount of my original thought; and in it I preserved entire reverence for the sacred writers.

As to miracles, scarcely anything staggered me. I received the strangest and the meanest prodigies of Scripture, with the same unhesitating faith, as if I had never understood a proposition of physical philosophy, nor a chapter of Hume and Gibbon.

CHAPTER III.

CALVINISM ABANDONED.

AFTER the excitement was past, I learned many things from the events which have been named.

First, I had found that the class of Christians with whom I had been joined had exploded the old Creeds in favour of another of their own, which was never given me upon authority, and yet was constantly slipping out, in the words, *Jesus is Jehovah*. It appeared to me certain that this would have been denounced as the Sabellian heresy by Athanasius and his contemporaries. I did not wish to run down Sabellians, much less to excommunicate them, if they would give me equality; but I felt it intensely unjust, when my adherence to the Nicene Creed was my real offence, that I should be treated as setting up some novel wickedness against all Christendom, and slandered by vague imputations which reached far and far beyond my power of answering or explaining. Mysterious aspersions were made even against my moral* character, and were alleged to me as additional reasons

---

* I afterwards learned that some of those gentlemen esteemed boldness of thought "a lust of the mind," and as such, an immorality. This enables them to persuade themselves that they do not reject a "heretic" for a matter of *opinion*, but for that which they have a right to call *immoral*. What immorality was imputed to me, I was not distinctly informed.

for refusing communion with me; and when I demanded a tribunal, and that my accuser would meet me face to face, all inquiry was refused, on the plea that it was needless and undesirable. I had much reason to believe that a very small number of persons had constituted themselves my judges, and used against me all the airs of the Universal Church; the many lending themselves easily to swell the cry of heresy, when they have little personal acquaintance with the party attacked. Moreover, when I was being condemned as in error, I in vain asked to be told what was the truth. "I accept the Scripture: that is not enough. I accept the Nicene Creed: that is not enough. Give me then your formula: where, what is it?" But no! those who thought it their duty to condemn me, disclaimed the pretensions of "making a Creed" when I asked for one. They reprobated my interpretation of Scripture as against that of the whole Church, but would not undertake to expound that of the Church. I felt convinced, that they could not have agreed themselves as to what was right: all that they could agree upon was, that I was wrong. Could I have borne to recriminate, I believed that I could have forced one of them to condemn another; but, oh! was divine truth sent us for discord and for condemnation? I sickened at the idea of a Church Tribunal, where none has any authority to judge, and yet to my extreme embarrassment I saw that no Church can safely dispense with judicial forms and other worldly apparatus for defending the reputation of individuals. At least none of the national and less spiritual institutions would have been so very unequitable towards me.

This idea enlarged itself into another,—*that spirituality is no adequate security for sound moral discernment.* These alienated friends did not know they were acting unjustly, cruelly, crookedly, or they would have hated themselves for it: they thought they were doing God service. The fervour of their love towards him was probably greater than mine; yet this did not make them superior to prejudice, or sharpen their logical faculties to see that they were idolizing words to which they attached no ideas. On several occasions I had distinctly perceived how serious alarm I gave by resolutely refusing to admit any shiftings and shufflings of language. I felt convinced, that if I would but have contradicted myself two or three times, and then have added, "That is the mystery of it," I could have passed as orthodox with many. I had been charged with a proud and vain determination to pry into divine mysteries, barely because I would not confess to propositions the meaning of which was to me doubtful,—or say and unsay in consecutive breaths. It was too clear, that a doctrine which muddles the understanding perverts also the power of moral discernment. If I had committed some flagrant sin, they would have given me a fair and honourable trial; but where they could not give me a public hearing, nor yet leave me unimpeached, without danger of (what they called) my infecting the Church, there was nothing left but to hunt me out unscrupulously.

Unscrupulously! did not this one word characterize *all* religious persecution? and then my mind wandered back over the whole melancholy tale of what is called Christian history. When Archbishop Cranmer overpowered the reluctance of young Edward VI. to burn to death the pious and innocent Joan of Kent, who moreover was as mystical and illogical as heart could wish, was Cranmer not actuated by deep religious convictions? None question his piety, yet it was an awfully wicked deed. What shall I say of Calvin, who burned Servetus? Why have I been so slow to learn, that religion is an impulse which animates us to execute our moral judgments, but an impulse which may be half blind? These brethren believe that I may cause the eternal ruin of others: how hard then is it for them to abide faithfully by the laws of morality and respect my rights! My rights! They are of course trampled down for the public good, just as a house is blown up to stop a conflagration. Such is evidently the theory of all persecution;—which is essentially founded on *Hatred*. As Aristotle says, "He who is angry, desires to punish somebody; but he who hates, desires the hated person not even to exist." Hence they cannot endure to see me face to face. That I may not infect the rest, they desire my non-existence; by fair means, if fair will succeed; if not, then by foul. And whence comes this monstrosity into such bosoms? Weakness of common sense, dread of the common understanding, an insufficient faith in common morality, are surely the disease: and e idently, nothing so exasperates this disease as consecrating religious tenets which forbid the exercise of common sense.

I now began to understand why it was peculiarly for unintelligible doctrines like Transubstantiation and the Tri-unity, that Christians had committed such execrable wickednesses. Now also for the first time I understood what had seemed not frightful only, but preternatural,—the sensualities and cruelties enacted as a part of religion in many of the old Paganisms. Religion and fanaticism are in the embryo but one and the same; to purify and elevate them we want a cultivation of the understanding, without which our moral code may be indefinitely depraved. Natural kindness and strong sense are aids and guides, which the most spiritual man cannot afford to despise.

I became conscious that I *had* despised "mere moral men," as they were called in the phraseology of my school. They were merged in the vague appellation of "the world," with sinners of every class; and it was habitually assumed, if not asserted, that they were necessarily Pharisaic, because they had not been born again. For some time after I had misgivings as to my fairness of judgment towards them, I could not disentangle myself from great bewilderment concerning their state in the sight of God: for it was an essential part of my Calvinistic Creed, that (as one of the 39 Articles states it) the very good works of the unregenerate "undoubtedly have the nature of sin," as indeed the very nature with which they were born "deserveth God's wrath and damnation." I began to mourn over the unlovely conduct into which I had been betrayed by this creed, long before I could thoroughly get rid of the creed that justified it: and a considerable time had to elapse, ere my new perceptions shaped themselves distinctly into the propositions: "Morality is the end, Spirituality is the means: Religion is the handmaid to Morals: we must be spiritual, in order that we may be in the highest and truest sense moral." Then at last I saw, that the deficiency of "mere moral men" is, that their morality is apt to be too external or merely negative, and therefore incomplete: that the man who worships a fiend for a God may be in some sense spiritual, but his spirituality will be a devilish fanaticism, having nothing in it to admire or approve: that the moral man deserves approval or love for all the absolute good that he has attained, though there be a higher good to which he aspires not; and that the truly and rightly spiritual is he who aims at an indefinitely high moral excellence, of which GOD is the embodiment to his heart and soul. If the absolute excellence of morality be denied, there is nothing for spirituality to aspire after, and nothing in God to worship. Years before I saw this as clearly as here stated; the general train of thought was very wholesome, in giving me increased kindliness of judgment towards the common world of men, who do not show any religious development. It was pleasant to me to look on an ordinary face, and see it light up into a smile, and think with myself: "*there* is one heart that will judge of me by what I am, and not by a Procrustean dogma." Nor only so, but I saw that the saints, without the world, would make a very bad world of it; and that as ballast is wanted to a ship, so the common and rather low interests, and the homely principles, rules, and ways of feeling, keep the church from foundering by the intensity of her own gusts.

Some of the above thoughts took a still more definite shape, as follows. It is clear that A. B. and X. Y. would have behaved towards me more kindly, more justly, and more wisely, if they had consulted their excellent strong sense and amiable natures, instead of following (what they suppose to be) the commands of the word of God. They have misinterpreted that word: true: but this very thing shows, that one may go wrong by trusting one's power of interpreting the book, rather than trusting one's common sense to judge without the book. It startled me to find, that I had exactly alighted on the Romish objection to Protestants, that an infallible book is useless, unless we have an infallible interpreter. But it was not for some time, that, after twisting the subject in all directions to avoid it, I brought out the conclusion, that "to go against one's common sense in obedience to Scripture is a most hazardous proceeding:" for the "rule of Scripture" means to each of us nothing but his own fallible interpretation; and to sacrifice common sense to this, is to mutilate one side of our mind at the command of another side. In the Nicene age, the Bible was in people's hands, and the Spirit of God surely was not withheld: yet I had read, in one of the Councils an insane anathema was passed: "If any one call Jesus Godman, instead of God and man, let him be accursed." Surely want of common sense, and dread of natural reason, will be confessed by our highest orthodoxy to have been the distemper of that day.

In all this I still remained theoretically convinced, that the contents of the Scriptures, rightly interpreted, were supreme and perfect truth; indeed, I had for several years accustomed myself to speak and think as if the Bible were our sole source of all moral knowledge: nevertheless, there were practically limits, beyond which I did not, and could not, even attempt to blind my moral sentiment at the dictation of the Scripture; and this had peculiarly frightened (as I afterwards found) the first friend who welcomed me from abroad. I was unable to admit the doctrine of "reprobation," as apparently taught in the 9th chapter of Paul's Epistle to the Romans;—that "God hardens in wickedness whomever He pleases, in order that He may show his long-suffering" in putting off their condemnation to a future dreadful day: and *especially*, that to all objectors it is a sufficient confutation—"Nay, but O man, who art thou, that repliest against God?" I told my friend, that I worshipped in God three great attributes, all independent,—Power, Goodness, and Wisdom: that in order to worship Him acceptably, I must discern these *as* realities with my inmost heart, and not merely take them for granted on authority: but that the argument which was here pressed upon me was an effort to supersede the necessity of my discerning Goodness in God: it bade me simply to *infer* Goodness from Power,—that is to say, establish the doctrine, "Might makes Right;" according to which, I might unawares worship a devil. Nay, nothing so much distinguished the spiritual truth of Judaism and Christianity from abominable heathenism, as this very discernment of God's purity, justice, mercy, truth, goodness; while the Pagan worshipped mere power, and had no discernment of moral excellence; but laid down the principle, that cruelty, impurity, or caprice in a God was to be treated reverentially, and called by some more decorous name. Hence, I said, it was undermining the very foundation of Christianity itself, to require belief of the validity of Rom. ix. 14—24, as my friend understood it. I acknowledged the difficulty of the passage, and of the whole argument. I was not prepared with an interpretation; but I revered St. Paul too much, to believe it possible that he could mean anything so obviously heathenish, as that first-sight meaning.—My friend looked grave and anxious; but I did not suspect how deeply I had shocked him, until many weeks after.

At this very time, moreover, ground was broken in my mind on a new subject, by opening in a gentleman's library a presentation-copy of a Unitarian treatise against the doctrine of Eternal Punishment. It was the first Unitarian book of which I had even seen the outside, and I handled it with a timid curiosity, as if by stealth. I had only time to dip into it here and there, and I should have been ashamed to possess the book; but I carried off enough to suggest important inquiry. The writer asserted that the Greek word αἰώνιος, (secular, or, belonging to the ages,) which we translate *everlasting and eternal*, is distinctly proved by the Greek translation of the Old Testament often to mean only *distant time*. Thus in Psalm lxxvi. 5, " I have considered the years of *ancient times*:" Isaiah lxiii. 11, " He remembered the days *of old*, Moses and his people;" in which, and in many similar places, the LXX have αἰώνιος. One striking passage is Exodus xv. 18; ("Jehovah shall reign for ever and ever;") where the Greek has τὸν αἰῶνα καὶ ἐπ' αἰῶνα καὶ ἔτι, which would mean " for eternity and still longer," if the strict rendering *eternity* were enforced. At the same time a suspicion as to the honesty of our translation presented itself in Micah v. 2, a controversial text, often used to prove the past eternity of the Son of God; where the translators give us,—" whose goings forth have been *from everlasting*," though the Hebrew is the same as they elsewhere render *from days of old*.

After I had at leisure searched through this new question, I found that it was impossible to make out any doctrine of a philosophical eternity in the whole Scriptures. The ordinary word for *eternal* (αἰώνιος), regarded as so very important in Matth. xxv. 46, is certainly used in Jude 6, of the fire which has been manifested against Sodom and Gomorrha. The last instance showed that allowance must be made for rhetoric; and that fire is called *eternal* or *unquenchable*, when it so destroys as to leave nothing unburnt. But on the whole, the very vocabulary of the Greek and Hebrew denoted that the idea of absolute eternity was unformed. The *hills* are called everlasting (secular?), by those who supposed them to have come into existence two or three thousand years before. —Only in two passages of the Revelations I could not get over the belief that the writer's energy was misplaced, if absolute eternity of torment was not intended: yet it seemed to me unsafe and wrong to found an important doctrine on a symbolic and confessedly obscure book of prophecy. Setting this aside, I found no proof of any *eternal* punishment.

As soon as the load of Scriptural authority was thus taken off from me, I had a vivid discernment of intolerable moral difficulties inseparable from the doctrine. First, that every sin is infinite in ill-desert and in result, *because* it is committed against an infinite Being. Thus the fretfulness of a child is an infinite evil! I was aghast that I could have believed it. Now that it was no longer laid upon me as a duty to uphold the infinitude of God's retaliation on sin, I saw that it was an immorality to teach that sin was measured by anything else than the heart and will of the agent. That a finite being should deserve infinite punishment, now was manifestly as incredible as that he should deserve infinite reward,—which I had never dreamed.—Again, I saw that the current orthodoxy made Satan eternal conqueror over Christ. In vain does the Son of God come from heaven and take human flesh and die on the cross. In spite of him, the devil carries off to hell the vast majority of mankind, in whom, not misery only, but *Sin* is triumphant for ever and ever. Thus Christ not only does not succeed in destroying the works of the devil, but even aggravates them.—Again: what sort of *gospel* or glad tidings had I been holding? Without this revelation no future state at all (I presumed) could be known. How much better no futurity for any, than that a few should be eternally in bliss, and the great majority* kept alive for eternal sin as well as eternal misery! My gospel then was bad tidings, nay, the worst of tidings! In a farther progress of thought, I asked, would it not have been better that the whole race of man had never come into existence? Clearly! And thus God was made out to be unwise in creating them. No *use* in the punishment was imaginable, without setting up Fear, instead of Love, as the ruling principle in the blessed. And what was the moral tendency of the doctrine? I had never borne to dwell upon it: but I before long suspected that it promoted malignity and selfishness, and was the real clue to the cruelties perpetrated under the name of religion. For he who does dwell on it, must comfort himself under the prospect of his brethren's eternal misery, by the selfish expectation of personal blessedness. When I asked whether I had been guilty of this selfishness, I remembered that I had often mourned, how small a part in my practical religion the future had ever borne. My heaven and my hell had been in the present, where my God was near me to smile or to frown. It had seemed to me a great weakness in my faith, that I never had any vivid imaginations or strong desires of heavenly glory:

---

* I really thought it needless to quote proof that but *few* will be saved, Matth. vii. 14. I know there is a class of Christians who believe in Universal salvation, and there are others who disbelieve eternal torment. They must not be angry with me for refuting the doctrine of other Christians, which they hold to be false.

ABANDONED.

yet now I was glad to observe, that it had at least saved me from getting so much harm from the wrong side of the doctrine of a future life.

Before I had worked out the objections so fully as here stated, I freely disclosed my thoughts to the friend last named, and to his wife, towards whom he encouraged me to exercise the fullest frankness. I confess, I said nothing about the Unitarian book; for something told me that I had violated Evangelical decorum in opening it, and that I could not calculate how it would affect my friend. Certainly no Romish hierarchy can so successfully exclude heretical books, as social enactment excludes those of Unitarians from our orthodox circles. The bookseller dares not to exhibit their books on his counter: all presume them to be pestilential: no one knows their contents or dares to inform himself. But to return. My friend's wife entered warmly into my new views; I have now no doubt that this exceedingly distressed him, and at length perverted his moral judgment: he himself examined the texts of the Old Testament, and attempted no answer to them. After I had left his neighbourhood, I wrote to him three affectionate letters, and at last got a reply—of vehement accusation. It can now concern no one to know, how many and deep wounds he planted in me. I forgave; but all was too instructive to forget.

For some years I rested in the belief that the epithet "*secular* punishment" either solely denoted punishment in a future age, or else only of long duration. This evades the horrible idea of eternal and triumphant Sin, and of infinite retaliation for finite offences. But still, I found my new creed uneasy, now that I had established a practice (if not a right) of considering the moral propriety of punishment. I could not so pare away the vehement words of the Scripture, as really to enable me to say that I thought transgressors *deserved* the fiery infliction. This had been easy, while I measured their guilt by God's greatness; but when that idea was renounced, how was I to think that a good-humoured voluptuary deserved to be raised from the dead in order to be tormented in fire for 100 years? and what shorter time could be called secular? Or if he was to be destroyed instantaneously, and "secular" meant only "in a future age," was he worth the effort of a divine miracle to bring him to life and again annihilate him? I was not willing to refuse belief to the Scripture on such grounds; yet I felt disquietude, that my moral sentiment and the Scripture were no longer in full harmony.

In this period I first discerned the extreme difficulty that there must essentially be, in applying to the Christian Evidences a principle, which, many years before, I had abstractedly received as sound, though it had been a dead letter with me in practice. The Bible (it seemed) contained two sorts of truth. Concerning one sort, man is bound to judge: the other sort is necessarily beyond his ken, and is received only by information from without. The first part of the statement cannot be denied. It would be monstrous to say that we know nothing of geography, history, or morals, except by learning them from the Bible. Geography, history, and other worldly sciences, lie beyond question. As to morals, I had been exceedingly inconsistent and wavering in my theory and in its application; but it now glared upon me, that if man had no independent power of judging, it would have been venial to think Barabbas more virtuous than Jesus. The hearers of Christ or Paul could not draw their knowledge of right and wrong from the New Testament. They had (or needed to have) an inherent power of discerning that his conduct was holy and his doctrine good. To talk about the infirmity or depravity of the human conscience is here quite irrelevant. The conscience of Christ's hearers may have been dim or twisted, but it was their best guide and only guide, as to the question, whether to regard him as a holy prophet: so likewise, as to ourselves, it is evident that we have no guide at all whether to accept or reject the Bible, if we distrust that inward power of judging, (whether called common sense, conscience, or the Spirit of God,)—which is independent of our belief in the Bible. To disparage the internally vouchsafed power of discerning truth without the Bible or other authoritative system, is, to endeavour to set up a universal moral scepticism. He who may not criticize cannot approve.— Well! Let it be admitted that we discern moral truth by a something within us, and that then, admiring the truth so glorious in the Scriptures, we are farther led to receive them as the word of God, and therefore to believe them absolutely in respect to the matters which are beyond our ken.

But two difficulties could no longer be dissembled: 1. How are we to draw the line of separation? For instance, would the doctrines of Reprobation and of lasting Fiery Torture with no benefit to the sufferers, belong to the moral part, which we freely criticize; or to the extra-moral part, as to which we passively believe? 2. What is to be done, if in the parts which indisputably lie open to criticism we meet with apparent error?—The second question soon became a practical one with me: but for the reader's convenience I defer it until my Fourth Period, to which it more naturally belongs: for in this Third Period I was principally exercised with controversies that do not vitally touch the *authority* of the Scripture. Of these the most important were matters contested between Unitarians and Calvinists.

When I had found how exactly the Nicene Creed summed up all that I myself gathered from John and Paul concerning the divine nature of Christ, I naturally referred to this creed, as expressing my convictions, when any unpleasant inquiry arose. I had recently gained the acquaintance of the late excellent Dr. Olinthus Gregory, a man of unimpeached orthodoxy; who met me by the frank avowal, that the Nicene Creed was "a great mistake." He said, that the Arian and the Athanasian difference was not very vital; and that the Scriptural truth lay *beyond* the Nicene doctrine, which fell short on the same side as Arianism had done. On the contrary, I had learned of an intermediate tenet, called Semi-Arianism, which appeared to me more scriptural than the views of either Athanasius or Arius. Let me bespeak my reader's patience for a little. Arius was judged by Athanasius (I was informed) to be erroneous in two points; 1. in teaching that the Son of God was a creature; *i. e.* that "begotten" and "made" were two words for the same idea: 2. in teaching, that he had an origin of existence in time; so that there was a distant period at which he was not. Of these two Arian tenets, the Nicene Creed condemned *the former* only; namely, in the words, "begotten, not made; being of one substance with the Father." But on *the latter* question the Creed is silent. Those who accepted the Creed, and hereby condemned the great error of Arius that the Son was of different substance from the Father, but nevertheless agreed with Arius in thinking that the Son had a beginning of existence, were called Semi-Arians; and were received into communion by Athanasius, in spite of this disagreement. To me it seemed to be a most unworthy shuffling with words, to say that the Son *was begotten, but was never begotten.* The very form of our past participle is invented to indicate an event in past time. If the Athanasians alleged that the phrase does not allude to "a coming forth" completed at a definite time, but indicates a process at no time begun and at no time complete, their doctrine could not be expressed by our past-perfect tense *begotten.* When they compared the derivation of the Son of God from the Father to the rays of light which ever flow from the natural sun, and argued that if that sun had been eternal, its emanations would be co-eternal, they showed that their true doctrine required the formula—"always being begotten, and as instantly perishing, in order to be rebegotten perpetually." They showed a real disbelief in our English statement "begotten, not made." I overruled the objection, that in the Greek it was not a participle, but a verbal adjective; for it was manifest to me, that a religion which could not be proclaimed in English could not be true; and the very idea of a Creed announcing that Christ was "*not begotten, yet begettive,*" roused in me an unspeakable loathing. Yet surely this would have been Athanasius's most legitimate form of denying Semi-Arianism. In short, the Scriptural phrase, *Son of God,* conveyed to us either a literal fact, or a metaphor. If literal, the Semi-Arians were clearly right, in saying that sonship implied a beginning of existence. If it was a metaphor, the Athanasians forfeited all right to press the literal sense in proof that the Son must be "of the same substance" as the Father.—Seeing that the Athanasians, in zeal to magnify the Son, had so confounded their good sense, I was certainly startled to find a man of Dr. Olinthus Gregory's moral wisdom treat the Nicenists as in obvious error for not having magnified Christ *enough.* On so many other sides, however, I met with the new and short creed, "Jesus is Jehovah," that I began to discern Sabellianism to be the prevalent view.

A little later, I fell in with a book of an American Professor, Moses Stuart of Andover, on the subject of the Trinity. Professor Stuart is a very learned man, and thinks for himself. It was a great novelty to me, to find him not only deny the orthodoxy of all the Fathers, (which was little more than Dr. Olinthus Gregory had done,) but avow that *from the change in speculative philosophy* it was simply impossible for any modern to hold the views prevalent in the third and fourth centuries. Nothing (said he) was clearer, than that with us the essential point in Deity is, to be unoriginated, underived; hence with us, *a derived God* is a self-contradiction, and the very sound of the phrase profane. On the other hand, it is certain that the doctrine of Athanasius, equally as of Arius, was, that the Father is the underived or self-existent God, but the Son is the derived subordinate God. This (argued Stuart) turned upon their belief in the doctrine of Emanations; but as *we* hold no such philosophical doctrine, the religious theory founded on it is necessarily inadmissible. Professor Stuart then develops his own creed, which appeared to me simple and undeniable Sabellianism.

That Stuart correctly represented the Fathers was clear enough to me; but I nevertheless thought that in this respect the Fathers had honestly made out the doctrine of the Scripture; and I did not at all approve of setting up a battery of modern speculative philosophy against Scriptural doctrine. "How are we to know that the doctrine of Emanations is false? (asked I.) If it is legitimately elicited from Scripture, it is true."—I refused to yield up my creed at this summons. Nevertheless, he left a wound upon me: for I now could not help seeing, that we moderns use the word *God* in a more limited sense than any ancient nations did. Hebrews and Greeks alike said *Gods*, to mean any superhuman beings; hence *derived God* did not sound to them absurd: but I could not deny that in good English it is absurd. This was a very disagreeable discovery: for now, if any one were to ask me whether I believed in the divinity of Christ, I saw it would be dishonest to say simply, *Yes;* for the interrogator means to ask, whether I hold Christ to be the eternal and underived Source of life: yet if I said *No*, he would care nothing for my professing to hold the Nicene Creed.

Might not then, after all, Sabellianism be the truth? No: I discerned too plainly what Gibbon states, that the Sabellian, if consistent, is only a concealed Ebionite, or as we now say, a Unitarian, Socinian. As we cannot admit that the Father was slain on the cross, or prayed to himself in the garden, he who will not allow the Father and the Son to be separate persons, but only two names for one person, *must divide the Son of God and Jesus into two persons*, and so fall back on the very heresy of Socinus which he is struggling to escape.

On the whole, I saw, that however people might call themselves Trinitarians, yet if, like Stuart and all the Evangelicals in Church and Dissent, they turn into a dead letter the *generation* of the Son of God, and *the procession* of the Spirit, nothing is possible but Sabellianism or Tritheism: or, indeed, Ditheism, if the Spirit's separate personality is not held. The modern creed is alternately the one or the other, as occasion requires. Sabellians would find themselves out to be mere Unitarians, if they always remained Sabellians: but in fact, they are half their lives Ditheists. They do not *aim* at consistency; would an upholder of the pseudo-Athanasian creed desire it? Why, that creed teaches, that the height of orthodoxy is to contradict oneself and protest that one does not. Now, however, rose on me the question: Why do I not take the Irish clergyman at his word, and attack him and others as idolaters and worshippers of three Gods? It was unseemly and absurd in him to try to force me into what he must have judged uncharitableness; but it was not the less incumbent on me to find a reply.

I remembered that in past years I had expressly disowned, as obviously unscriptural and absurd, prayers to the Holy Spirit, on the ground that the Spirit is evidently *God in the hearts of the faithful*, and nothing else: and it did not appear to me that any but a few extreme and rather fanatical persons could be charged with making the Spirit a third God or object of distinct worship. On the other hand, I could not deny that the Son and the Father were thus distinguished to the mind. So indeed John expressly avowed—" truly our fellowship is with the Father, and with his Son Jesus Christ." I myself also had prayed sometimes to God and sometimes to Christ, alternately and confusedly. Now, indeed, I was better taught! now I was more logical and consistent! I had found a triumphant answer to the charge of Ditheism, in that I believed the Son to be derived from the Father, and not to be the Unoriginated.—No doubt! yet, after all, could I seriously think that morally and spiritually I was either better or worse for this discovery? I could not pretend that I was.

This showed me, that if a man of partially unsound and visionary mind made the angel Gabriel a *fourth person* in the Godhead, it might cause no difference whatever in the actings of his spirit. The great question would be, whether he ascribed the same moral perfection to Gabriel as to the Father. If so, to worship him would be no degradation to the soul;

even if absolute omnipotence were not attributed, nay, nor a past eternal existence. It thus became clear to me, that Polytheism *as such* is not a moral and spiritual, but at most only an intellectual, error; and that its practical evil consists in worshipping beings whom we represent to our imaginations as morally imperfect. Conversely, one who imputes to God sentiments and conduct which in man he would call capricious or cruel, such a one, even if he be as monotheistic as a Mussulman, admits into his soul the whole virus of Idolatry.

Why then did I at all cling to the doctrine of Christ's superior nature, and not admit it among things indifferent? In obedience to the Scripture, I did actually affirm, that, as far as creed is concerned, a man should be admissible into the Church on the bare confession that *Jesus was the Christ*. Still, I regarded a belief in his superhuman origin as of first-rate importance, for many reasons, and among others, owing to its connexion with the doctrine of the Atonement; on which there is much to be said.

The doctrine which I used to read as a boy, taught that a vast sum of punishment was due to God for the sins of men. This vast sum was made up of all the woes due through eternity to the whole human race, or, as some said, to the elect. Christ on the cross bore this punishment himself, and thereby took it away: thus God is enabled to forgive without violating justice.—But I early encountered unanswerable difficulty on this theory, as to the question, whether Christ had borne the punishment of *all* or of *some* only. If of all, is it not unjust to inflict any of it on any? If of the elect only, what gospel have you to preach? for then you cannot tell sinners that God has provided a Saviour for them; for you do not know whether those whom you address are elect. Finding no way out of this, I abandoned the fundamental idea of *compensation in quantity*, as untenable; and rested in the vaguer notion, that God signally showed his abhorrence of sin, by laying tremendous misery on the Saviour who was to bear away sin.

I have already narrated, how at Oxford I was embarrassed as to the forensic propriety of transferring punishment at all. This however I received as matter of authority, and rested much on the wonderful exhibition made of the evil of sin, when *such* a being could be subjected to preternatural suffering as a vicarious sinbearer. To this view, a high sense of the personal dignity of Jesus was quite essential; and therefore I had always felt a great repugnance for Mr. Belsham, Dr. Priestley, and the Unitarians of that school, though I had not read a line of their writings.

A more intimate familiarity with St. Paul and an anxious harmonizing of my very words to the Scripture, led me on into a deviation from the popular creed, of the full importance of which I was not for some time aware. I perceived that it is not the *agonies* of mind or body endured by Christ, which in the Scriptures are said to take away sin, but his "death," his "laying down his life," or sometimes even his *resurrection*. I gradually became convinced, that when his "suffering," or more especially his "blood," is emphatically spoken of, nothing is meant but his *violent death*. In the Epistle to the Hebrews, where the analogy of Sacrifice is so pressed, we see that the pains which Jesus bore were in order that he might "learn obedience ;" but our redemption is effected by his dying as a voluntary victim : in which, death by bloodshed, not pain, is the cardinal point. So too the Paschal lamb (to which, though not properly a sacrifice, the dying Christ is compared by Paul) was not roasted alive, or otherwise put to slow torment, but was simply killed. I therefore saw that the doctrine of " vicarious agonies" was fundamentally unscriptural.

This being fully discerned, I at last became bold to criticize the popular tenet. What should we think of a judge, who, when a boy had deserved a stripe which would to him have been a sharp punishment, laid the very same blow on a strong man, to whom it was a slight infliction ? Clearly this would evade, not satisfy justice. To carry out the principle, the blow might be laid as well on a giant, an elephant, or on an inanimate thing. So, to lay our punishment on the infinite strength of Christ, who (they say) bore in six hours what it would have taken thousands of millions of men all eternity to bear, would be a similar evasion.—I farther asked, if we were to fall in with Pagans, who tortured their victims to death as an atonement, what idea of God should we think them to form ? and what should we reply, if they said, it gave them a wholesome view of his hatred of sin ? A second time I shuddered at the notions which I had once imbibed as a part of religion , and then got comfort from the inference, how much better men of this century are than their creed. Their creed was the product of ages of cruelty and credulity; and it sufficiently bears that stamp.

Thus I rested in the Scriptural doctrine, that the *death* of Christ is our atonement. To say the same of the death of Paul, was obviously unscriptural: it was, then, essential to believe the physical nature of Christ to be different from that of Paul. If otherwise, death was due to Jesus as the lot of nature: how could such death have anything to do with our salvation? On this ground the Unitarian doctrine was utterly untenable: I could see nothing between my own view and a total renunciation of the *authority of the doctrines* promulgated by Paul and John.

Nevertheless, my own view seemed more and more unmeaning the more closely it was interrogated. When I ascribed death to Christ, what did death mean? and what or whom did I suppose to die? Was it man that died, or God? If man only, how was that wonderful, or how did it concern us? Besides;—persons die, not natures: a *nature* is only a collection of properties: if Christ was one person, all Christ died. Did, then, God die, and man remain alive! For God to become non-existent is an unimaginable absurdity. But is this death a mere change of state, a renunciation of earthly life? Still it remains unclear how the parting with mere human life could be to one who possesses divine life either an atonement or a humiliation. Was it not rather an escape from humiliation, saving only the mode of death? So severe was this difficulty, that at length I unawares dropt from Semi-Arianism into pure Arianism, by *so* distinguishing the Son from the Father, as to admit the idea that the Son of God had actually been non-existent in the interval between death and resurrection: nevertheless, I more and more felt, that *to be able to define my own notions on such questions had exceedingly little to do with my spiritual state.* For me it was important and essential to know that God hated sin, and that God had forgiven my sin: but to know one particular manifestation of his hatred of sin, or the machinery by which He had enabled himself to forgive, was of very secondary importance. When He proclaims to me in his word, that He is forgiving to all the penitent, it is not for me to reply, that " I cannot believe that, until I hear how He manages to reconcile such conduct with his other attributes." Yet, I remembered, this was Bishop Beveridge's sufficient refutation of Mohammedism, which teaches no atonement.

At the same time great progress had been made in my mind towards the overthrow of the correlative dogma of the Fall of man and his total corruption. Probably for years I had been unawares anti-Calvinistic on this topic. Even at Oxford, I had held that human depravity is a *fact*, which it is absurd to argue against; a fact, attested by Thucydides, Polybius, Horace, and Tacitus, almost as strongly as by St. Paul. Yet in admitting man's total corruption, I interpreted this of *spiritual*, not of *moral*, perversion: for that there were kindly and amiable qualities even in the unregenerate, was quite as clear a fact as any other. Hence in result I did *not* attribute to man any great essential depravity, in the popular and moral sense of the word; and the doctrine amounted only to this, that "*spiritually*, man is paralyzed, until the grace of God comes freely upon him." How to reconcile this with the condemnation and punishment of man for being unspiritual, I knew not. I saw, and did not dissemble, the difficulty; but received it as a mystery hereafter to be cleared up.

But it gradually broke upon me, that when Paul said nothing stronger than heathen moralists had said about human wickedness, it was absurd to quote his words, any more than theirs, in proof of a *Fall*,—that is, of a permanent degeneracy induced by the first sin of the first man: and when I studied the 5th chapter of the Romans, I found it was *death*, not *corruption*, which Adam was said to have entailed. In short, I could scarcely find the modern doctrine of the "Fall" any where in the Bible. I then remembered that Calvin, in his Institutes, complains that all the Fathers are heterodox on this point; the Greek Fathers being grievously overweening in their estimate of human power; while of the Latin Fathers even Augustine is not always up to Calvin's mark of orthodoxy. This confirmed my rising conviction that the tenet is of rather recent origin. I afterwards heard, that both it and the doctrine of compensatory misery were first systematized by Archbishop Anselm, in the reign of our William Rufus: but I never took the pains to verify this.

For meanwhile I had been forcibly impressed with the following thought. Suppose a youth to have been carefully brought up at home, and every temptation kept out of his way: suppose him to have been in appearance virtuous, amiable, religious: suppose, farther, that at the age of twenty-one he goes out into the world, and falls into sin by the first temptation:—how will a Calvinistic teacher moralize over such a youth? Will he not say: "Behold a proof of the essential depravity of human nature! See the affinity of man for sin! How fair and deceptive was this young man's virtue, while he was sheltered from temptation; but oh! how rotten has it proved itself!"—Undoubtedly, the Calvinist would and must so moralize. But it struck me, that if I substituted the name of *Adam* for the youth, the argument proved the primitive corruption of Adam's nature. Adam fell by the first temptation: what greater proof of a fallen nature have *I* ever given? or what is it possible for any one to give?—I thus discerned that there was à *priori* impossibility of fixing on myself the imputation of *degeneracy*, without fixing the same on Adam. In short, Adam undeniably proved his primitive nature to be frail; so do we all: but as *he* was nevertheless not primitively corrupt, why should we call ourselves so? Frailty, then, is not corruption, and does not prove degeneracy.

"Original sin" (says one of the 39 Articles) "standeth not in the following of Adam, *as the Pelagians do vainly talk*," &c. Alas, then! was I become a Pelagian? certainly I could no longer see that Adam's first sin affected me more than his second or third, or so much as the sins of my immediate parents. A father who, for instance, indulges in furious passions and exciting liquors, may (I suppose) transmit violent passions to his son. In this sense I could not wholly reject the possibility of transmitted corruption; but it had nothing to do with the theological doctrine of the "Federal Headship" of Adam. Not that I could wholly give up this last doctrine; for I still read it in the 5th chapter of Romans. But it was clear to me, that whatever that meant, I could not combine it with the idea of degeneracy, nor could I find a proof of it in the *fact* of prevalent wickedness. Thus I received a shadowy doctrine on mere Scriptural *authority;* it had no longer any root in my understanding or heart.

Moreover, it was manifest to me that the Calvinistic view is based in a vain attempt to acquit God of having created a "sinful" being, while the broad Scriptural fact is, that he did create a being as truly "liable to sin" as any of us. If that needs no exculpation, how more does *our* state need it? Does it not suffice to say, that " every creature, because he is a creature and not God, must necessarily be frail?" But Calvin intensely aggravates whatever there is of difficulty: for he supposes God to have created the most precious thing on earth in *unstable equilibrium*, so as to tipple over irrecoverably at the first infinitesimal touch, and with it wreck for ever the spiritual hopes of all Adam's posterity. Surely all nature proclaims, that if God planted any spiritual nature at all in man, it was in *stable equilibrium*, able to right itself when deranged.

Lastly, I saw that the Calvinistic doctrine of human degeneracy teaches, that God disowns my nature (the only nature I ever had) as not his work, but the devil's work. He hereby tells me that he is *not* my Creator, and he disclaims his right over me, as a father who disowns a child. To teach this is to teach that I owe him no obedience, no worship, no trust; to sever the cords that bind the creature to the Creator, and to make all religion gratuitous and vain.

Thus Calvinism was found by me not only not to be Evangelical, but not to be logical, in spite of its high logical pretensions, and to be irreconcilable with any intelligent theory of religion. Of "gloomy Calvinism" I had often heard people speak with an emphasis, that annoyed me as highly unjust; for mine had not been a gloomy religion:—far, very far from it. On the side of eternal punishment, its theory, no doubt, had been gloomy enough; but human nature has a notable art of not realizing all the articles of a creed; moreover, *this* doctrine is equally held by Arminians. But I was conscious, that in dropping Calvinism I had lost nothing *Evangelical:* on the contrary, the gospel which I retained was as spiritual and deep-hearted as before, only more merciful.

Before this Third Period of my creed was completed, I made my first acquaintance with a Unitarian. This gentleman showed much sweetness of mind, largeness of charity, and a timid devoutness which I had not expected in such a quarter. His mixture of credulity and incredulity seemed to me capricious, and wholly incoherent. First, as to his incredulity, or rather, boldness of thought. Eternal punishment was a notion, which nothing could make him believe, and for which it would be useless to quote Scripture to him; for the doctrine (he said) darkened the moral character of God, and produced malignity in man. That Christ had any higher nature than we all have, was a tenet essentially inadmissible; first, because it destroyed all moral benefit from his example and sympathy, and next, because no one has yet succeeded in even stating the doctrine of the Incarnation without contradicting himself. If Christ was but one person, one mind, then that one mind could not be simultaneously finite and infinite, nor therefore simultaneously God and man. But when I came to hear more from this same gentleman, I found him to avow that no Trinitarian could have a higher conception than he of the present power and glory of Christ. He believed that the man Jesus is at the head of the whole moral creation of God; that all power in heaven and earth is given to him: that he will be Judge of all men, and is himself raised above all judgment. This was to me unimaginable from his point of view. Could he really think Jesus to be a mere man, and yet believe him to be sinless? On what did that belief rest? Two texts were quoted in proof, 1 Pet. ii. 21, and Heb. iv. 15. Of these, the former did not necessarily mean anything more than that Jesus was unjustly put to death; and the latter belonged to an Epistle, which my new friend had already rejected as unapostolic and not of first-rate authority, when speaking of the Atonement. Indeed, that the Epistle to the Hebrews is not from the hand of Paul, had very long seemed to me an obvious certainty,—as long as I had had any delicate feeling of Greek style.

That a human child, born with the nature of other children, and having to learn wisdom and win virtue through the same process, should grow up sinless, appeared to me an event so paradoxical, as to need the most amply decisive proof. Yet what kind of proof was possible? Neither Apollos, (if he was the author of the Epistle to the Hebrews,) nor yet Peter, had any power of *attesting* the sinlessness of Jesus, as a fact known to themselves personally: they could only learn it by some preternatural communication, to which, nevertheless, the passages before us implied no pretension whatever. To me it appeared an axiom,* that if Jesus was in physical origin a mere man,

* In this (second) edition, I have added an entire chapter expressly on the subject.

he was, like myself, a sinful man, and therefore certainly not my Judge, certainly not an omniscient reader of all hearts; nor on any account to be bowed down to as Lord. To exercise hope, faith, trust in him, seemed then an impiety. I did not mean to impute impiety to Unitarians; still I distinctly believed that English Unitarianism could never afford me a half hour's resting-place.

Nevertheless, from contact with this excellent person I learned how much tenderness of spirit a Unitarian may have; and it pleasantly enlarged my charity, although I continued to feel much repugnance for his doctrine, and was anxious and constrained in the presence of Unitarians. From the same collision with him, I gained a fresh insight into a part of my own mind. I had always regarded the Gospels (at least the three first) to be to the Epistles nearly as Law to Gospel; that is, the three gospels dealt chiefly in *precept*, the epistles in *motives* which act on the affections. This did not appear to me dishonourable to the teaching of Christ; for I supposed it to be a pre-determined development. But I now discovered that there was a deeper distaste in me for the details of the human life of Christ, than I was previously conscious of—a distaste which I found out, by a reaction from the minute interest felt in such details by my new friend. For several years more, I did not fully understand how and why this was; viz. that *my religion had always been Pauline.* Christ was to me the ideal of glorified human nature: but I needed some dimness in the portrait to give play to my imagination: if drawn too sharply historical, it sank into something not superhuman, and caused a revulsion of feeling. As all paintings of the miraculous used to displease and even disgust me from a boy by the unbelief which they inspired; so if any one dwelt on the special proofs of tenderness and love exhibited in certain words or actions of Jesus, it was apt to call out in me a sense, that from day to day equal kindness might often be met. The imbecility of preachers, who would dwell on such words as "Weep not," as if nobody else ever uttered such,— had always annoyed me. I felt it impossible to obtain a worthy idea of Christ from studying any of the details reported concerning him. If I dwelt too much on these, I got a finite object; but I yearned for an infinite one: hence my preference for John's mysterious Jesus. Thus my Christ was not the figure accurately painted in the narrative, but one kindled in my imagination by the allusions and (as it were) poetry of the New Testament. I did not wish for vivid historical realization: relics I could never have valued: pilgrimages to Jerusalem had always excited in me more of scorn than of sympathy;—and I make no doubt such was fundamentally Paul's* feeling. On the contrary, it began to appear to me (and I believe not unjustly) that the Unitarian mind revelled peculiarly in "Christ after the flesh," whom Paul resolved not to know. Possibly in this circumstance will be found to lie the strong and the weak points of the Unitarian religious character, as contrasted with that of the Evangelical, far more truly than in the doctrine of the Atonement. I can testify that the Atonement may be dropt out of Pauline religion without affecting its quality; so may Christ be spiritualized into God, and identified with the Father: but I suspect that a Pauline faith could not, without much violence and convulsion, be changed into devout admiration of a clearly drawn historical character; as though any full and unsurpassable embodiment of God's moral perfections could be exhibited with ink and pen.

A reviewer, who has since made his name known, has pointed to the preceding remarks, as indicative of my deficiency in *imagination* and my tendency to *romance*. My dear friend is undoubtedly right in the former point; I am destitute of (creative) poetical imagination: and as to the latter point, his insight into character is so great, that I readily believe him to know me better than I know myself. Nevertheless, I think he has mistaken the nature of the preceding argument. I am, on the contrary, almost disposed to say, that those have a tendency to romance who can look at a picture with men flying into the air, or on an angel with a brass trumpet, and dead men rising out of their graves with good stout muscles, and *not* feel that the picture suggests unbelief. Nor do I confess to romance, in my desire of something *more* than historical and daily human nature in the character of Jesus; for all Christendom, between

---

* The same may probably be said of all the apostles, and their whole generation. If they had looked on the life of Jesus with the same tender and human affection as modern Unitarians and pious Romanists do, the church would have swarmed with *holy coats* and other relics in the very first age. The mother of Jesus and her little establishment would at once have swelled into importance. This certainly was not the case; which may make it doubtful whether the other apostles dwelt at all more on the *human personality* of Jesus than Paul did. Strikingly different as James is from Paul, he is in this respect perfectly agreed with him.

the dates A.D. 100 to A.D. 1850, with the exception of small eccentric coteries, has held Jesus to be essentially superhuman. Paul and John so taught concerning him. To believe their doctrine (I agree with my friend) is, in some sense, a weakness of understanding; but it is a weakness to which minds of every class have been for ages liable.

Such had been the progress of my mind, towards the end of what I will call my Third Period. In it the authority of the Scriptures as to some details (which at length became highly important) had begun to be questioned; of which I shall proceed to speak: but hitherto this was quite secondary to the momentous revolution which lay Calvinism prostrate in my mind, which opened my heart to Unitarians, and, I may say, to unbelievers; which enlarged all my sympathies, and soon set me to practise free moral thought, at least as a necessity, if not as a duty. Yet I held fast an unabated reverence for the moral and spiritual teaching of the New Testament, and had not the most remote conception that anything could ever shatter my belief in its great miracles. In fact, during this period, I many times yearned to proceed to India, whither my friend Groves had transferred his labours and his hopes; but I was thwarted by several causes, and was again and again damped by the fear of bigotry from new quarters. Otherwise, I thought I could succeed in merging as needless many controversies. In all the workings of my mind about Tri-unity, Incarnation, Atonement, the Fall, Resurrection, Immortality, Eternal Punishment, how little had any of these to do with the inward exercises of my soul towards God! He was still the same, immutably glorious: not one feature of his countenance had altered to my gaze, or could alter. This surely was the God whom Christ came to reveal, and bring us into fellowship with: this is that, about which Christians ought to have no controversy, but which they should unitedly, concordantly, themselves enjoy and exhibit to the heathen. But oh, Christendom! what dost thou believe and teach? The heathen cry out to thee,—Physician, heal thyself.

CHAPTER IV.

THE RELIGION OF THE LETTER RENOUNCED.

It has been stated that I had already begun to discern that it was impossible with perfect honesty to defend every tittle contained in the Bible. Most of the points which give moral offence in the book of Genesis I had been used to explain away by the doctrine of Progress; yet every now and then it became hard to deny that God is represented as giving an actual *sanction* to that which we now call sinful. Indeed, up and down the Scriptures very numerous texts are scattered, which are notorious difficulties with commentators. These I had habitually *overruled* one by one: but again of late, since I had been forced to act and talk less and think more, they began to encompass me. But I was for a while too full of other inquiries to follow up coherently any of my doubts or perceptions, until my mind became at length nailed down to the definite study of one well-known passage.

This passage may be judged of extremely secondary importance in itself, yet by its remoteness from all properly spiritual and profound questions, it seemed to afford to me the safest of arguments. The *genealogy* with which the gospel of Matthew opens, I had long known to be a stumbling-block to divines, and I had never been satisfied with their explanations. On reading it afresh, after long intermission, and comparing it for myself with the Old Testament, I was struck with observing that the corruption of the two names Ahaziah and Uzziah into the same sound (Oziah) has been the cause of merging four generations into one; as the similarity of Jehoiakim to Jehoiachin also led to blending them both in the name Jeconiah. In consequence, there ought to be 18 generations where Matthew has given us only 14: yet we cannot call this an error of a transcriber; for it is distinctly remarked, that the genealogy consists of 14 three times repeated. Thus there were but 14 names inserted by Matthew: yet it ought to have been 18: and he was under manifest mistake. This surely belongs to a class of knowledge, of which man has cognizance: it would not be piety, but grovelling superstition, to avow before God that I distrust my powers of counting, and, in obedience to the written word, I believe that 18 is 14 and 14 is 18. Thus it is impossible to deny, that there is cognizable error in the first chapter of Matthew. Consequently, that gospel is not all dictated by the Spirit of God, and (unless we can get rid of the first chapter as no part of the Bible) the doctrine of the verbal infallibility of the whole Bible, or indeed of the New Testament, is demonstrably false.

After I had turned the matter over often, and had become accustomed to the thought, this single instance at length had great force to give boldness to my mind within a very narrow range. I asked whether, if the chapter were now proved to be spurious, that would save the infallibility of the Bible. The reply was: not of the Bible as it is; but only of the Bible when cleared of that *and of all other* spurious additions. If by independent methods, such as an examination of manuscripts, the spuriousness of the chapter could now be shown, *this would verify the faculty of criticism* which has already objected to its contents: thus it would justly urge us to apply similar criticism to other passages.

I farther remembered, and now brought together under a single point of view, other undeniable mistakes. The genealogy of the nominal father of Jesus in Luke is inconsistent with that in Matthew, in spite of the flagrant dishonesty with which divines seek to deny this; and neither evangelist gives the genealogy of Mary, which alone is wanted.—In Acts vii. 16, the land which *Jacob* bought of the children of Hamor,* is confounded with that which *Abraham* bought of Ephron the Hittite. In Acts v. 36, 37, Gamaliel is made to say that Theudas was earlier in time than Judas of Galilee. Yet in fact, Judas of Galilee preceded Theudas: and the revolt of Theudas had not yet taken place when Gamaliel spoke, so the error is not Gamaliel's, but Luke's. Of both the insurgents we have a clear and unimpeached historical account in Josephus.—The slaughter of the infants by Herod, if true, must, I thought, needs have been recorded by the same historian.—So again, in regard to the allusion made by Jesus to Zacharias, son of Barachias, as *last of the martyrs*, it was difficult for me to shake off the suspicion, that a gross error had been committed, and that the person intended is the "Zacharias son of Baruchus," who, as we know from Josephus, was martyred *within the courts of the temple* during the siege of Jerusalem by Titus, about 40 years after the crucifixion. The

* See Gen. xxxiii. 19, and xlix. 29 32, xxiii.

well-known prophet Zechariah was indeed son of Berechiah ; but he was not last of the martyrs,* if indeed he was martyred at all. On the whole, the persuasion stuck to me, that words had been put into the mouth of Jesus, which he could not possibly have used.—The impossibility of settling the names of the twelve apostles struck me as a notable fact.—I farther remembered the numerous difficulties of harmonizing the four gospels; how, when a boy at school, I had tried to incorporate all four into one history, and the dismay with which I had found the insoluble character of the problem,—the endless discrepancies and perpetual uncertainties. These now began to seem to me inherent in the materials, and not to be ascribable to our want of intelligence.

I had also discerned in the opening of Genesis things which could not be literally received. The geography of the rivers in Paradise is inexplicable, though it assumes the tone of explanation. The curse on the serpent, who is to go on his belly—(how else did he go before?)—and eat dust, is a capricious punishment on a race of brutes, one of whom the Devil chose to use as his instrument. That the painfulness of childbirth is caused, not by Eve's sin, but by artificial habits and a weakened nervous system, seems to be proved by the twofold fact, that savage women and wild animals suffer but little, and tame cattle often suffer as much as human females. —About this time also, I had perceived (what I afterwards learned the Germans to have more fully investigated) that the two different accounts of the Creation are distinguished by the appellations given to the divine Creator. I did not see how to resist the inference that the book is made up of heterogeneous documents, and was not put forth by the direct dictation of the Spirit to Moses.

A new stimulus was after this given to my mind by two short conversations with the late excellent Dr. Arnold at Rugby. I had become aware of the difficulties encountered by physiologists in believing the whole human race to have proceeded in about 6000 years from a single Adam and Eve; and that the longevity (not miraculous, but ordinary) attributed to the patriarchs was another stumbling-block. The geological difficulties of the Mosaic cosmogony were also at

* Some say, that Zechariah, son of Jehoaida, named in the Chronicles, is meant ; that he is *confounded* with the prophet, the son of Berechiah, and was *supposed* to be the last of the martyrs, because the Chronicles are placed last in the Hebrew Bible. This is a plausible view; but it saves the Scripture only by imputing error to Jesus.

that time exciting attention. It was a novelty to me, that Arnold treated these questions as matters of indifference to religion; and did not hesitate to say, that the account of Noah's deluge was evidently mythical, and the history of Joseph "a beautiful poem." I was staggered at this. If all were not descended from Adam, what became of St. Paul's parallel between the first and second Adam, and the doctrine of Headship and Atonement founded on it? If the world was not made in six days, how could we defend the Fourth Commandment as true, though said to have been written in stone by the very finger of God? If Noah's deluge was a legend, we should at least have to admit that Peter did not know this: what too would be said of Christ's allusion to it? I was unable to admit Dr. Arnold's views; but to see a vigorous mind, deeply imbued with Christian devoutness, so convinced, both reassured me that I need not fear moral mischiefs from free inquiry, and indeed laid that inquiry upon me as a duty.

Here, however, was a new point started. Does the question of the derivation of the human race from two parents belong to things cognizable by the human intellect, or to things about which we must learn submissively? Plainly to the former. It would be monstrous to deny that such inquiries legitimately belong to physiology, or to proscribe a free study of this science. If so, there was an *à priori* possibility, that what is in the strictest sense called "religious doctrine" might come into direct collision, not merely with my ill-trained conscience, but with legitimate science; and that this would call on me to ask: "Which of the two certainties is stronger? that the religious parts of the Scripture are infallible, or that the science is trustworthy?" and I then first saw, that while science had (within however limited a range of thought) demonstration or severe verifications, it was impossible to pretend to anything so cogent in favour of the infallibility of any or some part of the Scriptures; a doctrine which I was accustomed to believe, and felt to be a legitimate presumption; yet one of which it grew harder and harder to assign any proof, the more closely I analyzed it. Nevertheless, I still held it fast, and resolved not to let it go until I was forced.

A fresh strain fell on the Scriptural infallibility, in contemplating the origin of Death. Geologists assured us, that death went on in the animal creation many ages before the existence of man. The rocks formed of the shells of animals testify that death is a phenomenon thousands of thousand years old: to refer the death of animals to the sin of Adam and Eve is evidently impossible. Yet, if not, the analogies of the human to the brute form make it scarcely credible that man's body can ever have been intended for immortality. Nay, when we consider the conditions of birth and growth to which it is subject, the wear and tear essential to life, the new generations intended to succeed and supplant the old,—so soon as the question is proposed as one of physiology, the reply is inevitable that death is no accident introduced by the perverse will of our first parents, nor any way connected with man's sinfulness; but is purely a result of the conditions of animal life. On the contrary, St. Paul rests most important conclusions on the fact, that one man Adam by personal sin brought death upon all his posterity. If this was a fundamental error, religious doctrine also is shaken.

In various attempts at compromise,—such as conceding the Scriptural fallibility in human science, but maintaining its spiritual perfection,—I always found the division impracticable. At last it pressed on me, that if I admitted morals to rest on an independent basis, it was dishonest to shut my eyes to any apparent collisions of morality with the Scriptures. A very notorious and decisive instance is that of Jael.— Sisera, when beaten in battle, fled to the tent of his friend Heber, and was there warmly welcomed by Jael, Heber's wife. After she had refreshed him with food, and lulled him to sleep, she killed him by driving a nail into his temples; and for this deed, (which now-a-days would be called a perfidious murder,) the prophetess Deborah, in an inspired psalm, pronounces Jael to be "blessed above women," and glorifies her act by an elaborate description of its atrocity. As soon as I felt that I was bound to pass a moral judgment on this, I saw that as regards the Old Testament the battle was already lost. Many other things, indeed, instantly rose in full power upon me, especially the command to Abraham to slay his son. Paul and James agree in extolling Abraham as the pattern of faith; James and the author of the Epistle to the Hebrews specify the sacrifice of Isaac as a firstrate fruit of faith: yet if the voice of morality is allowed to be heard, Abraham was (in heart and intention) not less guilty than those who sacrificed their children to Molech.

Thus at length it appeared, that I must choose between two courses. I must EITHER blind my moral sentiment, my powers of criticism, and my scientific knowledge, (such as they were,) in order to accept the Scripture entire; OR I must encounter the problem, however arduous, of adjusting the relative claims of human knowledge and divine revelation. As to the former method, to name it was to condemn it; for it would put every system of Paganism on a par with Christianity. If one system of religion may claim that we blind our hearts and eyes in its favour, so may another; and there is precisely the same reason for becoming a Hindoo in religion as a Christian. We cannot be both; therefore the principle is *demonstrably* absurd. It is also, of course, morally horrible, and opposed to countless passages of the Scriptures themselves. Nor can the argument be evaded by talking of external evidences; for these also are confessedly moral evidences, to be judged of by our moral faculties. Nay, according to all Christian advocates, they are God's test of our moral temper. To allege, therefore, that our moral faculties are not to judge, is to annihilate the evidences for Christianity.—Thus, finally, I was lodged in three inevitable conclusions:

1. The moral and intellectual powers of man must be acknowledged as having a right and duty to criticize the contents of the Scripture:

2. When so exerted, they condemn portions of the Scripture as erroneous and immoral:

3. The assumed infallibility of the *entire* Scripture is a proved falsity, not merely as to physiology, and other scientific matters, but also as to morals: and it remains for farther inquiry how to discriminate the trustworthy from the untrustworthy within the limits of the Bible itself.

When distinctly conscious, after long efforts to evade it, that this was and must henceforth be my position, I ruminated on the many auguries which had been made concerning me by frightened friends. "You will become a Socinian," had been said of me even at Oxford: "You will become an infidel," had since been added. My present results, I was aware, would seem a sadly triumphant confirmation to the clearsighted instinct of orthodoxy. But the animus of such prophecies had always made me indignant, and I could not admit that there was any merit in such clearsightedness. What! (used I to say,) will you shrink from truth, lest it lead to error? If following truth must bring us to Socinianism, let us by all means become Socinians, or anything else. Surely we do not love our doctrines more than the truth, but because they are the truth. Are we not exhorted to "prove all things, and hold fast that which is good?"—But to my discomfort, I generally found that this (to me so convincing) argument for feeling no alarm, only caused more and more alarm, and gloomier omens concerning me. On considering all this in leisurely retrospect, I began painfully to doubt, whether after all there is much love of truth even among those who have an undeniable strength of religious feeling. I questioned with myself, whether love of truth is not a virtue demanding a robust mental cultivation; whether mathematical or other abstract studies may not be practically needed for it. But no: for how then could it exist in some feminine natures? how in rude and unphilosophical times? On the whole, I rather concluded, that there is in nearly all English education a positive repressing of a young person's truthfulness; for I could distinctly see, that in my own case there was always need of defying authority and public opinion,—not to speak of more serious sacrifices,—if I was to follow truth. All society seemed so to hate novelties of thought, as to prefer the chances of error in the old.—Of course! why, how could it be otherwise, while Test Articles were maintained?

Yet surely if God is truth, none sincerely aspire to him, who dread to lose their present opinions in exchange for others truer.—I had not then read a sentence of Coleridge, which is to this effect: "If any one begins by loving Christianity more than the truth, he will proceed to love his Church more than Christianity, and will end by loving his own opinions better than either." A dim conception of this was in my mind; and I saw that the genuine love of God was essentially connected with loving truth as truth, and not truth as our own accustomed thought, truth as our old prejudice; and that the real saint can never be afraid to let God teach him one lesson more, or unteach him one more error. Then I rejoiced to feel how right and sound had been our principle, that no creed can possibly be used as the touchstone of spirituality: for man morally excels man, as far as creeds are concerned, not by assenting to true propositions, but by loving them because they are discerned to be true, and by possessing a faculty of discernment sharpened by the love of truth. Such are God's true apostles, differing enormously in attainment and elevation, but all born to ascend. For these to quarrel between themselves because they do not agree in opinions, is monstrous. *Sentiment*, surely, not *opinion*, is the bond of the Spirit; and as the love of God, so the love of truth is a high and sacred sentiment, in comparison to which our creeds are mean.

Well, I had been misjudged; I had been absurdly measured by other men's creed: but might I not have similarly misjudged others, since I had from early youth been under similar influences? How many of my seniors at Oxford I had virtually despised because they were not evangelical! Had I had opportunity of testing their spirituality? or had I the faculty of so doing? Had I not really condemned them as unspiritual, barely because of their creed? On trying to reproduce the past to my imagination, I could not condemn myself quite as sweepingly as I wished; but my heart smote me on account of one. I had a brother, with whose name all England was resounding for praise or blame: from his sympathies, through pure hatred of Popery, I had long since turned away. What was this but to judge him by his creed? True, his whole theory was nothing but Romanism transferred to England: but what then? I had studied with the deepest interest Mrs. Schimmelpenninck's account of the Portroyalists, and though I was aware that she exhibits only the bright side of her subject, yet the absolute excellencies of her nuns and priests showed that Romanism *as such* was not fatal to spirituality. They were persecuted: this did them good perhaps, or certainly exhibited their brightness. So too my brother surely was struggling after truth, fighting for freedom to his own heart and mind, against church articles and stagnancy of thought. For this he deserved both sympathy and love: but I, alas! had not known and seen his excellence. But now God had taught me more largeness by bitter sorrow working the peaceable fruit of righteousness; at last then I might admire my brother. I therefore wrote to him a letter of contrition. Some change, either in his mind or in his view of my position, had taken place; and I was happy to find him once more able, not only to feel fraternally, as he had always done, but to act also fraternally. Nevertheless, to this day it is to me a painfully unsolved mystery, how a mind can claim its freedom in order to establish bondage.

For the *peculiarities* of Romanism I feel nothing, and I can pretend nothing, but contempt, hatred, disgust, or horror. But this system of falsehood, fraud, unscrupulous and unrelenting ambition, will never be destroyed, while Protestants keep up their insane anathemas against opinion. These are the outworks of the Romish citadel: until they are razed to the ground, the citadel will defy attack. If we are to blind our eyes, in order to accept an article of King Edward VI., or an argument of St. Paul's, why not blind them so far as to accept the Council of Trent? If we are to pronounce that a man "without doubt shall perish everlastingly," unless he believes the self-contradictions of the pseudo-Athanasian Creed, why should we shrink from a similar anathema on those who reject the self-contradictions of Transsubstantiation? If one man is cast out of God's favour for eliciting error while earnestly searching after truth, and another remains in favour by passively receiving the word of a Church, of a Priest, or of an Apostle, then to search for truth is dangerous; apathy is safer; then the soul does not come directly into contact with God and learn of him, but has to learn from, and unconvincedly submit to, some external authority. This is the germ of Romanism: its legitimate development makes us Pagans outright.

But in what position was I now, towards the apostles? Could I admit their inspiration, when I no longer thought them infallible? Undoubtedly. What could be clearer on every hypothesis, than that they were inspired on and after the day of Pentecost, and *yet* remained ignorant and liable to mistake about the relation of the Gentiles to the Jews? The moderns have introduced into the idea of inspiration that of infallibility, to which either *omniscience* or *dictation* is essential. That there was no dictation, (said I,) is proved by the variety of style in the Scriptural writers; that they were not omniscient, is manifest. In truth, if human minds had not been left to them, how could they have argued persuasively? was not the superior success of their preaching to that of Christ, perhaps due to their sharing in the prejudices of their contemporaries? An orator is most persuasive, when he is lifted above his hearers on those points only on which he is to reform their notions. The apostles were not omniscient: granted: but it cannot hence be inferred that they did not know the message given them by God. Their knowledge however perfect, must yet in a human mind have coexisted with ignorance; and nothing (argued I) but a perpetual miracle could prevent ignorance from now and then exhibiting itself in some error. But hence to infer that they are not inspired, and are not messengers from God, is quite gratuitous. Who indeed imagines that John or Paul understood astronomy so well as Sir William Herschel? Those who believe that the apostles might err in human science, need not the less revere their moral and spiritual wisdom.

At the same time it became a matter of duty to me, if possible, to discriminate the authoritative from the unauthoritative in the Scripture, or at any rate avoid to accept and propagate as true that which is false, even if it be false only as science and not as religion. I unawares,—more perhaps from old habit than from distinct conviction,—started from the assumption that my fixed point of knowledge was to be found in the sensible or scientific, not in the moral. I still retained from my old Calvinistic doctrine a way of proceeding, as if purely moral judgment were my weak side, at least in criticizing the Scripture: so that I preferred never to appeal to direct moral and spiritual considerations, except in the most glaringly necessary cases. Thus, while I could not accept the panegyric on Jael, and on Abraham's intended sacrifice of his son, I did not venture unceremoniously to censure the extirpation of the Canaanites by Joshua: of which I barely said to myself, that it "certainly needed very strong proof" of the divine command to justify it. I still went so far in timidity as to hesitate to reject on internal evidence the account of heroes or giants begotten by angels, who, enticed by the love of women, left heaven for earth. The narrative in Gen. vi. had long appeared to me undoubtedly to bear this sense; and to have been so understood by Jude and Peter (2 Pet. ii.), as, I believe, it also was by the Jews and early Fathers. I did at length set it aside as incredible; not however from moral repugnance to it, (for I feared to trust the soundness of my instinct,) but because I had slid into a new rule of interpretation,—that *I must not obtrude miracles on the Scripture narrative.* The writers tell their story without showing any consciousness that it involves physiological difficulties. To invent a miracle in order to defend this, began to seem to me unwarrantable.

It had become notorious to the public, that Geologists rejected the idea of a universal deluge as physically impossible. Whence could the water come, to cover the highest mountains? Two replies were attempted: 1. The flood of Noah is not described as universal: 2. The flood was indeed universal, but the water was added and removed by miracle.—Neither reply however seemed to me valid. First, the language respecting the universality of the flood is as strong as any that could be written: moreover it is stated that the tops of the high hills *were all covered*, and after the water subsides, the ark settles on the mountains of Armenia. Now in Armenia, of necessity numerous peaks would be seen, unless the water covered them, and especially Ararat. But a flood that covered Ararat would overspread all the continents, and leave only a few summits above. If then the account in Genesis is to be received, the flood was universal. Secondly: the narrator represents the surplus water to have come from the clouds and perhaps from the sea, and again to drain back into the sea. Of a miraculous *creation and destruction* of water, he evidently does not dream.

Other impossibilities came forward: the insufficient dimensions of the ark to take in all the creatures; the unsuitability of the same climate to arctic and tropical animals for a full year; the impossibility of feeding them and avoiding pestilence; and especially, the total disagreement of the modern facts of the dispersion of animals, with the idea that they spread anew from Armenia as their centre. We have no right to call in a series of miracles to solve difficulties, of which the writer was unconscious. The ark itself was expressly devised to economize miracle, by making a fresh creation of animals needless.

Different in kind was the objection which I felt to the story, which is told twice concerning Abraham and once concerning Isaac, of passing off a wife as a sister. Allowing that such a thing was barely not impossible, the improbability was so intense, as to demand the strictest and most cogent proof: yet when we asked, Who testifies it? no proof appeared that it was Moses; or, supposing it to be he, what his sources of knowledge were. And this led to the far wider remark, that nowhere in the book of Genesis is there a line to indicate who is the writer, or a sentence to imply that the writer believes himself to write by special information from God. Indeed, it is well known that there are numerous small phrases which denote a later hand than that of Moses. The kings of Israel are once alluded to historically, Gen. xxxvi. 31.

Why then was anything improbable to be believed on the

writer's word? as, for instance, the story of Babel and the confusion of tongues? One reply only seemed possible; namely, that we believe the Old Testament in obedience to the authority of the New: and this threw me again to consider the references to the Old Testament in the Christian Scriptures.

But here, the difficulties soon became manifestly more and more formidable. In opening Matthew, we meet with quotations from the Old Testament applied in the most startling way. First is the prophecy about the child Immanuel; which in Isaiah no unbiassed interpreter would have dreamed could apply to Jesus. Next; the words of Hosea, "Out of Egypt have I called my son," which do but record the history of Israel, are imagined by Matthew to be prophetic of the return of Jesus from Egypt. This instance moved me much; because I thought, that if the text were "spiritualized," so as to make Israel mean *Jesus*, Egypt also ought to be spiritualized and mean *the world*, not retain its geographical sense, which seemed to be carnal and absurd in such a connection: for Egypt is no more to Messiah than Syria or Greece.—One of the most decisive testimonies to the Old Testament which the New contains, is in John x. 35, where I hardly knew how to allow myself to characterize the reasoning. The case stands thus. The 82nd Psalm rebukes *unjust* governors; and at length says to them: "I have said, Ye are gods, and all of you are children of the most high: but ye shall die like men, and fall like one of the princes." In other words:—"though we are apt *to think* of rulers *as if* they were superhuman, yet they shall meet the lot of common men." Well: how is this applied in John?—Jesus has been accused of blasphemy, for saying that "He and his Father are one;" and in reply, he quotes the verse, "I have said, Ye are gods," as his sufficient justification for calling himself Son of God: for "the Scripture cannot be broken." I dreaded to precipitate myself into shocking unbelief, if I followed out the thoughts that this suggested: and (I know not how) for a long time yet put it off.

The quotations from the Old Testament in St. Paul had always been a mystery to me. The more I now examined them, the clearer it appeared that they were based on untenable Rabbinical principles. Nor are those in the Acts and in the Gospels any better. If we take free leave to canvass them, it may appear that not one quotation in ten is sensible and appropriate. And shall we then accept the decision of the New Testament writers as final, concerning the value and credibility of the Old Testament, when it is so manifest that they most imperfectly understood that book?

In fact the appeal to them proved too much. For Jude quotes the book of Enoch as an inspired prophecy, and yet, since Archbishop Laurence has translated it from the Ethiopian, we know that book to be a fable undeserving of regard, and undoubtedly not written by "Enoch, the seventh from Adam." Besides, it does not appear that any peculiar divine revelation taught them that the Old Testament is perfect truth. In point of fact, they only reproduce the ideas on that subject current in their age. So far as Paul deviates from the common Jewish view, it is in the direction of disparaging the Law as essentially imperfect. May it not seem that his remaining attachment to it was still exaggerated by old sentiment and patriotism?

I farther found that not only do the Evangelists give us no hint that they thought themselves divinely inspired, or that they had any other than human sources of knowledge, but Luke most explicitly shows the contrary. He opens by stating to Theophilus, that since many persons have committed to writing the things handed down from eye-witnesses, it seemed good to him also to do the same, since he had "accurately attended to every thing from its sources ($ἄνωθεν$)." He could not possibly have written thus, if he had been conscious of superhuman aids. How absurd then of us, to pretend that we know more than Luke knew of his own inspiration!

In truth, the arguments of theologians to prove the inspiration (i. e. infallibility) of Matthew, Mark, and Luke, are sometimes almost ludicrous. My lamented friend, John Sterling, has thus summed up Dr. Henderson's arguments about Mark. "Mark was probably inspired, *because he was an acquaintance of Peter;* and because Dr. Henderson would be reviled by other Dissenters, if he doubted it."

About this time, the great phenomenon of these three gospels,—the casting out of devils,—pressed forcibly on my attention. I now dared to look full into the facts, and saw that the disorders described were perfectly similar to epilepsy, mania, catalepsy, and other known maladies. Nay, the deaf, the dumb, the hunchbacked, are spoken of as devil-ridden. I farther knew that such diseases are still ascribed to evil genii in Mussulman countries: even a vicious horse is believed by the Arabs to be *majnūn*, possessed by a Jin or Genie. Devils also are cast out in Abyssinia to this day. Having fallen in with Farmer's treatise on the Demoniacs, I carefully studied it; and found it to prove unanswerably, that a belief in demoniacal possession is a superstition not more respectable than that of witchcraft. But Farmer did not at all convince me, that the three Evangelists do not share the vulgar error. Indeed, the instant we believe that the imagined possessions were only various forms of disease, we are forced to draw conclusions of the utmost moment, most damaging to the credit of the narrators.*

Clearly, they are then convicted of misstating facts, under the influence of superstitious credulity. They represent demoniacs as having a supernatural acquaintance with Jesus, which, it now becomes manifest, they cannot have had. The devils cast out of two demoniacs (or one) are said to have entered into a herd of swine. This must have been a credulous fiction. Indeed, the casting out of devils is so very prominent a part of the miraculous agency ascribed to Jesus, as at first sight to impair our faith in his miracles altogether.

I however took refuge in the consideration, that when Jesus wrought one great miracle, popular credulity would inevitably magnify it into ten; hence the discovery of foolish exaggerations is no disproof of a real miraculous agency: nay, perhaps the contrary. Are they not a sort of false halo round a disc of glory,—a halo so congenial to human nature, that the absence of it might be even wielded as an objection? Moreover, John tells of no demoniacs: does not this show his freedom from popular excitement? Observe the great miracles narrated by John,—the blind man,—and Lazarus—

---

* My Eclectic Reviewer says (p. 276): "Thus because the evangelists held an erroneous *medical* theory, Mr. Newman suffered a breach to be made in the credit of the Bible." No; but as the next sentence states, "because they are convicted of *misstating facts*," under the influence of this erroneous medical theory. Even this reviewer—candid for an orthodox critic, and not over-orthodox either—cannot help garbling me.

how different in kind from those on demoniacs! how incapable of having been mistaken! how convincing! His statements cannot be explained away: their whole tone, moreover, is peculiar. On the contrary, the three first gospels contain much that (after we see the writers to be credulous) must be judged legendary.

The two first chapters of Matthew abound in dreams. Dreams? Was indeed the "immaculate conception" merely told to Joseph in a *dream?* a dream which not he only was to believe, but we also, when reported to us by a person wholly unknown, who wrote 70 or 80 years after the fact, and gives us no clue to his sources of information! Shall I reply that he received his information by miracle? But why more than Luke? and Luke evidently was conscious only of human information. Besides, inspiration has not saved Matthew from error about demons; and why then about Joseph's dream and its highly important contents?

In former days, I had never dared to let my thoughts dwell inquisitively on the *star*, which the wise men saw in the East, and which accompanied them, and pointed out the house where the young child was. I now thought of it, only to see that it was a legend fit for credulous ages; and that it must be rejected in common with Herod's massacre of the children, —an atrocity unknown to Josephus. How difficult it was to reconcile the flight into Egypt with the narrative of Luke, I had known from early days: I now saw that it was waste time to try to reconcile them.

But perhaps I might say:—" That the writers should make errors about the *infancy* of Jesus was natural; they were distant from the time: but that will not justly impair the credit of events, to which they may possibly have been contemporaries or even eye-witnesses."—How then would this apply to the Temptation, at which certainly none of them were present? Is it accident, that the same three, who abound in the demoniacs, tell also the scene of the Devil and Jesus on a pinnacle of the temple; while the same John who omits the demoniacs, omits also this singular story? It being granted that the writers are elsewhere mistaken, to criticize the tale was to reject it.

In near connexion with this followed the discovery, that many other miracles of the Bible are wholly deficient in that moral dignity, which is supposed to place so great a chasm between them and ecclesiastical writings. Why should I look with more respect on the napkins taken from Paul's body (Acts xix. 12), than on pocket-handkerchiefs dipped in the blood of martyrs ? How could I believe, on this same writer's hearsay, that "the Spirit of the Lord caught away Philip" (viii. 39), transporting him through the air; as oriental genii are supposed to do ? Or what moral dignity was there in the curse on the barren fig-tree,—about which, moreover, we are so perplexingly told, that it was *not* the time for figs ? What was to be said of a cure, wrought by touching the hem of Jesus' garment, which drew physical *virtue* from him without his will ? And how could I distinguish the genius of the miracle of tribute-money in the fish's mouth, from those of the apocryphal gospels ? What was I to say of useless miracles, like that of Peter and Jesus walking on the water,—or that of many saints coming out of the graves to show themselves, or of a poetical sympathy of the elements, such as the earthquake and rending of the temple-veil when Jesus died ? Altogether, I began to feel that Christian advocates commit the flagrant sophism of treating every objection as an isolated "cavil," and overrule each as obviously insufficient, with the same confidence as if it were the only one. Yet, in fact, the objections collectively are very powerful, and cannot be set aside by supercilious airs, and by calling unbelievers "superficial," any more than by harsh denunciations.

Pursuing the same thought to the Old Testament, I discerned there also no small sprinkling of grotesque or unmoral miracles. A dead man is raised to life, when his body by accident touches the bones of Elisha: as though Elisha had been a Romish saint, and his bones a sacred relic. Uzzah, when the ark is in danger of falling, puts out his hand to save it, and is struck dead for his impiety ! Was this the judgment of the Father of mercies and God of all comfort ? What was I to make of God's anger with Abimelech (Gen. xx.), whose sole offence was, the having believed Abraham's lie ? for which a miraculous barrenness was sent on all the females of Abimelech's tribe, and was bought off only by splendid presents to the favoured deceiver.—Or was it at all credible that the lying and fraudulent Jacob should have been so specially loved by God, more than the rude animal Esau ?—Or could I any longer overlook the gross imagination of antiquity, which made Abraham and Jehovah dine on the same carnal food, like Tantalus with the gods;—which fed Elijah by ravens, and set angels to bake cakes for him ? Such is a specimen of the flood of difficulties which poured in, through the great breach which the demoniacs had made in the credit of Biblical marvels.

While I was in this stage of progress, I had a second time the advantage of meeting Dr. Arnold, and had satisfaction in finding that he rested the main strength of Christianity on the gospel of John. The great similarity of the other three seemed to him enough to mark that they flowed from sources very similar, and that the first gospel had no pretensions to be regarded as the actual writing of Matthew. This indeed had been for some time clear to me, though I now cared little about the author's name, when he was proved to be credulous. —Arnold regarded John's gospel as abounding with smaller touches which marked the eye-witness, and, altogether, to be the vivid and simple picture of a divine reality, undeformed by credulous legend. In this view I was gratified to repose, in spite of a few partial misgivings, and returned to investigations concerning the Old Testament.

For some time back I had paid special attention to the book of Genesis; and I had got aid in the analysis of it from a German volume. That it was based on *at least* two different documents, technically called the Elohistic and Jehovistic, soon became clear to me: and an orthodox friend who acknowledged the fact, regarded it as a high recommendation of the book, that it was conscientiously made out of pre-existing materials, and was not a fancy that came from the brain of Moses. My good friend's argument was not a happy one: no written record could exist of things and times which preceded the invention of writing. After analyzing this book with great minuteness, I now proceeded to Exodus and Numbers; and was soon assured, that these had not, any more than Genesis, come forth from one primitive witness of the facts. In all these books is found the striking phenomenon of *duplicate* or even *triplicate narratives*. The creation of man is three times told. The account of the Flood is made up out of two discrepant originals, marked by the names Elohim and Jehovah; of which one makes Noah take into the ark *seven* pairs of clean, and *single* (or double?) pairs of unclean beasts; while the other gives him two and two of all kinds, without distinguishing the clean. The two documents may indeed in this narrative be almost re-discovered by mechanical separation. The triple statement of Abraham and Isaac passing off a wife for a sister was next in interest; and here also the two which concern Abraham are contrasted as Jehovistic and

Elohistic. A similar double account is given of the origin of circumcision, of the names Isaac, Israel, Bethel, Beersheba. Still more was I struck by the positive declaration in Exodus (vi. 3) that *God was* NOT *known to Abraham, Isaac, and Jacob by the name Jehovah;* while the book of Genesis abounds with the contrary fact. This alone convinced me beyond all dispute, that these books did not come from one and the same hand, but are conglomerates formed out of older materials, unartistically and mechanically joined.

Indeed a fuller examination showed in Exodus and Numbers a twofold miracle of the quails, of which the latter is so told as to indicate entire unacquaintance with the former. There is a double description of the manna, a needless second appointment of Elders of the congregation: water is twice brought out of the rock by the rod of Moses, whose faith is perfect the first time and fails the second time. The name of Meribah is twice bestowed. There is a double promise of a guardian angel, a double consecration of Aaron and his sons: indeed, I seemed to find a double or even threefold* copy of the Decalogue. Comprising Deuteronomy within my view, I met two utterly incompatible accounts of Aaron's death; for Deuteronomy makes him die *before* reaching Meribah Kadesh, where, according to Numbers, he sinned and incurred the penalty of death (Num. xx. 24, Deut. x. 6: cf. Num. xxxiii. 31, 38).

That there was error on a great scale in all this, was undeniable; and I began to see at least one *source* of the error. The celebrated miracle of "the sun standing still" has long been felt as too violent a derangement of the whole globe to be used by the most High as a means of discomfiting an army: and I had acquiesced in the idea that the miracle was *ocular* only. But in reading the passage, (Josh. x. 12—14,) I for the first time observed that the narrative rests on the authority of a poetical book which bears the name of Jasher.† He who composed—" Sun, stand thou still upon Gibeon; and thou, Moon, in the valley of Ajalon!"—like other poets, called on the Sun and Moon to stand and look on Joshua's deeds; but he could not anticipate that his words would be hardened into

---

* I have explained this in my " Hebrew Monarchy."

† This poet celebrated also the deeds of David (2 Sam. i. 18) according to our translation : if so, he was many centuries later than Joshua · however, the sense of the Hebrew is a little obscure.

fact by a prosaic interpreter, and appealed to in proof of a stupendous miracle. The commentator could not tell what *the Moon* had to do with it; yet he has quoted honestly.— This presently led me to observe other marks that the narrative has been made up, at least in part, out of old poetry. Of these the most important are in Exodus xv. and Num. xxi., in the latter of which three different poetical fragments are quoted, and one of them is expressly said to be from " the book of the wars of Jehovah," apparently a poem descriptive of the conquest of Canaan by the Israelites. As for Exodus xv. it appeared to me (in that stage, and after so abundant proof of error,) almost certain that Moses' song is the primitive authority, out of which the prose narrative of the passage of the Red Sea has been worked up. Especially since, after the song, the writer adds: v. 19. " For the horse of Pharaoh went in with his chariots and with his horsemen into the sea, and the Lord brought again the waters of the sea upon them: but the children of Israel went on dry land in the midst of the sea." This comment scarcely could have been added, if the detailed account of ch. xiv. had been written previously. The song of Moses *implies no miracle at all :* it is merely high poetry. A later prosaic age took the hyperbolic phrases of v. 8 literally, and so generated the comment of v. 19, and a still later time expanded this into the elaborate 14th chapter.

Other proofs crowded upon me, that cannot here be enlarged upon. Granting then (for argument) that the four first books of the Pentateuch are a compilation, made long after the event, I tried for a while to support the very arbitrary opinion, that Deuteronomy (all but its last chapter) which seemed to be a more homogeneous composition, was alone and really the production of Moses. This however needed some 'definite proof: for if tradition was not sufficient to guarantee the whole Pentateuch, it could not guarantee to me Deuteronomy alone. I proceeded to investigate the external history of the Pentateuch, and in so doing, came to the story, how the book of the Law was *found* in the reign of the young king Josiah, nearly at the end of the Jewish monarchy. As I considered the narrative, my eyes were opened. If the book had previously been the received sacred law, it could not possibly have been so lost, that its contents were unknown, and the fact of its loss forgotten: it was therefore evidently *then first compiled*, or at least then first produced and made authoritative to the nation.* And with this the general course of the history best agrees, and all the phenomena of the books themselves.

Many of the Scriptural facts were old to me: to the importance of the history of Josiah I had perhaps even become dim-sighted by familiarity. Why had I not long ago seen that my conclusions ought to have been different from those of prevalent orthodoxy?—I found that I had been cajoled by the primitive assumptions, which though not clearly *stated*, are unceremoniously *used*. Dean Graves, for instance, always takes for granted, that, *until the contrary shall be demonstrated*, it is to be firmly believed that the Pentateuch is from the pen of Moses. He proceeds to set aside, *one by one*, as not demonstrative, the indications that it is of later origin: and when other means fail, he says that the particular verses remarked on were added by a later hand! I considered that if we were debating the antiquity of an Irish book, and in one page of it were found an allusion to the Parliamentary Union with England, we should at once regard the whole book, *until the contrary should be proved*, as the work of this century; and not endure the reasoner, who, in order to uphold a theory that it is five centuries old, pronounced that sentence "evidently to be from a later hand." Yet in this arbitrary way Dean Graves and all his coadjutors set aside, one by one, the texts which point at the date of the Pentateuch. I was possessed with indignation. Oh sham science! Oh false-named Theology!

> O mihi tam longæ maneat pars ultima vitæ,
> Spiritus et, quantum sat erit tua dicere facta!

Yet I waited some eight years longer, lest I should on so grave a subject write anything premature. Especially I felt that it was necessary to learn more of what the erudition of Germany had done on these subjects. Michaelis on the New Testament had fallen into my hands several years before, and I had found the greatest advantage from his learning and candour. About this time I also had begun to get more or less aid from four or five living German divines; but none produced any strong impression on me but De Wette. The two grand lessons which I learned from him, were, the greater recency of Deuteronomy, and the very untrustworthy character of the book of Chronicles; with which discovery, the true

* I have fully discussed this in my "Hebrew Monarchy."

origin of the Pentateuch becomes still clearer.* After this, I heard of Hengstenberg as the most learned writer on the opposite side, and furnished myself with his work in defence of the antiquity of the Pentateuch: but it only showed me how hopeless a cause he had undertaken.

In this period I came to a totally new view of many parts of the Bible; and not to be tedious, it will suffice here to sum up the results.

The first books which I looked at as doubtful, were the Apocalypse and the Epistle to the Hebrews. From the Greek style I felt assured that the former was not by John,† nor the latter by Paul. In Michaelis I first learnt the interesting fact of Luther having vehemently repudiated the Apocalypse, so that he not only declared its spuriousness in the Preface of his Bible, but solemnly charged his successors not to print his translation of the Apocalypse without annexing this avowal: —a charge which they presently disobeyed. Such is the habitual unfairness of ecclesiastical corporations. I was afterwards confirmed by Neander in the belief that the Apocalypse is a false prophecy. The only chapter of it which is interpreted,—the 17th,—appears to be a political speculation suggested by the civil war of Otho, Vitellius and Vespasian; and erroneously opines that the eighth emperor of Rome is to be the last, and is to be one of the preceding emperors restored, —probably Nero, who was believed to have escaped to the kings of the East.—As for the Epistle to the Hebrews, (which I was disposed to believe Luther had well guessed to be the production of Apollos,) I now saw quite a different genius in it from that of Paul, as more artificial and savouring of rhetorical culture. As to this, the learned Germans are probably unanimous.

Next to these, the Song of Solomon fell away. I had been accustomed to receive this as a sacred representation of the loves of Christ and the Church: but after I was experimentally

---

* The English reader may consult Theodore Parker's translation of De Wette's Introduction to the Canon of Scripture. I have also amply exhibited the vanity of the *Chronicles* in my "Hebrew Monarchy." De Wette has a separate treatise on the Chronicles.

† If the date of the Apocalypse is twenty years earlier than that of the fourth Gospel, I now feel no such difficulty in their being the composition of the same writer.

acquainted with the playful and extravagant genius of man's love for woman, I saw the Song of Solomon with new eyes. and became entirely convinced that it consists of fragments of love-songs, some of them rather voluptuous.

After this, it followed that the so-called *Canon* of the Jews could not guarantee to us the value of the writings. Consequently, such books as Ruth and Esther, (the latter indeed not containing one religious sentiment,) stood forth at once in their natural insignificance. Ecclesiastes also seemed to me a meagre and shallow production. Chronicles I now learned to be not credulous only, but unfair, perhaps so far as to be actually dishonest. Not one of the historical books of the Old Testament could approve itself to me as of any high antiquity or of any spiritual authority; and in the New Testament I found the first three books and the Acts to contain many doubtful and some untrue accounts, and many incredible miracles.

Many persons, after reading thus much concerning me, will be apt to say: "Of course then you gave up Christianity?"— Far from it. I gave up all that was clearly untenable, and clung the firmer to all that still appeared sound. I had found out that the Bible was not to be my religion, nor its perfection any tenet of mine: but what then? Did Paul go about preaching the Bible? nay, but he preached Christ. The New Testament did not as yet exist: to the Jews he necessarily argued from the Old Testament; but that "faith in the book" was no part of Paul's gospel, is manifest from his giving no list of sacred books to his Gentile converts. Twice indeed in his epistles to Timothy, he recommends the Scriptures of the Old Testament; but even in the more striking passage, (on which such exaggerated stress has been laid,) the spirit of his remark is essentially apologetic. "Despise not, oh Timothy," (is virtually his exhortation) "the Scriptures that you learned as a child. Although now you have the Spirit to teach you, yet that does not make the older writers useless: for *"every divinely inspired writing is also profitable for instruction,* &c." In Paul's religion, respect for the Scriptures was a means, not an end. The Bible was made for man, not man for the Bible.

Thus the question with me was: "May I still receive Christ as a Saviour from sin, a Teacher and Lord sent from heaven, and can I find an adequate account of what He came to do or teach?" And my reply was, Yes. The gospel of John alone gave an adequate account of him: the other three, though often erroneous, had clear marks of simplicity, and in so far confirmed the general belief in the supernatural character and works of Jesus. Then the conversion of Paul was a powerful argument. I had Peter's testimony to the resurrection, and to the transfiguration. Many of the prophecies were eminently remarkable, and seemed unaccountable except as miraculous. The origin of Judaism and spread of Christianity appeared to be beyond common experience, and were perhaps fairly to be called supernatural. Broad views such as these did not seem to be affected by the special conclusions at which I had arrived concerning the books of the Bible. I conceived myself to be resting under an Indian Figtree, which is supported by certain grand stems, but also lets down to the earth many small branches, which seem to the eye to prop the tree, but in fact are supported by it. If they were cut away, the tree would not be less strong. So neither was the tree of Christianity weakened by the loss of its apparent props. I might still enjoy its shade, and eat of its fruits, and bless the hand that planted it.

In the course of this period I likewise learnt how inadequate allowance I had once made for the repulsion produced by my own dogmatic tendency on the sympathies of the unevangelical. I now often met persons of Evangelical opinion, but could seldom have any interchange of religious sentiment with them, because every word they uttered warned me that I could escape controversy only while I kept them at a distance: moreover, if any little difference of opinion led us into amicable argument, they uniformly reasoned by quoting texts. This was now inadmissible with me, but I could only have done mischief by going farther than a dry disclaimer; after which indeed I saw I was generally looked on as "an infidel." No doubt the parties who so came into collision with me, approached me often with an earnest desire and hope to find some spiritual good in me, but withdrew disappointed, finding me either cold and defensive, or (perhaps they thought) warm and disputatious. Thus, as long as artificial tests of spirituality are allowed to exist, their erroneousness is not easily exposed by the mere wear and tear of life. When the collision of opinion is very strong, two good men may meet, and only be confirmed in their prejudices against one another: for in order that one may elicit the spiritual sympathies of the other, a certain liberality is prerequisite. Without this, each prepares to shield himself from attack, or even holds out weapons of offence. Thus "articles of Communion" are essentially articles of Disunion.—On the other hand, if all tests of opinion in a church were heartily and truly done away, then the principles of spiritual affinity and repulsion would act quite undisturbed. Surely therefore this was the only right method?—Nevertheless, I saw the necessity of *one* test, "Jesus is the Son of God," and felt unpleasantly that one article tends infallibly to draw another after it. But I had too much, just then, to think of in other quarters, to care much about Church Systems.

CHAPTER V.

FAITH AT SECOND HAND FOUND TO BE VAIN.

I RECKON my fifth period to begin from the time when I had totally abandoned the claims of "the Canon" of Scripture, however curtailed, to be received as the object of faith, as free from error, or as something raised above moral criticism; and looked out for some deeper foundation for my creed than any sacred Letter. But an entirely new inquiry had begun to engage me at intervals, viz., *the essential logic of these investigations.* Ought we in any case to receive moral truth in obedience to an apparent miracle of sense? or conversely, ought we ever to believe in sensible miracles because of their recommending some moral truth? I perceived that the endless jangling which goes on in detailed controversy, is inevitable, while the disputants are unawares at variance with one another, or themselves wavering, as to these pervading principles of evidence.—I regard my fifth period to come to an end with the decision of this question. Nevertheless, many other important lines of inquiry were going forward simultaneously.

I found in the Bible itself,—and even in the very same book, as in the Gospel of John,—great uncertainty and inconsistency on this question. In one place, Jesus reproves* the demand of a miracle, and blesses those who believe without† miracles; in another, he requires that they will submit to his doctrine because‡ of his miracles. Now, this is intelligible, if

---
* Matt. xii. 39, xvi. 4. † John xx. 29.
‡ John xiv. 11. In x. 37, 38, the same idea seems to be intended. So xv. 24.

blind external obedience is the end of religion, and not Truth and inward Righteousness. An ambitious and unscrupulous *Church*, that desires, by fair means or foul, to make men bow down to her, may say, " Only believe; and all is right. The end being gained,—Obedience to us,—we do not care about your reasons." But *God* cannot speak thus to man; and to a divine teacher we should peculiarly look for aid in getting clear views of the grounds of faith; because it is by a knowledge of these that we shall both be rooted on the true basis, and saved from the danger of false beliefs.

It, therefore, peculiarly vexed me to find so total a deficiency of clear and sound instruction in the New Testament, and eminently in the gospel of John, on so vital a question. The more I considered it, the more it appeared, as if Jesus were solely anxious to have people believe in Him, without caring on what grounds they believed, although that is obviously the main point. When to this was added the threat of "damnation" on those who did not believe, the case became far worse: for I felt that if such a threat were allowed to operate, I might become a Mohammedan or a Roman Catholic. Could I in any case rationally assign this as a ground for believing in Christ,—" because I am frightened by his threats"—?

Farther thought showed me that a question of *logic*, such as I here had before me, was peculiarly one on which the propagator of a new religion could not be allowed to dictate; for if so, every false system could establish itself. Let Hindooism dictate our logic,—let us submit to its tests of a divine revelation, and its mode of applying them,—and we may, perhaps, at once find ourselves necessitated to "become little children" in a Brahminical school. Might not then this very thing account for the Bible not enlightening us on the topic? namely, since Logic, like Mathematics, belongs to the common intellect.—Possibly so: but still, it cannot reconcile us to *vacillations* and *contradictions* in the Bible on so critical a point.

Gradually I saw that deeper and deeper difficulties lay at bottom. If Logic *cannot* be matter of authoritative revelation, so long as the nature of the human mind is what it is,—if it appears, as a fact, that in the writings and speeches of the New Testament the logic is far from lucid,—if we are to compare Logic with Mathematics and other sciences, which grew up with civilization and long time,—we cannot doubt that the apostles imbibed the logic, like the astronomy, of their own day, with all its defects. Indeed, the same is otherwise plain. Paul's reasonings are those of a Gamaliel, and often are indefensible by our logical notions. John, also (as I had been recently learning,) has a wonderful similarity to Philo. This being the case, it becomes of deep interest to us to know,—if we are to accept results *at second hand* from Paul and John,—*what was the sort of evidence which convinced them ?* The moment this question is put, we see the essential defect to which we are exposed, in not being able to cross-examine them. Paul says that "Christ appeared to him:" elsewhere, that he has "received of the Lord" certain facts, concerning the Holy Supper: and that his Gospel was "given to him by revelation." If any modern made such statements to us, and on this ground demanded our credence, it would be allowable, and indeed obligatory, to ask many questions of him. What does he *mean*, by saying that he has had a "revelation?" Did he see a sight, or hear a sound? or was it an inward impression? and how does he distinguish it as divine?* Until these questions are fully answered, we have no materials at all before us for deciding to accept his results: to believe him, merely because he is earnest and persuaded, would be judged to indicate the weakness of inexperience. How then can it be pretended that we have, or can possibly get, the means of assuring ourselves that the apostles held correct principles of evidence and applied them justly, when we are not able to interrogate them?

Farther, it appears that *our* experience of delusion forces us to enact a very severe test of supernatural revelation. No doubt, we can conceive that which is equivalent to a *new sense* opening to us; but then it must have verifications connecting it with the other senses. Thus, a particularly vivid sort of dream recurring with special marks, and communicating at once heavenly and earthly knowledge, of which the latter was otherwise verified, would probably be admitted as a valid sort of evidence: but so intense would be the interest and duty to have all unravelled and probed to the bottom, that we should think it impossible to verify the new sense too anxiously, and

---

* A reviewer erroneously treats this as inculcating a denial of the possibility of inward revelation. It merely says, that *some answer* is needed to these questions; and *none is given*. We can make out (in my opinion) that dreams and inward impressions were the form of suggestion trusted to; but we do not learn what precautions were used against foolish credulity.

we should demand the fullest particulars of the divine transaction. On the contrary, it is undeniable that all such severity of research is rebuked in the Scriptures as unbelief. The deeply interesting *process* of receiving supernatural revelation.—a revelation, *not* of moral principles, but of outward facts and events, supposed to be communicated in a mode wholly peculiar and unknown to common men,—this process, which ought to be laid open and analyzed under the fullest light, *if we are to believe the results at second hand*, is always and avowedly shrouded in impenetrable darkness. There surely is something here, which denotes that it is dangerous to resign ourselves to the conclusions of the apostles, when their logical notions are so different from ours.

I farther inquired, what sort of miracle I could conceive, that would alter my opinion on a moral question. Hosea was divinely ordered to go and unite himself to an impure woman: could I possibly think that God ordered *me* to do so, if I heard a voice in the air commanding it? Should I not rather disbelieve my hearing, than disown my moral perceptions? If not, where am I to stop? I may practise all sorts of heathenism. A man who, in obedience to a voice in the air, kills his innocent wife or child, will either be called mad, and shut up for safety, or will be hanged as a desperate fanatic: do I dare to condemn this modern judgment of him? Would any conceivable miracle justify my slaying my wife? God forbid! It *must* be morally right, to believe moral rather than sensible perceptions. No outward impressions on the eye or ear can be so valid an assurance to me of God's will, as my inward judgment. How amazing, then, that a Paul or a James could look on Abraham's intention to slay his son, as indicating a praiseworthy faith!—And yet not amazing: it does but show, that apostles in former days, like ourselves, scrutinized antiquity with different eyes from modern events. If Paul had been ordered by a supernatural voice to slay Peter, he would have attributed the voice to the devil, "the prince of the power of the air," and would have despised it. He praises the faith of Abraham, but he certainly would never have imitated his conduct. Just so, the modern divines who laud Joseph's piety towards Mary, would be very differently affected, if events and persons were transported to the present day.

But to return. Let it be granted that no sensible miracle would authorize me so to violate my moral perceptions as to slay (that is, to murder) my innocent wife. May it, nevertheless, authorize me to invade a neighbour country, slaughter the people and possess their cities, although, without such a miracle, the deed would be deeply criminal? It is impossible to say that here, more than in the former case, miracles* can turn aside the common laws of morality. Neither, therefore, could they justify Joshua's war of extermination on the Canaanites, nor that of Samuel on the Amalekites; nor the murder of misbelievers by Elijah and by Josiah. If we are shocked at the idea of God releasing Mohammed from the vulgar law of marriage, we must as little endure relaxation in the great laws of justice and mercy. Farther, if only a *small* immorality is concerned, shall we then say that a miracle may justify it? Could it authorise me to plait a whip of small cords, and flog a preferment-hunter out of the pulpit? or would it justify me in publicly calling the Queen and her ministers "a brood of vipers, who cannot escape the damnation of hell"?† Such questions go very deep into the heart of the Christian claims.

I had been accustomed to overbear objections of this sort by replying, that to allow of their being heard would amount to refusing leave to God to give commands to his creatures. For, it seems, if he *did* command, we, instead of obeying, should discuss whether the command was right and reasonable; and if we thought it otherwise, should conclude that God never gave it. The extirpation of the Canaanites is compared by divines to the execution of a criminal; and it is insisted, that if the voice of society may justify the executioner, much more may the voice of God.—But I now saw the analogy to be insufficient and unsound. Insufficient, because no executioner is justified in slaying those whom his conscience tells him to be innocent; and it is a barbarous morality alone, which pretends that he may make himself a passive tool of slaughter. But next, the analogy *assumes*, (what none of my very dictatorial and insolent critics make even the faintest effort to prove to be a fact,) that God, like

---

* If miracles were vouchsafed on the scale of *a new sense*, it is of course conceivable that they would reveal new masses of fact, tending to modify our moral judgments of particular actions: but nothing of this can be made out in Judaism or Christianity.

† A friendly reviewer derides this passage as a very feeble objection to the doctrine of the Absolute Moral perfections of Jesus. It is here rather feebly *stated*, because at that period I had not fully worked out the thought. He seems to have forgotten that I am narrating.

man, speaks from without: that what we call Reason and Conscience is *not* his mode of commanding and revealing his will, but that words to strike the ear, or symbols displayed before the senses, are emphatically and exclusively "Revelation." Besides all this, the command of slaughter to the Jews is not directed against the seven nations of Canaan only, as modern theologians often erroneously assert: it is a *universal* permission of avaricious massacre and subjugation of "the cities which are very far off from thee, which are *not* of the cities of these nations," Deut. xx. 15.

The thoughts which here fill but a few pages, occupied me a long while in working out; because I consciously, with caution more than with timidity, declined to follow them rapidly. They came as dark suspicions or as flashing possibilities; and were again laid aside for reconsideration, lest I should be carried into antagonism to my old creed. For it is clear that great error arises in religion, by the undue ardour of converts, who become bitter against the faith which they have left, and outrun in zeal their new associates. So also successive centuries oscillate too far on the right and on the left of truth. But so happy was my position, that I needed not to hurry: no practical duty forced me to rapid decision, and a suspense of judgment was not an unwholesome exercise. Meanwhile, I sometimes thought Christianity to be to me, like the great river Ganges to a Hindoo. Of its value he has daily experience: he has piously believed that its sources are in heaven, but of late the report has come to him, that it only flows from very high mountains of this earth. What is he to believe? He knows not exactly: he cares not much: in any case the river is the gift of God to him: its positive benefits cannot be affected by a theory concerning its source.

Such a comparison undoubtedly implies that he who uses it discerns for himself a moral excellence in Christianity, and *submits to it only so far as this discernment commands*. I had practically reached this point, long before I concluded my theoretical inquiries as to Christianity itself: but in the course of this fifth period numerous other overpowering considerations crowded upon me which I must proceed to state in outline.

All pious Christians feel, and all the New Testament proclaims, that Faith is a moral act and a test of the moral and spiritual that is within us; so that he who is without faith, (faithless, unfaithful, "infidel,") is morally wanting and is cut off from God. To assent to a religious proposition *solely* in obedience to an outward miracle, would be Belief; but would not be Faith, any more than is scientific conviction. Bishop Butler and all his followers can insist with much force on this topic, when it suits them, and can quote most aptly from the New Testament to the same effect. They deduce, that a really overpowering miraculous proof would have destroyed the moral character of Faith: yet they do not see that the argument supersedes the authoritative force of outward miracles entirely. It had always appeared to me very strange in these divines, to insist on the stupendous character and convincing power of the Christian miracles, and then, in reply to the objection that they were *not* quite convincing, to say that the defect was purposely left "to try people's Faith." Faith in what? Not surely in the confessedly ill-proved miracle, but in the truth as discernible by the heart *without aid of miracle*.

I conceived of two men, Nathaniel and Demas, encountering a pretender to miracles, a Simon Magus of the scriptures. Nathaniel is guileless, sweet-hearted and of strong moral sense, but in worldly matters rather a simpleton. Demas is a sharp man, who gets on well in the world, quick of eye and shrewd of wit, hard-headed and not to be imposed upon by his fellows; but destitute of any high religious aspirations or deep moral insight. The juggleries of Simon are readily discerned by Demas, but thoroughly deceive poor Nathaniel: what then is the latter to do? To say that we are to receive true miracles and reject false ones, avails not, unless the mind is presumed to be capable of discriminating the one from the other. The wonders of Simon are as divine as the wonders of Jesus to a man, who, like Nathaniel, can account for neither by natural causes. If we enact the rule, that men are to "submit their understandings" to apparent prodigies, and that "revelation" is a thing of the outward senses, we alight on the unendurable absurdity, that Demas has faculties better fitted than those of Nathaniel for discriminating religious truth and error, and that Nathaniel, in obedience to eye and ear, which he knows to be very deceivable organs, is to abandon his moral perceptions.

Nor is the case altered, if instead of Simon in person, a huge thing called a Church is presented as a claimant of authority to Nathaniel. Suppose him to be a poor Spaniard, surrounded by false miracles, false erudition, and all the apparatus of reigning and unopposed Romanism. He cannot cope with the priests in cleverness,—detect their juggleries,—refute their historical falsehoods, disentangle their web of sophistry : but if he is truehearted, he may say : "You bid me not to keep faith with heretics : you defend murder, exile, imprisonment, fines, on men who will not submit their consciences to your authority : this I see to be wicked, though you ever so much pretend that God has taught it you." So, also, if he be accosted by learned clergymen, who undertake to prove that Jesus wrought stupendous miracles, or by learned Moolahs who allege the same of Mohammed or of Menu, he is quite unable to deal with them on the grounds of physiology, physics, or history.—In short, nothing can be plainer, than that *the moral and spiritual sense is the only religious faculty of the poor man;* and that as Christianity in its origin was preached to the poor, so it was to the inward senses that its first preachers appealed, as the supreme arbiters in the whole religious question. Is it not then absurd to say that in the act of conversion the convert is to trust his moral perception, and is ever afterwards to distrust it?

An incident had some years before come to my knowledge, which now seemed instructive. An educated, highly acute and thoughtful person, of very mature age, had become a convert to the Irving miracles, from an inability to distinguish them from those of the Pauline epistles ; or to discern anything of falsity which would justify his rejecting them. But after several years he totally renounced them as a miserable delusion, *because* he found that a system of false doctrine was growing up and was propped by them. Here was a clear case of a man with all the advantages of modern education and science, who yet found the direct judgment of a professed miracle, that was acted before his senses, too arduous for him! He was led astray while he trusted his power to judge of miracle: he was brought right by trusting to his moral perceptions.

When we farther consider, that a knowledge of Natural Philosophy and Physiology not only does not belong to the poor, but comes later in time to mankind than a knowledge of morals;—that a Miracle can only be judged of by Philosophy,—that it is not easy even for philosophers to define what is a "miracle"—that to discern "a deviation from the course of nature," implies a previous certain knowledge of what *the course of nature* is,—and that illiterate and early ages certainly have not this knowledge, and often have hardly even the idea,—it becomes quite a monstrosity to imagine that sensible and external miracles constitute the necessary process and guarantee of divine revelation.

Besides, if an angel appeared to my senses, and wrought miracles, how would that assure me of his moral qualities? Such miracles might prove his power and his knowledge, but whether malignant or benign, would remain doubtful, until by purely moral evidence, which no miracles could give, the doubt should be solved.* This is the old difficulty about diabolical wonders. The moderns cut the knot, by denying that any but God can possibly work real miracles. But to establish their principle, they make their definition and verification of a miracle so strict, as would have amazed the apostles; and after all, the difficulty recurs, that miraculous phenomena will never prove the goodness and veracity of God, if we do not know these qualities in Him without miracle. There is then a deeper and an earlier revelation of God, which sensible miracles can never give.

We cannot distinctly learn what was Paul's full idea of a divine revelation; but I can feel no doubt that he conceived it to be, in great measure, an *inward* thing. Dreams and visions were not excluded from influence, and more or less affected his moral judgment; but he did not, consciously and on principle, beat down his conscience in submission to outward impressions. To do so, is indeed to destroy the moral character of Faith, and lay the axe to the root, not of Christian doctrine only, but of every possible spiritual system.

Meanwhile, new breaches were made in those citadels of my creed which had not yet surrendered.

One branch of the Christian Evidences concerns itself with the *history* and *historical effects* of the faith, and among Pro-

---

* An ingenious gentleman, well versed in history, has put forth a volume called "The Restoration of Faith," in which he teaches that *I have no right to a conscience or to a God*, until I adopt his historical conclusions. I leave his co-religionists to confute his portentous heresy; but in fact it is already done more than enough in a splendid article of the "Westminster Review," July, 1852.

testants the efficacy of the Bible to enlighten and convert has been very much pressed. The disputant, however, is apt to play "fast and loose." He adduces the theory of Christianity when the history is unfavourable, and appeals to the history if the theory is impugned. In this way, just so much is picked out of the mass of facts as suits his argument, and the rest is quietly put aside.

I. In the theory of my early creed, (which was that of the New Testament, however convenient it may be for my critics to deride it as fanatical and *not* Christian,) cultivation of mind and erudition were classed with worldly things, which might be used where they pre-existed, (as riches and power may subserve higher ends,) but which were quite extraneous and unessential to the spiritual kingdom of Christ. A knowledge of the Bible was assumed to need only an honest heart and God's Spirit, while science, history, and philosophy were regarded as doubtful and dangerous auxiliaries. But soon after the first reflux of my mind took place towards the Common Understanding, as a guide of life legitimately co-ordinate with Scripture, I was impressed with the consideration that *Free Learning* had acted on a great scale for the improvement of spiritual religion. I had been accustomed to believe that *the Bible** brought about the Protestant Reformation; and until my twenty-ninth year probably it had not occurred to me to question this. But I was first struck with the thought, that the Bible did not prevent the absurd iniquities of the Nicene and Post Nicene controversy, and that the Church, with the Bible in her hands, sank down into the gulf of Popery. How then was the Bible a sufficient explanation of her recovering out of Popery?

Even a superficial survey of the history shows, that the first improvement of spiritual doctrine in the tenth and eleventh centuries, came from a study of the moral works of Cicero and Boethius;—a fact notorious in the common historians. The Latin moralists effected, what (strange to think!) the New Testament alone could not do.

In the fifteenth century, when Constantinople was taken

---

* I seem to have been understood now to say that a knowledge of the Bible was not a pre-requisite of the Protestant Reformation. What I say is, that at this period I learned the study of the Classics to have caused and determined that it should then take place; moreover, I say, that a free study of *other books than sacred ones* is essential, and always was, to conquer superstition.

by the Turks, learned Greeks were driven out to Italy and to other parts of the West, and the Roman Catholic world began to read the old Greek literature. All historians agree, that the enlightenment of mind hence arising was a prime mover of religious Reformation; and learned Protestants of Germany have even believed, that the overthrow of Popish error and establishment of purer truth would have been brought about more equably and profoundly, if Luther had never lived, and the passions of the vulgar had never been stimulated against the externals of Romanism.

At any rate, it gradually opened upon me, that the free cultivation of the *understanding*, which Latin and Greek literature had imparted to Europe and our freer public life, were chief causes of our religious superiority to Greek, Armenian, and Syrian Christians. As the Greeks in Constantinople under a centralized despotism retained no free intellect, and therefore the works of their fathers did their souls no good; so in Europe, just in proportion to the freedom of learning, has been the force of the result. In Spain and Italy the study of miscellaneous science and independent thought were nearly extinguished; in France and Austria they were crippled; in Protestant countries they have been freest. And then we impute all their effects to the Bible!*

I at length saw how untenable is the argument drawn from the inward history of Christianity in favour of its superhuman origin. In fact: this religion cannot pretend to *self-sustaining power*. Hardly was it started on its course, when it began to be polluted by the heathenism and false philosophy around it. With the decline of national genius and civil culture it became more and more debased. So far from being able to uphold the existing morality of the best Pagan teachers, it became barbarized itself, and sank into deep superstition and manifold moral corruption. From ferocious men it learnt ferocity. When civil society began to coalesce into order, Christianity also turned for the better, and presently learned to use the wisdom, first of Romans, then of Greeks: such studies opened men's eyes to new apprehensions of the Scrip-

* I am asked why *Italy* witnessed no improvement of spiritual doctrine. The reply is, that *she did*. The Evangelical movement there was quelled only by the Imperial arms and the Inquisition. I am also asked, why Pagan Literature did not save the ancient church from superstition. I have always understood that the vast majority of Christian teachers during the decline were unacquainted with Pagan literature, and that the Church at an early period *forbade* it.

ture and of its doctrine. By gradual and human means, Europe, like ancient Greece, grew up towards better political institutions; and Christianity improved with them,—the Christianity of the more educated. Beyond Europe, where there have been no such institutions, there has been no Protestant Reformation:—that is in the Greek, Armenian, Syrian, Coptic churches. Not unreasonably then do Franks in Turkey disown the title Nazarene, as denoting *that* Christianity which has not been purified by European laws and European learning. Christianity rises and sinks with political and literary influences: in so far,* it does not differ from other religions.

The same applied to the origin and advance of Judaism. It began in polytheistic and idolatrous barbarism: it cleared into a hard monotheism, with much superstition adhering to it. This was farther improved by successive psalmists and prophets, until Judaism culminated. The Jewish faith was eminently grand and pure; but there is nothing† in this history which we can adduce in proof of preternatural and miraculous agency.

II. The facts concerning the outward spread of Christianity have also been disguised by the party spirit of Christians, as though there were something essentially *different in kind* as to the mode in which it began and continued its conquests, from the corresponding history of other religions. But no such distinction can be made out. It is general to all religions to begin by moral means, and proceed farther by more worldly instruments.

Christianity had a great moral superiority over Roman paganism, in its humane doctrine of universal brotherhood, its unselfishness, its holiness; and thereby it attracted to itself

---

* My friend James Martineau, who insists that "a self-sustaining power" in a religion is a thing *intrinsically inconceivable*, need not have censured me for coming to the conclusion that it does not exist in Christianity. In fact, I entirely agree with him; but at the time of which I here write, I had only taken the first step in his direction; and I barely drew a negative conclusion, to which he perfectly assents. To my dear friend's capacious and kindling mind, all the thoughts here expounded are prosaic and common; being to him quite obvious, so far as they are true. He is right in looking down upon them; and, I trust, by his aid, I have added to my wisdom since the time of which I write. Yet they were to me discoveries once, and he must not be displeased at my making much of them in this connexion.

† It is the fault of my critics that I am forced to tell the reader this is exhibited in my "Hebrew Monarchy."

(among other and baser materials) all the purest natures and most enthusiastic temperaments. Its first conquests were noble and admirable. But there is nothing *superhuman* or unusual in this. Mohammedism in the same way conquers those Pagan creeds which are morally inferior to it. The Seljuk and the Ottoman Turks were Pagans, but adopted the religion of Tartars and Persians whom they subjugated, because it was superior and was blended with a superior civilization; exactly as the German conquerors of the Western Empire of Rome adopted some form of Christianity.

But if it is true that *the sword* of Mohammed was the influence which subjected Arabia, Egypt, Syria and Persia to the religion of Islam, it is no less true that the Roman empire was finally conquered to Christianity by the sword. Before Constantine, Christians were but a small fraction of the empire. In the preceding century they had gone on deteriorating in good sense and most probably therefore in moral worth, and had made no such rapid progress in numbers as to imply that by the mere process of conversion they would ever Christianize the empire. That the conversion of Constantine, such as it was, (for he was baptized only just before death,) was dictated by mere worldly considerations, few modern Christians will deny. Yet a great fact is here implied; viz., that Christianity was adopted as a state-religion, because of the great *political* power accruing from the organization of the churches and the devotion of Christians to their ecclesiastical citizenship. Roman statesmen well knew that a hundred thousand Roman citizens devoted to the interests of Rome, could keep in subjection a population of ten millions who were destitute of any intense patriotism and had no central objects of attachment. The Christian church had shown its immense resisting power and its tenacious union, in the persecution by Galerius; and Constantine was discerning enough to see the vast political importance of winning over such a body; which, though but a small fraction of the whole empire, was the only party which could give coherence to that empire, the only one which had enthusiastic adherents in every province, the only one on whose resolute devotion it was possible for a partizan to rely securely. The bravery and faithful attachment of Christian regiments was a lesson not lost upon Constantine; and we may say, in some sense, that the Christian soldiers in his armies conquered the empire (that is, the imperial appointments) for Christianity. But Paganism subsisted, even in spite of imperial allurements, until at length the sword of Theodosius violently suppressed heathen worship. So also, it was the spear of Charlemagne which drove the Saxons to baptism, and decided the extirpation of Paganism from Teutonic Europe. There is nothing in all this to distinguish the outward history of Christianity from that of Mohammedism. Barbarous tribes, now and then, venerating the superiority of our knowledge, adopt our religion: so have Pagan nations in Africa voluntarily become Mussulmans. But neither we nor they can appeal to any case, where an old State-religion has yielded without warlike compulsion to the force of heavenly truth,—" charm we never so wisely." The whole influence which Christianity exerts over the world at large depends on the political history of modern Europe. The Christianity of Asia and Abyssinia is perhaps as pure and as respectable in this nineteenth century as it was in the fourth and fifth, yet no good or great deeds come forth out of it, of such a kind that Christian disputants dare to appeal to them with triumph. The politico-religious and very peculiar history of *European* Christendom has alone elevated the modern world; and as Gibbon remarks, this whole history has directly depended on the fate of the great battles of Tours between the Moors and the Franks. The defeat of Mohammedism by Christendom certainly has not been effected by spiritual weapons. The soldier and the statesman have done to the full as much as the priest to secure Europe for Christianity, and win a Christendom of which Christians can be proud. As for the Christendom of Asia, the apologists of Christianity simply ignore it. With these facts, how can it be pretended that the external history of Christianity points to an exclusively divine origin?

The author of the "Eclipse of Faith" has derided me for despatching in two paragraphs what occupied Gibbon's whole fifteenth chapter; but this author, here as always, misrepresents me. Gibbon is exhibiting and developing the deep-seated causes of the spread of Christianity before Constantine, and he by no means exhausts the subject. I am comparing the ostensible and notorious facts concerning the outward conquest of Christianity with those of other religions. To *account* for the early growth of any religion, Christian, Mussulman, or Mormonite, is always difficult.

III. The moral advantages which we owe to Christianity have been exaggerated by the same party spirit, as if there were in them anything miraculous.

1. We are told that Christianity is the decisive influence which has raised *womankind:* this does not appear to be true. The old Roman matron was, relatively to her husband,* morally as high as in modern Italy: nor is there any ground for supposing that modern women have advantage over the ancient in Spain and Portugal, where Germanic have been counteracted by Moorish influences. The relative position of the sexes in Homeric Greece exhibits nothing materially different from the present day. In Armenia and Syria perhaps Christianity has done the service of extinguishing polygamy: this is creditable, though nowise miraculous. Judaism also unlearnt polygamy, and made an unbidden improvement upon Moses. In short, only in countries where Germanic sentiment has taken root, do we see marks of any elevation of the female sex superior to that of Pagan antiquity; and as this elevation of the German woman in her deepest Paganism was already striking to Tacitus and his contemporaries, it is highly unreasonable to claim it as an achievement of Christianity.

In point of fact, Christian doctrine, as propounded by Paul, is not at all so honourable to woman as that which German soundness of heart has established. With Paul† the *sole* reason for marriage, is, that a man may gratify instinct without sin. He teaches, that *but* for this object it would be better not to marry. He wishes that all were in this respect as free as himself, and calls it a special gift of God. He does not encourage a man to desire a mutual soul intimately to share griefs and joys; one in whom the confiding heart can repose, whose smile shall reward and soften toil, whose voice shall beguile sorrow. He does not seem aware that the fascinations of woman refine and chasten society; that virtuous attachment has in it an element of respect, which abashes and purifies, and which shields the soul, even when marriage is deferred; nor yet, that the union of two persons who have no previous affection can seldom yield the highest fruits of

---

* It is not to the purpose to urge the *political* minority of the Roman wife. This was a mere inference from the high power of the head of the household. The father had right of death over his son, and (as the lawyers stated the case) the wife was on the level of one of the children.
† 1 Cor. vii. 2—9.

matrimony, but often leads to the severest temptations. How *should* he have known all this? Courtship before marriage did not exist in the society open to him: hence he treats the propriety of giving away a maiden, as one in which *her* conscience, *her* likes and dislikes, are not concerned: 1 Cor. vii. 37, 38. If the law leaves the parent "power over his own will" and imposes no "necessity" to give her away, Paul decidedly advises to keep her unmarried.

The author of the Apocalypse, a writer of the first century, who was received in the second as John the apostle, holds up a yet more degrading view of the matrimonial relation. In one of his visions he exhibits 144,000 chosen saints, perpetual attendants of "the Lamb," and places the cardinal point of their sanctity in the fact, that "they were not defiled with women, but were virgins." Marriage, therefore, is defilement! Protestant writers struggle in vain against this obvious meaning of the passage. Against all analogy of Scriptural metaphor, they gratuitously pretend that *women* mean *idolatrous religions:* namely, because in the Old Testament the Jewish Church is personified as a virgin betrothed to God, and an idol is spoken of as her paramour.

As a result of the apostolic doctrines, in the second, third, and following centuries, very gross views concerning the relation of the sexes prevailed, and have been everywhere transmitted where men's morality is exclusively* formed from the New Testament. The marriage service of the Church of England, which incorporates the Pauline doctrine, is felt by English brides and bridegrooms to contain what is so offensive and degrading, that many clergymen mercifully make unlawful omissions. Paul had indeed expressly denounced *prohibitions* of marriage. In merely *dissuading* it, he gave advice, which, from his limited horizon and under his expectation of the speedy return of Christ, was sensible and good; but when this advice, with all its reasons, was made an oracle of eternal wisdom, it generated the monkish notions concerning womanhood. If the desire of a wife is a weakness, which the apostle would gladly have forbidden, only that he feared worse consequences, an enthusiastic youth cannot but infer that it is a higher state of perfection *not* to desire a wife, and therefore

---

* Namely, in the Armenian, Syrian, and Greek churches, and in the Romish church in exact proportion as Germanic and poetical influences have been repressed; that is, in proportion as the hereditary Christian doctrine has been kept pure from modern innovations.

aspires to "the crown of virginity." Here at once is full-grown monkery. Hence that debasement of the imagination, which is directed perpetually to the lowest, instead of the highest side of the female nature. Hence the disgusting admiration and invocation of Mary's perpetual virginity. Hence the transcendental doctrine of her immaculate conception from Anne, the "grandmother of God."

In the above my critics have represented me to say that Christianity has done *nothing* for women. I have not said so, but that what it has done has been exaggerated. I say: If the *theory* of Christianity is to take credit from the *history* of Christendom, it must also receive discredit. Taking in the whole system of nuns and celibates, and the doctrine which sustains it, the root of which is apostolic, I doubt whether any balance of credit remains over from this side of Christian history. I am well aware that the democratic doctrine of "the equality of souls" has a *tendency* to elevate women,—and the poorer orders too; but this is not the whole of actual Christianity, which is a very heterogeneous mass.

2. Again: the modern doctrine, by aid of which West Indian slavery has been exterminated, is often put forward as Christian; but I had always discerned that it was not Biblical, and that, in respect to this great triumph, undue credit has been claimed for the fixed Biblical and authoritative doctrine. As I have been greatly misunderstood in my first edition, I am induced to expand this topic. Sir George Stephen,* after describing the long struggle in England against the West Indian interest and other obstacles, says, that for some time, "worst of all, we found the people, not actually against us, but apathetic, lethargic, incredulous, indifferent. It was then, and *not till then*, that we sounded the right note, and touched a chord that never ceased to vibrate. *To uphold slavery was a crime against God!* It was a NOVEL DOCTRINE, but it was a cry that was heard, for it would be heard. The national conscience was awakened to inquiry, and inquiry soon produced conviction." Sir George justly calls the doctrine novel. As developed in the controversy, it laid down the general proposition, that *men and women are not, and cannot be chattels;* and that all human enactments which decree this are *morally null and void,* as sinning against the higher law of nature and of God. And the reason of this lies in the

* In a tract republished from the *Northampton Mercury.* Longman, 1853.

essential contrast of a moral personality and a chattel. Criminals may deserve to be bound and scourged, but they do not cease to be persons, nor indeed do even the insane. Since every man is a person, he cannot be a piece of property, nor has an "owner" any just and moral claim to his services. Usage, so far from conferring this claim, increases the total amount of injustice; the longer an innocent man is *forcibly* kept in slavery, the greater the reparation to which he is entitled for the oppressive immorality. This doctrine I now believe to be irrefutable truth, but I disbelieved it while I thought the Scripture authoritative; because I found a very different doctrine there—a doctrine which is the argumentative stronghold of the American slaveholder. Paul sent back the fugitive Onesimus to his master Philemon, with kind recommendations and apologies for the slave, and a tender charge to Philemon, that he would receive Onesimus as a brother in the Lord, since he had been converted by Paul in the interval; but this very recommendation, full of affection as it is, virtually recognizes the moral rights of Philemon to the services of his slave; and hinting that if Onesimus stole anything, Philemon should now forgive him, Paul shows perfect insensibility to the fact that the master who detains a slave in captivity against his will, is guilty himself of a continual theft. What says Mrs. Beecher Stowe's Cassy to this? "Stealing!—They who steal body and soul need not talk to us. Every one of these bills is stolen—stolen from poor starving, sweating creatures." Now Onesimus, in the very act of taking to flight, showed that he had been submitting to servitude against his will, and that the house of his owner had previously been a prison to him. To suppose that Philemon has a pecuniary interest in the return of Onesimus to work without wages, implies that the master habitually steals the slave's earnings; but if he loses nothing by the flight, he has not been wronged by it. Such is the modern doctrine, developed out of the fundamental fact that persons are not chattels; but it is to me wonderful that it should be needful to prove to any one, that this is *not* the doctrine of the New Testament. Paul and Peter deliver excellent charges to masters in regard to the treatment of their slaves, but without any hint to them that there is an injustice in claiming them as slaves at all. That slavery, *as a system*, is essentially immoral, no Christian of those days seems to have suspected. Yet it existed in its worst forms under Rome. Whole gangs of slaves were mere tools of capitalists, and were numbered like cattle, with no moral relationship to the owner; young women of beautiful person were sold as articles of voluptuousness. Of course every such fact was looked upon by Christians as hateful and dreadful; yet, I say, it did not lead them to that moral condemnation of slavery, *as such*, which has won the most signal victory in modern times, and is destined, I trust, to win one far greater.

A friendly reviewer replies to this, that the apathy of the early Christians to the intrinsic iniquity of the slave system rose out of "their expectation of an immediate close of this world's affairs. The only reason why Paul sanctioned contentment with his condition in the converted slave, was, that for so short a time it was not worth while for any man to change his state." I agree to this; but it does not alter my fact: on the contrary, it confirms what I say,—that the Biblical morality is not final truth. To account for an error surely is not to deny it.

Another writer has said on the above: "Let me suppose you animated to go as missionary to the East to preach this (Mr. Newman's) spiritual system: would you, in addition to all this, publicly denounce the social and political evils under which the nations groan? If so, your spiritual projects would soon be perfectly understood, and *summarily dealt with.*—It is vain to say, that, if commissioned by Heaven, and endowed with power of working miracles, you would do so; for you cannot tell under what limitations your commission would be given: it is pretty certain, that *it would leave you to work a moral and spiritual system by moral and spiritual means*, and not allow you to turn the world upside down, and *mendaciously* tell it that you came only to preach peace, while every syllable you uttered would be an incentive to sedition."—*Eclipse of Faith*, p. 419.

This writer supposes that he is attacking *me*, when every line is an attack on Christ and Christianity. Have *I* pretended power of working miracles? Have I imagined or desired that miracle would shield me from persecution? Did Jesus *not* "publicly denounce the social and political evils" of Judæa? was he not "summarily dealt with"? Did he not know that his doctrine would send on earth "not peace, but a sword"? and was he *mendacious* in saying, "Peace I leave unto you?" or were the angels mendacious in proclaiming, "Peace on earth, goodwill among men"? Was not "every syllable that Jesus uttered" in the discourse of Matth. xxiii., "an incentive to sedition?" and does this writer judge it to be *mendacity*, that Jesus opened by advising to OBEY the very men, whom he proceeds to vilify at large as immoral, oppressive, hypocritical, blind, and destined to the damnation of hell? Or have I anywhere blamed the apostles because they did *not* exasperate wicked men by direct attacks? It is impossible to answer such a writer as this; for he elaborately misses to touch what I have said. On the other hand, it is rather too much to require me to defend Jesus from his assault.

Christian preachers did not escape the imputation of turning the world upside down, and at length, in some sense, effected what was imputed. It is matter of conjecture, whether any greater convulsion would have happened, if the apostles had done as the Quakers in America. No Quaker holds slaves: why not? Because the Quakers teach their members that it is an essential immorality. The slave-holding states are infinitely more alive and jealous to keep up their "peculiar institution," than was the Roman government; yet the Quakers have caused no political convulsion. I confess, to me it seems, that if Paul, and John, and Peter, and James, had done as these Quakers, the imperial administration would have looked on it as a harmless eccentricity of the sect, and not as an incentive* to sedition. But be this as it may, I did not say what else the apostles might have succeeded to enforce; I merely pointed out what it was that they actually taught, and that, *as a fact*, they did *not* declare slavery to be an immorality and the basest of thefts. If any one thinks their course was more wise, he may be right or wrong, but his opinion is in itself a concession of my fact.

As to the historical progress of Christian practice and doctrine on this subject, it is, as usual, mixed of good and evil. The humanity of good Pagan emperors softened the harshness of the laws of bondage, and manumission had always been extremely common amongst the Romans. Of course, the more humane religion of Christ acted still more powerfully in the same direction, especially in inculcating the propriety of freeing *Christian* slaves. This was creditable, but not peculiar,

---

* The Romans practised fornication at pleasure, and held it ridiculous to blame them. If Paul had claimed authority to hinder them, they might have been greatly exasperated; but they had not the least objection to his denouncing fornication as immoral to Christians. Why not slavery also?

and is not a fact of such a nature as to add to the exclusive claims of Christianity. To every *proselyting* religion the sentiment is so natural, that no divine spirit is needed to originate and establish it. Mohammedans also have a conscience against enslaving Mohammedans, and generally bestow freedom on a slave as soon as he adopts their religion. But no zeal for *human* freedom has ever grown out of the purely biblical and ecclesiastical system, any more than out of the Mohammedan. In the middle ages, zeal for the liberation of serfs first rose in the breasts of the clergy, after the whole population had become nominally Christian. It was not men, but Christians, whom the clergy desired to make free: it is hard to say, that they thought Pagans to have any human rights at all, even to life. Nor is it correct to represent ecclesiastical influences as the sole agency which overthrew slavery and serfdom. The desire of the kings to raise up the chartered cities as a bridle to the barons, was that which chiefly made rustic slavery untenable in its coarsest form; for a "villain" who escaped into the free cities could not be recovered. In later times, the first public act against slavery came from republican France, in the madness of atheistic enthusiasm; when she declared black and white men to be equally free, and liberated the negroes of St. Domingo. In Britain, the battle of social freedom has been fought chiefly by that religious sect which rests least on the letter of Scripture. The bishops, and the more learned clergy, have consistently been apathetic to the duty of overthrowing the slave system.—I was thus led to see, that here also the New Testament precepts must not be received by me as any final and authoritative law of morality.

But I meet opposition in a quarter from which I had least expected it;—from one who admits the imperfection of the morality actually attained by the apostles, but avows that Christianity, as a divine system, is not to be identified with apostolic doctrine, but with the doctrine *ultimately developed* in the Christian Church; moreover, the ecclesiastical doctrine concerning slavery he alleges to be truer than mine,—I mean, truer than that which I have expounded as held by modern abolitionists. He approves of the principle of claiming freedom, not for *men*, but for *Christians.* He says: "That Christianity opened its arms at all to the servile class was enough; for in its embrace was the sure promise of emancipation . . . . . . Is it imputed as a disgrace, that Christianity put conversion before manumission, and *brought them to God, ere it trusted*

them with themselves? .... It created the simultaneous obligation to make the Pagan a convert, and the convert free."
..... "If our author had made his attack from the opposite side, and contended that its doctrines 'proved too much' against servitude, and *assumed with too little qualification the capacity of each man for self-rule,* we should have felt more hesitation in expressing our dissent."

I feel unfeigned surprize at these sentiments from one whom I so highly esteem and admire; and considering that they were written at first anonymously, and perhaps under pressure of time, for a review, I hope it is not presumptuous in me to think it possible that they are hasty, and do not wholly express a deliberate and final judgment. I must think there is some misunderstanding; for I have made no high claims about capacity for *self-rule,* as if laws and penalties were to be done away. But the question is, shall human beings, who (as all of us) are imperfect, be controlled by public law, or by individual caprice? Was not my reviewer intending to advocate some form of *serfdom* which is compatible with legal rights, and recognizes the serf as a man; not *slavery* which pronounces him a chattel? Serfdom and apprenticeship we may perhaps leave to be reasoned down by economists and administrators; slavery proper is what I attacked as essentially immoral.

Returning then to the arguments, I reason against them as if I did not know their author.—I have distinctly avowed, that the effort to liberate Christian slaves was creditable: I merely add, that in this respect Christianity is no better than Mohammedism. But is it really no moral fault,—is it not a moral enormity,—to deny that Pagans have human rights? "That Christianity opened its arms *at all* to the servile class, *was enough.*" Indeed! Then either unconverted men have no natural right to freedom, or Christians may withhold a natural right from them. Under the plea of "bringing them to God," Christians are to deny by law, to every slave who refuses to be converted, the rights of husband and father, rights of persons, rights of property, rights over his own body. Thus manumission is a bribe to make hypocritical converts, and Christian superiority a plea for depriving men of their dearest rights. Is not freedom older than Christianity? Does the Christian recommend his religion to a Pagan by stealing his manhood and all that belongs to it? Truly, if only Christians have a right to personal freedom, what harm is there in hunting and catching Pagans to make slaves of them ? And this was exactly the "development" of thought and doctrine in the Christian church. The same priests who taught that *Christians* have moral rights to their sinews and skin, to their wives and children, and to the fruit of their labour, which *Pagans* have not, consistently developed the same fundamental idea of Christian superiority into the lawfulness of making war upon the heathen, and reducing them to the state of domestic animals. If Christianity is to have credit from the former, it must also take the credit of the latter. If cumulative evidence of its divine origin is found in the fact, that Christendom has liberated Christian slaves, must we forget the cumulative evidence afforded by the assumed right of the Popes to carve out the countries of the heathen, and bestow them with their inhabitants on Christian powers ? Both results flow logically out of the same assumption, and were developed by the same school.

But, I am told, a man must not be freed, until we have ascertained his capacity for self-rule ! This is indeed a tyrannical assumption: *vindiciæ secundum servitutem*. Men are not to have their human rights, until we think they will not abuse them ! Prevention is to be used against the hitherto innocent and injured ! The principle involves all that is arrogant, violent, and intrusive, in military tyranny and civil espionage. Self-rule ? But abolitionists have no thought of exempting men from the penalties of common law, if they transgress the law; we only desire that all men shall be equally subjected to the law, and equally protected by it. It is truly a strange inference, that because a man is possibly deficient in virtue, therefore he shall not be subject to public law, but to private caprice: as if this were a school of virtue, and not eminently an occasion of vice. Truer far is Homer's morality, who says, that a man loses half his virtue on the day he is made a slave. As to the pretence that slaves are not fit for freedom, those Englishmen who are old enough to remember the awful predictions which West Indian planters used to pour forth about the bloodshed and confusion which would ensue, if they were hindered by law from scourging black men and violating black women, might, I think, afford to despise the danger of *enacting* that men and women shall be treated as men and women, and not made tools of vice and victims of cruelty. If ever sudden emancipation ought to have produced violences and wrong from the emancipated, it was in Jamaica, where the oppression and ill-will was so great; yet the freed blacks have not in fifteen years inflicted on the whites as much lawless violence as they suffered themselves in six months of apprenticeship. It is the *masters* of slaves, not the slaves, who are deficient in self-rule; and slavery is doubly detestable, because it depraves the masters.

What degree of "worldly moderation and economical forethought" is needed by a practical statesman in effecting the liberation of slaves, it is no business of mine to discuss. I however feel assured, that no constitutional statesman, having to contend against the political votes of numerous and powerful slave-owners, who believe their fortunes to be at stake, will ever be found to undertake the task *at all*, against the enormous resistance of avarice and habit, unless religious teachers pierce the conscience of the nation by denouncing slavery as an essential wickedness. Even the petty West Indian interests —a mere fraction of the English empire—were too powerful, until this doctrine was taught. Mr. Canning in parliament spoke emphatically against slavery, but did not dare to bring in a bill against it. When such is English experience, I cannot but expect the same will prove true in America.

In replying to objectors, I have been carried beyond my narrative, and have written from my *present* point of view; I may therefore here complete this part of the argument, though by anticipation.

The New Testament has beautifully laid down Truth and Love as the culminating virtues of man; but it has imperfectly discerned that Love is impossible where Justice does not go first. Regarding this world as destined to be soon burnt up, it despaired of improving the foundations of society, and laid down the principle of Non-resistance, even to Injurious force, in terms so unlimited, as practically to throw its entire weight into the scale of tyranny. It recognizes individuals who call themselves kings or magistrates (however tyrannical and usurping), as Powers ordained of God: it does *not* recognize nations as Communities ordained of God, or as having any power and authority whatsoever, as against pretentious individuals. To obey a king, is strenuously enforced; to resist a usurping king, in a patriotic cause, is not contemplated in the New Testament as under any circumstances an imaginable duty. Patriotism has no recognized existence in the Christian records. I am well aware of the *cause* of this: I do not say that it reflects any dishonour on the Christian apostles: I merely remark on it as a calamitous fact, and deduce that their precepts cannot and must not be made the sufficient rule of life, or they will still be (as they always have hitherto been) a mainstay of tyranny. The rights of Men and of Nations are wholly ignored* in the New Testament, but the authority of Slave-owners and of Kings is very distinctly recorded for solemn religious sanction. If it had been wholly silent, no one could have appealed to its decision : but by consecrating mere Force, it has promoted Injustice, and in so far has made that Love impossible, which it desired to establish.

It is but one part of this great subject, that the apostles absolutely command a slave to give obedience to his master in all things, "as to the Lord." It is in vain to deny, that *the most grasping of slave-owners asks nothing more of abolitionists than that they would all adopt Paul's creed;* viz., acknowledge the full authority of owners of slaves, tell them that they are responsible to God alone, and charge them to use their power righteously and mercifully.

3. LASTLY : it is a lamentable fact, that not only do superstitions about Witches, Ghosts, Devils, and Diabolical Miracles derive a strong support from the Bible, (and in fact have been exploded by nothing but the advance of physical philosophy,)—but what is far worse, the Bible alone has nowhere sufficed to establish an enlightened religious toleration. This is at first seemingly unintelligible : for the apostles certainly would have been intensely shocked at the thought of punishing men, in body, purse, or station, for not being Christians or not being orthodox. Nevertheless, not only does the Old Testament justify bloody persecution, but the New teaches † that God will visit men with fiery vengeance *for holding an erroneous creed;*—that vengeance indeed is his, not ours ; but

---

* I fear it cannot be denied that the zeal for Christianity which began to arise in our upper classes sixty years ago, was largely prompted by a feeling that its precepts repress all speculations concerning the rights of man. A similar cause now influences despots all over Europe. The *Old* Testament contains the elements which they dread, and these gave a political creed to our Puritans.

† More than one critic flatly denies the fact. It is sufficient for me here to say, that such is the obvious interpretation, and such *historically has been* the interpretation of various texts,—for instance, 2 Thess. i. 7: "The Lord Jesus shall be revealed, ... in flaming fire, taking vengeance on them *that know not God, and that obey not the Gospel;* who shall be punished with everlasting destruction," &c. Such again is the sense which all popular minds receive and must receive from Heb. x. 25—31.—I am willing to change *teaches* into *has always been understood to teach,* if my critics think anything is gained by it.

that still the punishment is deserved. It would appear, that wherever this doctrine is held, possession of power for two or three generations inevitably converts men into persecutors; and in so far, we must lay the horrible desolations which Europe has suffered from bigotry, at the doors, not indeed of the Christian apostles themselves, but of that Bibliolatry which has converted their earliest records into a perfect and eternal law.

IV. "Prophecy" is generally regarded as a leading evidence of the divine origin of Christianity. But this also had proved itself to me a more and more mouldering prop, whether I leant on those which concerned Messiah, those of the New Testament, or the miscellaneous predictions of the Old Testament.

1. As to the Messianic prophecies, I began to be pressed with the difficulty of proving against the Jews that "Messiah was to suffer." The Psalms generally adduced for this purpose can in no way be fixed on Messiah. The prophecy in the 9th chapter of Daniel looks specious in the authorized English version, but has evaporated in the Greek translation and is not acknowledged in the best German renderings. I still rested on the 53rd chapter of Isaiah, as alone fortifying me against the Rabbis: yet with an unpleasantly increasing perception that the system of " double interpretation" in which Christians indulge, is a playing fast and loose with prophecy, and is essentially dishonest. *No one dreams of a " second sense until the primary sense proves false:* all false prophecy may be thus screened. The three prophecies quoted (Acts xiii. 33—35) in proof of the resurrection of Jesus, are simply puerile, and deserve no reply.—I felt there was something unsound in all this.

2. The prophecies of the New Testament are not many. First, we have that of Jesus in Matt xxiv. concerning the destruction of Jerusalem. It is marvellously exact, down to the capture of the city and miserable enslavement of the population; but at this point it becomes clearly and hopelessly false: namely, it declares, that "*immediately after* that tribulation, the sun shall be darkened, &c. &c., and then shall appear the sign of the Son of Man in heaven, and then shall all the tribes of the earth mourn, and they shall see the Son of Man coming in the clouds of heaven with power and great glory. And he shall send his angels with a great sound of a trumpet, and they shall gather together his elect," &c. This

is a manifest description of the Great Day of Judgment : and the prophecy goes on to add : "Verily I say unto you, This generation shall not pass, till all these things be fulfilled." When we thus find a prediction to break down suddenly in the middle, we have the well-known mark of its earlier part being written after the event : and it becomes unreasonable to doubt that the detailed annunciations of this 24th chapter of Matthew, were first composed *very soon after* the war of Titus, and never came from the lips of Jesus at all. Next: we have the prophecies of the Apocalypse. Not one of these can be interpreted certainly of any human affairs, except one in the 17th chapter, which the writer himself has explained to apply to the emperors of Rome : and that is proved false by the event.—Farther, we have Paul's prophecies concerning the apostacy of the Christian Church. These are very striking, as they indicate his deep insight into the moral tendencies of the community in which he moved. They are high testimonies to the prophetic soul of Paul; and as such, I cannot have any desire to weaken their force. But there is nothing in them that can establish the theory of supernaturalism, in the face of his great mistake as to the speedy return of Christ from heaven.

3. As for the Old Testament, if all its prophecies about Babylon and Tyre and Edom and Ishmael and the four Monarchies were both true and supernatural, what would this prove? That God had been pleased to reveal something of coming history to certain eminent men of Hebrew antiquity. That is all. We should receive this conclusion with an otiose faith. It could not order or authorize us to submit our souls and consciences to the obviously defective morality of the Mosaic system in which these prophets lived; and with Christianity it has nothing to do.

At the same time I had reached the conclusion that large deductions must be made from the credit of these old prophecies.

First, as to the Book of Daniel: the 11th chapter is closely historical down to Antiochus Epiphanes, after which it suddenly becomes false ; and according to different modern expositors, leaps away to Mark Antony, or to Napoleon Buonaparte, or to the Papacy. Hence we have a *primâ facie* presumption that the book was composed in the reign of that Antiochus: nor can it be proved to have existed earlier: nor is there in it one word of prophecy which can be shown to have been fulfilled in regard to any later era. Nay, the 7th chapter also is confuted by the event; for the great Day of Judgment has not followed upon the fourth* Monarchy.

Next, as to the prophecies of the Pentateuch. They abound, as to the times which precede the century of Hezekiah; higher than which we cannot trace the Pentateuch.† No prophecy of the Pentateuch can be proved to have been fulfilled, which had not been already fulfilled before Hezekiah's day.

Thirdly, as to the prophecies which concern various nations, —some of them are remarkably verified, as that against Babylon; others failed, as those of Ezekiel concerning Nebuchadnezzar's wars against Tyre and Egypt. The fate predicted against Babylon was delayed for five centuries, so as to lose all moral meaning as a divine infliction on the haughty city.— On the whole, it was clear to me, that it is a vain attempt to forge polemical weapons out of these old prophets, for the service of modern creeds.‡

V. My study of John's gospel had not enabled me to sustain Dr. Arnold's view, that it was an impregnable fortress of Christianity.

In discussing the Apocalypse, I had long before felt a doubt whether we ought not rather to assign that book to John the apostle in preference to the Gospel and Epistles: but this remained only as a doubt. The monotony also of the Gospel had often excited my *wonder*. But I was for the first time *offended*, on considering with a fresh mind an old fact,—the great similarity of the style and phraseology in the third chapter, in the testimony of the Baptist, as well as in Christ's address to Nicodemus, that of John's own epistle. As the three first gospels have their family likeness, which enables us on hearing a text to know that it comes out of one of the three, though we perhaps know not which; so is it with the Gospel and Epistles of John. When a verse is read, we know that it is either from an epistle of John, or else from the

---

* The four monarchies in chapters ii. and vii. are, probably, the Babylonian, the Median, the Persian, the Macedonian. Interpreters however blend the Medes and Persians into one, and then pretend that the Roman empire is *still in existence*.

† The first apparent reference is by Micah (vi. 5) a contemporary of Hezekiah; which proves that an account contained in our Book of Numbers was already familiar.

‡ I have had occasion to discuss most of the leading prophecies of the Old Testament in my "Hebrew Monarchy."

Jesus of John; but often we cannot tell which. On contemplating the marked character of this phenomenon, I saw it infallibly* to indicate that John has made both the Baptist and Jesus speak, as John himself would have spoken; and that we cannot trust the historical reality of the discourses in the fourth gospel.

That narrative introduces an entirely new phraseology, with a perpetual discoursing about the Father and the Son; of which there is barely the germ in Matthew:—and herewith a new doctrine concerning the heaven-descended personality of Jesus. That the divinity of Christ cannot be proved from the three first gospels, was confessed by the early Church, and is proved by the labouring arguments of the modern Trinitarians. What then can be clearer, than that John has put into the mouth of Jesus the doctrines of half a century later, which he desired to recommend?

When this conclusion pressed itself first on my mind, the name of Strauss was only beginning to be known in England, and I did not read his great work until years after I had come to a final opinion on this whole subject. The contemptuous reprobation of Strauss in which it is fashionable for English writers to indulge, makes it a duty to express my high sense of the lucid force with which he unanswerably shows that the fourth gospel (whoever the author was) is no faithful exhibition of the discourses of Jesus. Before I had discerned this so vividly in all its parts, it had become quite certain to me that the secret colloquy with Nicodemus, and the splendid testimony of the Baptist to the Father and the Son, were wholly modelled out of John's own imagination. And no sooner had I felt how severe was the shock to John's general veracity, than a new and even graver difficulty rose upon me.

The stupendous and public event of Lazarus's resurrection, —the circumstantial cross-examination of the man born blind and healed by Jesus,—made those two miracles, in Dr. Arnold's view, grand and unassailable bulwarks of Christianity. The more I considered them, the mightier their superiority seemed

---

* A critic is pleased to call this a mere *suspicion* of my own; in so writing, people simply evade my argument. I do not ask them to adopt my conviction; I merely communicate it as mine, and wish them to admit that it is *my duty* to follow my own conviction. It is with me no mere "suspicion," but a certainty. When they cannot possibly give, or pretend, any *proof* that the long discourses of the fourth gospel have been accurately reported, they ought to be less supercilious in their claims of unlimited belief. If it is right for them to follow their judgment on a purely literary question, let them not carp at me for following mi

to those of the other gospels. They were wrought at Jerusalem, under the eyes of the rulers, who did their utmost to detect them, and could not; but in frenzied despair, plotted to kill Lazarus. How different from the frequently vague and wholesale statements of the other gospels concerning events which happened where no enemy was watching to expose delusion! many of them in distant and uncertain localities.

But it became the more needful to ask, How was it that the other writers omitted to tell of such decisive exhibitions? Were they so dull in logic, as not to discern the superiority of these? Can they possibly have known of such miracles, wrought under the eyes of the Pharisees, and defying all their malice, and yet have told in preference other less convincing marvels? The question could not be long dwelt on, without eliciting the reply: "It is necessary to believe, at least until the contrary shall be proved, that the three first writers either had never heard of these two miracles, or disbelieved them." Thus the account rests on the unsupported evidence of John, with a weighty presumption against its truth.

When, where, and in what circumstances did John write? It is agreed, that he wrote half a century after the events; when the other disciples were all dead; when Jerusalem was destroyed, her priests and learned men dispersed, her nationality dissolved, her coherence annihilated:—he wrote in a tongue foreign to the Jews of Palestine, and for a foreign people, in a distant country, and in the bosom of an admiring and confiding church, which was likely to venerate him the more, the greater marvels he asserted concerning their Master. He told them miracles of firstrate magnitude, which no one before had recorded. Is it possible for me to receive them *on his word*, under circumstances so conducive to delusion, and without a single check to ensure his accuracy? Quite impossible; when I have already seen how little to be trusted is his report of the discourses and doctrine of Jesus.

But was it necessary to impute to John conscious and wilful deception? By no means absolutely necessary;—as appeared by the following train* of thought. John tells us that Jesus promised the Comforter, *to bring to their memory* things that concerned him: oh that one could have the satisfaction of cross-examining John on this subject! Let me suppose him put into the witness-box; and I will speak to him thus: "O

---

* I am told that this defence of John is fanciful. It satifies me provisionally; but I do not hold myself bound to satisfy others, or to explain John's delusiveness.

aged Sir, we understand that you have two memories, a natural and a miraculous one: with the former you retain events as other men; with the latter you recall what had been totally forgotten. Be pleased to tell us now. Is it from your natural or from your supernatural memory that you derive your knowledge of the miracle wrought on Lazarus and the long discourses which you narrate?" If to this question John were frankly to reply, "It is solely from my supernatural memory,—from the special action of the Comforter on my mind:" then should I discern that he was perfectly true-hearted. Yet I should also see, that he was liable to mistake a reverie, a meditation, a day-dream, for a resuscitation of his memory by the Spirit. In short, a writer who believes such a doctrine, and does not think it requisite to warn us how much of his tale comes from his natural, and how much from his supernatural memory, forfeits all claim to be received as an historian, witnessing by the common senses to external fact. His work may have religious value, but it is that of a novel or romance, not of a history. It is therefore superfluous to name the many other difficulties in detail which it contains.

Thus was I flung back to the three first gospels, as, with all their defects,—their genealogies, dreams, visions, devil-miracles, and prophecies written after the event,—yet on the whole, more faithful as a picture of the true Jesus, than that which is exhibited in John.

And now my small root of supernaturalism clung the tighter to Paul, whose conversion still appeared to me a guarantee, that there was at least some nucleus of miracle in Christianity, although it had not pleased God to give us any very definite and trustworthy account. Clearly it was an error, to make miracles our *foundation;* but might we not hold them as a result? Doctrine must be our foundation; but perhaps we might believe the miracles for the sake of it.—And in the epistles of Paul I thought I saw various indications that he took this view. The practical soundness of his eminently sober understanding had appeared to me the more signal, the more I discerned the atmosphere of erroneous philosophy which he necessarily breathed. But he also proved a broken reed, when I tried really to lean upon him as a main support.

1. The first thing that broke on me concerning Paul, was, that his moral sobriety of mind was no guarantee against his mistaking extravagances for miracle. This was manifest to me in his treatment of *the gift of tongues.*

So long ago as in 1830, when the Irving "miracles" commenced in Scotland, my particular attention had been turned to this subject, and the Irvingite exposition of the Pauline phenomena appeared to me so correct, that I was vehemently predisposed to believe the miraculous tongues. But my friend " the Irish clergyman" wrote me a full account of what he heard with his own ears; which was to the effect—that none of the sounds, vowels or consonants, were foreign;—that the strange words were moulded after the Latin grammar, ending in -abus, -obus, -ebat, -avi, &c., so as to denote poverty of invention rather than spiritual agency;—and *that there was no interpretation*. The last point decided me, that any belief which I had in it must be for the present unpractical. Soon after, a friend of mine applied by letter for information as to the facts to a very acute and pious Scotchman, who had become a believer in these miracles. The first reply gave us no facts whatever, but was a declamatory exhortation to believe. The second was nothing but a lamentation over my friend's unbelief, because he asked again for the facts. This showed me, that there was excitement and delusion: yet the general phenomena appeared so similar to those of the church of Corinth, that I supposed the persons must unawares have copied the exterior manifestations, if, after all, there was no reality at bottom.

Three years sufficed to explode these tongues; and from time to time I had an uneasy sense, how much discredit they cast on the Corinthian miracles. Neander's discussion on the 2nd Chapter of the Acts first opened to me the certainty, that Luke (or the authority whom he followed) has exaggerated into a gift of languages what cannot have been essentially different from the Corinthian, and in short from the Irvingite, tongues. Thus Luke's narrative has transformed into a splendid miracle, what in Paul is no miracle at all. It is true that Paul speaks of *interpretation of tongues* as possible, but without a hint that any verification was to be used. Besides, why should a Greek not speak Greek in an assembly of his own countrymen? Is it credible, that the Spirit should inspire one man to utter unintelligible sounds, and a second to interpret these, and then give the assembly endless trouble to find out whether the interpretation was pretence or reality, when the whole difficulty was gratuitous? We grant that there *may* be good reasons for what is paradoxical; but we need the stronger proof that it is a reality. Yet what in fact is there? and why should the gift of tongues in Corinth, as described by Paul, be treated with more respect than in Newman Street, London? I could find no other reply, than that Paul was too sober-minded: yet his own description of the tongues is that of a barbaric jargon, which makes the church appear as if it "were mad," and which is only redeemed from contempt by miraculous interpretation. In the Acts we see that this phenomenon pervaded all the Churches; from the day of Pentecost onward it was looked on as the standard mark of "the descent of the Holy Spirit;" and in the conversion of Cornelius it was the justification of Peter for admitting uncircumcised Gentiles: yet not once is "interpretation" alluded to, except in Paul's epistle. Paul could not go against the whole Church. He held a logic too much in common with the rest, to denounce the tongues as *mere* carnal excitement; but he does anxiously degrade them as of lowest spiritual value, and wholly prohibits them where there is "no interpreter." To carry out this rule, would perhaps have suppressed them entirely.

This however showed me, that I could not rest on Paul's practical wisdom, as securing him against speculative hallucinations in the matter of miracles; for indeed he says: "I thank my God, that I speak with tongues *more than ye all*."

2. To another broad fact I had been astonishingly blind, though the truth of it flashed upon me as soon as I heard it named;—that Paul shows total unconcern to the human history and earthly teaching of Jesus, never quoting his doctrine or any detail of his actions. The Christ with whom Paul held communion was a risen, ascended, exalted Lord, a heavenly being, who reigned over arch-angels, and was about to appear as Judge of the world: but of Jesus in the flesh Paul seems to know nothing beyond the bare fact that he *did** "humble himself" to become man, and "pleased not himself." Even in the very critical controversy about meat and drink, Paul omits to quote Christ's doctrine, "Not that which goeth into the mouth defileth the man," &c. He surely, therefore, must have been wholly and contentedly ignorant of the oral teachings of Jesus.

3. This threw a new light on the *independent* position of Paul. That he anxiously refused to learn from the other

---

* Phil. ii. 5—8; Rom. xv. 3. The last suggests it was from the Psalms (viz from Ps. lxix. 9) that Paul learned the *fact* that Christ pleased not himself.

postles, and "conferred not with flesh and blood," — not having received his gospel of man, but by the revelation of Jesus Christ"—had seemed to me quite suitable to his high pretensions. Any novelties which might be in his doctrine, I had regarded as mere developments, growing out of the common stem, and guaranteed by the same Spirit. But I now saw that this independence invalidated his testimony. He may be to us a supernatural, but he certainly is not a natural, witness to the truth of Christ's miracles and personality. It avails not to talk of the *opportunities* which he had of searching into the truth of the resurrection of Christ, for we see that he did not choose to avail himself of the common methods of investigation. He learned his gospel *by an internal revelation.** He even recounts the appearance of Christ to him, years after his ascension, as evidence co-ordinate to his appearance to Peter and to James, and to 500 brethren at once. 1 Cor. xv. Again the thought is forced on us,—how different was his logic from ours!

To see the full force of the last remark, we ought to conceive how many questions a Paley would have wished to ask of Paul; and how many details Paley himself, if *he* had had the sight, would have felt it his duty to impart to his readers. Had Paul ever seen Jesus when alive? How did he recognize the miraculous apparition to be the person whom Pilate had crucified? Did he see him as a man in a fleshly body, or as a glorified heavenly form? Was it in waking, or sleeping, and if the latter, how did he distinguish his divine vision from a common dream? Did he see only, or did he also handle? If it was a palpable man of flesh, how did he assure himself that it was a person risen from the dead, and not an ordinary living man?

Now as Paul *is writing specially*† *to convince the incredulous or to confirm the wavering*, it is certain that he would have dwelt on these details, if he had thought them of value

---

* Here, again, I have been erroneously understood to say that there cannot be *any* internal revelation of *anything*. Internal truth may be internally communicated, though even so it does not become authoritative, or justify the receiver in saying to other men, "Believe, *for* I guarantee it." But a man who, on the strength of an *internal* revelation believes an *external event*, (past, present, or future,) is not a valid witness of it. Not Paley only, nor Priestley, but James Martineau also, would disown his pretence to authority; and the more so, the more imperious his claim that we believe on his word.

† This appears in v. 2, " by which ye are saved.—*unless ye have believed in vain*," &c. So v. 17-19

to the argument. As he wholly suppresses them, we must infer that he held them to be immaterial; and therefore that the evidence with which he was satisfied, in proof that a man was risen from the dead, was either totally different in kind from that which we should now exact, or exceedingly inferior in rigour. It appears, that he believed in the resurrection of Christ, first, on the ground of prophecy:* secondly, (I feel it is not harsh or bold to add,) on very loose and wholly unsifted testimony. For since he does not afford to us the means of sifting and analyzing his testimony, he cannot have judged it our duty so to do; and therefore is not likely himself to have sifted very narrowly the testimony of others.

Conceive farther how a Paley would have dealt with so astounding a fact, so crushing an argument, as the appearance of the risen Jesus *to 500 brethren at once.* How would he have extravagated and revelled in proof! How would he have worked the topic, that "this could have been no dream, no internal impression, no vain fancy, but a solid indubitable fact!" How he would have quoted his authorities, detailed their testimonies, and given their names and characters! Yet Paul dispatches the affair in one line, gives no details and no special declarations, and seems to see no greater weight in this decisive appearance, than in the vision to his single self. He expects us to take his very vague announcement of the 500 brethren as enough, and it does not seem to occur to him that his readers (if they need to be convinced) are entitled to expect fuller information. Thus if Paul does not intentionally supersede human testimony, he reduces it to its minimum of importance.

How can I believe *at second hand*, from the word of one whom I discern to hold so lax notions of evidence? Yet *who* of the Christian teachers was superior to Paul? He is regarded as almost the only educated man of the leaders. Of his activity of mind, his moral sobriety, his practical talents, his profound sincerity, his enthusiastic self-devotion, his spiritual insight, there is no question: but when his notions of

---

* 1 Cor. xv. "He rose again the third day *according to the Scriptures.*" This must apparently be a reference to Hosea vi. 2, to which the margin of the Bible refers. There is no other place in the existing Old Testament from which we can imagine him to have elicited the rising *on the third day.* Some refer to the type of Jonah. Either of the two suggests how marvellously weak a proof satisfied him.

evidence are infected with the errors of his age, what else can we expect of the eleven, and of the multitude?

4. Paul's neglect of the earthly teaching of Jesus might in part be imputed to the nonexistence of written documents and the great difficulty of learning with certainty what he really had taught.—This agreed perfectly well with what I already saw of the untrustworthiness of our gospels; but it opened a chasm between the doctrine of Jesus and that of Paul, and showed that Paulinism, however good in itself, is not assuredly to be identified with primitive Christianity. Moreover, it became clear, why James and Paul are so contrasted. James retains with little change the traditional doctrine of the Jerusalem Christians; Paul has superadded or substituted a gospel of his own. This was, I believe, pointedly maintained 25 years ago by the author of "Not Paul, but Jesus;" a book which I have never read.

VII. I had now to ask,—Where are *the twelve men* of whom Paley talks, as testifying to the resurrection of Christ? Paul cannot be quoted as a witness, but only as a believer. Of the twelve we do not even know the names, much less have we their testimony. Of James and Jude there are two epistles, but it is doubtful whether either of these is of the twelve apostles; and neither of them declare themselves eyewitnesses to Christ's resurrection. In short, Peter and John are the only two. Of these however, Peter does not attest the *bodily*, but only the *spiritual*, resurrection of Jesus; for he says that Christ was* "put to death in flesh, but made alive in spirit," 1 Pet. iii. 18: yet if this verse had been lost, his opening address (i. 3) would have seduced me into the belief that Peter taught the bodily resurrection of Jesus. So dangerous is it to believe miracles, on the authority of words quoted from a man whom we cannot cross-examine! Thus, once more, John is left alone in his testimony; and how insufficient that is, has been said.

The question also arose, whether Peter's testimony to the transfiguration (2 Pet. i. 18), was an important support. A first objection might be drawn from the sleep ascribed to the three disciples in the gospels; if the narrative were at all

---

* Such is the most legitimate translation. That in the received version is barely a possible meaning. There is no such distinction of prepositions as *in* and *by* in this passage.

trustworthy. But a second and greater difficulty arises in the doubtful authenticity of the second Epistle of Peter.

Neander positively decides against that epistle. Among many reasons, the similarity of its second chapter to the Epistle of Jude is a cardinal fact. Jude is supposed to be original; yet his allusions show him to be post-apostolic. If so, the second Epistle of Peter is clearly spurious.—Whether this was certain, I could not make up my mind: but it was manifest that where such doubts may be honestly entertained, no basis exists to found a belief of a great and significant miracle.

On the other hand, both the Transfiguration itself, and the fiery destruction of Heaven and Earth prophesied in the third chapter of this epistle, are open to objections so serious, as mythical imaginations, that the name of Peter will hardly guarantee them to those with whom the general evidence for the miracles in the gospels has thoroughly broken down.

On the whole, one thing only was clear concerning Peter's faith;—that he, like Paul, was satisfied with a kind of evidence for the resurrection of Jesus which fell exceedingly short of the demands of modern logic: and that it is absurd in us to believe, barely *because* they believed.

CHAPTER VI.

HISTORY DISCOVERED TO BE NO PART OF RELIGION.

AFTER renouncing any "Canon of Scripture" or Sacred Letter at the end of my fourth period, I had been forced to abandon all "Second-hand Faith" by the end of my fifth. If asked *why* I believed this or that, I could no longer say, "*Because* Peter, or Paul, or John believed, and I may thoroughly trust that they cannot mistake." The question now pressed hard, whether this was equivalent to renouncing Christianity.

Undoubtedly, my positive belief in its miracles had evaporated; but I had not arrived at a positive *dis*belief. I still felt the actual benefits and comparative excellencies of this religion too remarkable a phenomenon to be scorned for defect of proof. In Morals likewise it happens, that the ablest practical expounders of truth may make strange blunders as to the foundations and ground of belief: why was this impossible as to the apostles ? Meanwhile, it did begin to appear to myself remarkable, that I continued to love and have pleasure in so much that I certainly disbelieved. I perused a chapter of Paul or of Luke, or some verses of a hymn, and although they appeared to me to abound with error, I found satisfaction and profit in them. Why was this ? was it all fond prejudice, —an absurd clinging to old associations ?

A little self-examination enabled me to reply, that it was no ill-grounded feeling or ghost of past opinions; but that my religion always had been, and still was, *a state of sentiment* toward God, far less dependent on articles of a creed, than once I had unhesitatingly believed. The Bible is pervaded by a sentiment,* which is implied everywhere,—viz. *the intimate sympathy of the Pure and Perfect God with the heart of each faithful worshipper.* This is that which is wanting in Greek philosophers, English Deists, German Pantheists, and all formalists. This is that which so often edifies me in Christian writers and speakers, when I ever so much disbelieve the letter of their sentences. Accordingly, though I saw more and more of moral and spiritual imperfection in the Bible, I by no means ceased to regard it as a quarry whence I might dig precious metal, though the ore needed a refining analysis: and I regarded this as the truest essence and most vital point in Christianity,—to sympathize with the great souls from whom its spiritual eminence has flowed;—to love, to hope, to rejoice, to trust with them ;—and *not*, to form the same interpretations of an ancient book and to take the same views of critical argument.

My historical conception of Jesus had so gradually melted into dimness, that he had receded out of my practical religion, I knew not exactly when. I believe that I must have disused any distinct prayers to him, from a growing opinion that he ought not to be the *object* of worship, but only the *way* by whom we approach to the Father; and as in fact we need no such "way" at all, this was (in the result) a change from practical Ditheism to pure Theism. His "mediation" was to me always a mere name, and, as I believe, would otherwise

* A critic presses me with the question, how I can doubt that doctrine so holy *comes from God*. He professes to review my book on the Soul; yet, apparently because he himself *disbelieves* the doctrine of the Holy Spirit taught alike in the Psalms and Prophets, and in the New Testament,—he cannot help forgetting that I profess to believe it. He is not singular in his dulness. That the sentiment above is necessarily independent of Biblical *authority*, see p. 133.

have been mischievous.*—Simultaneously a great uncertainty had grown on me, how much of the discourses put into the mouth of Jesus was really uttered by him; so that I had in no small measure to form him anew to my imagination.

But if religion is addressed to, and must be judged by, our moral faculties, how could I believe in that painful and gratuitous personality,—The Devil?—He also had become a waning phantom to me, perhaps from the time that I saw the demoniacal miracles to be fictions, and still more when proofs of manifold mistake in the New Testament rose on me. This however took a solid form of positive *dis*belief, when I investigated the history of the doctrine,—I forget exactly in what stage. For it is manifest, that the old Hebrews believed only in evil spirits sent *by God* to do *his bidding*, and had no idea of a rebellious Spirit that rivalled God. That idea was first imbibed in the Babylonish captivity, and apparently therefore must have been adopted from the Persian Ahriman, or from the "Melek Taous," the "Sheitan" still honoured by the Yezidi with mysterious fear. That *the serpent* in the early part of Genesis denoted the same Satan, is probable enough; but this only goes to show, that that narrative is a legend imported from farther East; since it is certain that the subsequent Hebrew literature has no trace of such an Ahriman. The Book of Tobit and its demon show how wise in these matters the exiles in Nineveh were beginning to be. The Book of Daniel manifests, that by the time of Antiochus Epiphanes the Jews had learned each nation to have its guardian spirit, good or evil; and that the fates of nations depend on the invisible conflict of these tutelary powers. In Paul the same idea is strongly brought out. Satan is the prince of the power of the air; with principalities and powers beneath him; over all of whom Christ won the victory on his cross. In the Apocalypse we read the Oriental doctrine of the "*seven angels* who stand before God." As the Christian tenet thus rose among the Jews from their contact with Eastern superstition, and was propagated and expanded while prophecy was mute, it cannot be ascribed to "divine supernatural revelation" as the source. The ground of it is clearly seen in infant speculations on the cause of moral evil and of national calamities.

Thus Christ and the Devil, the two poles of Christendom, had faded away out of my spiritual vision; there were left the

* I do not here enlarge on this, as it is discussed in my treatise on The Soul, 2nd edition, p. 76, or 3rd edition, p. 52.

more vividly, God and Man. Yet I had not finally renounced the *possibility*, that Jesus might have had a divine mission to stimulate all our spiritual faculties, and to guarantee to us a future state of existence. The abstract arguments for the immortality of the soul had always appeared to me vain trifling; and I was deeply convinced that nothing could *assure* us of a future state but a divine communication. In what mode this might be made, I could not say *à priori:* might not this really be the great purport of Messiahship? was not this, if any, a worthy ground for a divine interference? On the contrary, to heal the sick did not seem at all an adequate motive for a miracle; else, why not the sick of our own day? Credulity had exaggerated, and had represented Jesus to have wrought miracles: but that did not wholly *dis*prove the miracle of resurrection (whether bodily or of whatever kind), said to have been wrought by God *upon* him, and of which so very intense a belief so remarkably propagated itself. Paul indeed believed it* from prophecy; and, as we see this to be a delusion, resting on Rabbinical interpretations, we may perhaps *account* thus for the belief of the early church, without in any way admitting the fact.—Here, however, I found I had the clue to my only remaining discussion, the primitive Jewish controversy. Let us step back to an earlier stage than John's or Paul's or Peter's doctrine. We cannot doubt that Jesus claimed to be Messiah: what then was Messiah to be? and, did Jesus (though misrepresented by his disciples) truly fulfil his own claims?

The really Messianic prophecies appeared to me to be far fewer than is commonly supposed. I found such in the 9th and 11th of Isaiah, the 5th of Micah, the 9th of Zechariah, in the 72nd Psalm, in the 37th of Ezekiel, and, as I supposed, in the 50th and 53rd of Isaiah. To these nothing of moment could be certainly added; for the passage in Dan. ix. is ill-translated in the English version, and I had already concluded that the Book of Daniel is a spurious fabrication. From Micah and Ezekiel it appeared, that Messiah was to come from Bethlehem and either be David himself, or a spiritual David: from Isaiah it is shown that he is a rod out of the stem of Jesse.—It is true, I found no proof that Jesus did come from Bethlehem or from the stock of David; for the tales in Matthew and Luke refute one another, and have clearly been generated by a desire to verify the prophecy.

* 1 Cor. xv. 3. Compare Acts xiii. 33, 34, 35 · also Acts ii. 27, 34.

But genealogies for or against Messiahship seemed to me a mean argument; and the fact of the prophets demanding a carnal descent in Messiah struck me as a worse objection than that Jesus had not got it,—if this could be ever proved. The Messiah of Micah, however, was not Jesus; for he was to deliver Israel from *the Assyrians*, and his whole description is literally warlike. Micah, writing when the name of Sennacherib was terrible, conceived of a powerful monarch on the throne of David who was to subdue him: but as this prophecy was not verified, the imaginary object of it was looked for as "Messiah," even after the disappearance of the formidable Assyrian power. This undeniable vanity of Micah's prophecy extends itself also to that in the 9th chapter of his contemporary Isaiah,—if indeed that splendid passage did not really point at the child Hezekiah. Waiving this doubt, it is at any rate clear that the marvellous child on the throne of David was to break the yoke of the oppressive Assyrian; and none of the circumstantials are at all appropriate to the historical Jesus.

In the 37th of Ezekiel the (new) David is to gather Judah and Israel " from the heathen whither they be gone" and to "make them one nation *in the land, on the mountains of Israel:*" and Jehovah adds, that they shall " dwell in the land *which I gave unto Jacob my servant, wherein your fathers dwelt:* and they shall dwell therein, they and their children and their children's children for ever: and my servant David shall be their prince for ever." It is trifling to pretend that *the land promised to Jacob, and in which the old Jews dwelt*, was a spiritual, and not the literal Palestine; and therefore it is impossible to make out that Jesus has fulfilled any part of this representation. The description however that follows (Ezekiel xl. &c.) of the new city and temple, with the sacrifices offered by "the priests the Levites, of the seed of Zadok," and the gate of the sanctuary for the prince (xliv. 3), and his elaborate account of the borders of the land (xlviii. 13-23), place the earnestness of Ezekiel's literalism in still clearer light.

The 72nd Psalm, by the splendour of its predictions concerning the grandeur of some future king of Judah, earns the title of Messianic, *because* it was never fulfilled by any historical king. But it is equally certain, that it has had no appreciable fulfilment in Jesus.

But what of the 11th of Isaiah? Its portraiture is not so

much that of a king, as of a prophet endowed with superhuman power. "He shall smite the earth with the rod of his mouth, and with the breath of his lips he shall slay the wicked." A Paradisiacal state is to follow.—This general description *may* be verified by Jesus *hereafter;* but we have no manifestation, which enables us to call the fulfilment a fact. Indeed, the latter part of the prophecy is out of place for a time so late as the reign of Augustus; which forcibly denotes that Isaiah was predicting only that which was his immediate political aspiration: for in this great day of Messiah, Jehovah is to gather back his dispersed people from Assyria, Egypt, and other parts; he is *to reconcile Judah and Ephraim,* (who had been perfectly reconciled centuries before Jesus was born.) and as a result of this Messianic glory, the people of Israel "shall fly upon the shoulders of the *Philistines* towards the west; they shall spoil them of the east together: they shall lay their hand on *Edom* and *Moab,* and the children of *Ammon* shall obey them." But Philistines, Moab and Ammon, were distinctions entirely lost before the Christian era.—Finally, the Red Sea is to be once more passed miraculously by the Israelites, returning (as would seem) to their fathers' soil. Take all these particulars together, and the prophecy is neither fulfilled in the past nor possible to be fulfilled in the future.

The prophecy which we know as Zechariah ix.-xi. is believed to be really from a prophet of uncertain name, contemporaneous with Isaiah. It was written while Ephraim was still a people, *i. e.* before the capture of Samaria by Shalmanezer; and xi. 1-3 appears to howl over the recent devastations of Tiglathpilezer. The prophecy is throughout full of the politics of that day. No part of it has the most remote or imaginable* similarity to the historical life of Jesus, except that he once rode into Jerusalem on an ass; a deed which cannot have been peculiar to him, and which Jesus moreover appears to have planned with the express† purpose of assimilating himself to the lowly king here described. Yet such an isolated act is surely a carnal and beggarly fulfilment. To

* I need not except the *potter* and the thirty pieces of silver (Zech. xi. 13), for the *potter* is a mere absurd error of text or translation. The Septuagint has the *foundry,* De Wette has the *treasury,* with whom Hitzig and Ewald agree. So Winer (Simoni's Lexicon).

† Some of my critics are very angry with me for saying this; but * Matthew himself (xxi. 4) almost says it:—"*All this was done, that it might be fulfilled,*" &c. Do my critics mean to tell me that Jesus was

ride on an ass is no mark of humility in those who must ordinarily go on foot. The prophet clearly means that the righteous king is not to ride on a warhorse and trust in cavalry, as Solomon and the Egyptians, (see Ps. xx. 7. Is. xxxi. 1-3, xxx. 16,) but is to imitate the lowliness of David and the old judges, who rode on young asses; and is to be a lover of peace.

Chapters 50 and 53 of the pseudo-Isaiah remained; which contain many phrases so aptly descriptive of the sufferings of Christ, and so closely knit up with our earliest devotional associations, that they were the very last link of my chain that snapt. Still, I could not conceal from myself, that no exactness in this prophecy, however singular, could avail to make out that Jesus was the Messiah of Hezekiah's prophets. There must be *some* explanation; and if I did not see it, that must probably arise from prejudice and habit.—In order therefore to gain freshness, I resolved to peruse the entire prophecy of the pseudo-Isaiah in Lowth's version, from ch. xl. onward, at a single sitting.

This prophet writes from Babylon, and has his vision full of the approaching restoration of his people by Cyrus, whom he addresses by name. In ch. xliii. he introduces to us an eminent and "chosen servant of God," whom he invests with all the evangelical virtues, and declares that he is to be a light to the Gentiles. In ch. xliv. (v. 1—also v. 21) he is named as "*Jacob* my servant, and *Israel* whom I have chosen." The appellations recur in xlv. 4: and in a far more striking passage, xlix. 1-12, which is eminently Messianic to the Christian ear, *except* that in v. 3, the speaker distinctly declares himself to be (not Messiah, but) Israel. The same speaker continues in ch. l., which is equally Messianic in sound. In ch. lii. the prophet speaks *of* him, (vv. 13-15) but the subject of the chapter is *restoration from Babylon;* and from this he runs on into the celebrated ch. liii.

It is essential to understand the *same* "elect servant" all along. He is many times called Israel, and is often addressed in a tone quite inapplicable to Messiah, viz. as one needing salvation himself; so in ch. xliii. Yet in ch. xlix. this elect Israel is distinguished from Jacob and Israel at large: thus there is an entanglement. Who can be called on to risk his eternal hopes on his skilful unknotting of it? It appeared

not aware of the prophecy? or if Jesus did know of the prophecy, will they tell me *that he was not designing* to fulfil it? I feel such carping to be little short of hypocrisy.

however to me most probable, that as our high Churchmen distinguish "mother Church" from the individuals who compose the Church, so the "Israel" of this prophecy is the idealizing of the Jewish Church; which I understood to be a current Jewish interpretation. The figure perhaps embarrasses us, only because of the male sex attributed to the ideal servant of God; for when "Zion" is spoken of by the same prophet in the same way, no one finds difficulty, or imagines that a female person of superhuman birth and qualities must be intended.

It still remained strange that in Isaiah liii. and Pss. xxii. and lxix. there should be *coincidences* so close with the sufferings of Jesus: but I reflected, that I had no proof that the narrative had not been strained by credulity,* to bring it into artificial agreement with these imagined predictions of his death. And herewith my last argument in favour of views for which I once would have laid down my life, seemed to be spent.

Nor only so: but I now reflected that the falsity of the prophecy in Dan. vii. (where the coming of "a Son of Man" to sit in universal judgment follows immediately upon the break-up of the Syrian monarchy,)—to say nothing of the general proof of the spuriousness of the whole Book of Daniel, —ought perhaps long ago to have been seen by me as of more cardinal importance. For if we believe anything at all about the discourses of Christ, we cannot doubt that he selected "*Son of Man*" as his favourite title; which admits no interpretation so satisfactory, as, that he tacitly refers to the seventh chapter of Daniel, and virtually bases his pretensions upon it. On the whole, it was no longer defect of proof which presented itself, but positive disproof of the primitive and fundamental claim.

I could not for a moment allow weight to the topic, that "it is dangerous to *dis*believe wrongly;" for I felt, and had always felt, that it gave a premium to the most boastful and tyrannizing superstition:—as if it were not equally dangerous to *believe* wrongly! Nevertheless, I tried to plead for farther delay, by asking: Is not the subject too vast for me to decide upon?—Think how many wise and good men have fully examined, and have come to a contrary conclusion. What a

---

* Apparently on these words of mine, a reviewer builds up the inference that I regard "the Evangelical narrative as a mythical fancy-piece imitated from David and Isaiah." I feel this to be a great caricature. My words are carefully limited to a few petty details of one part of the narrative.

grasp of knowledge and experience of the human mind it requires! Perhaps too I have unawares been carried away by a love of novelty, which I have mistaken for a love of truth.

But the argument recoiled upon me. Have I not been 25 years a reader of the Bible? have I not full 18 years been a student of Theology? have I not employed 7 of the best years of my life, with ample leisure, in this very investigation;—without any intelligible earthly bribe to carry me to my present conclusion, against all my interests, all my prejudices and all my education? There are many far more learned men than I,—many men of greater power of mind; but there are also a hundred times as many who are my inferiors; and if I have been seven years labouring in vain to solve this vast literary problem, it is an extreme absurdity to imagine that the solving of it is imposed by God on the whole human race. Let me renounce my little learning; let me be as the poor and simple: what then follows? Why, then, *still the same thing follows*, that difficult literary problems concerning distant history cannot afford any essential part of my religion.

It is with hundreds or thousands a favourite idea, that "they have an inward witness of the truth of (*the historical and outward facts of*) Christianity." Perhaps the statement would bring its own refutation to them, if they would express it clearly. Suppose a biographer of Sir Isaac Newton, after narrating his sublime discoveries and ably stating some of his most remarkable doctrines, to add, that Sir Isaac was a great magician, and had been used to raise spirits by his arts, and finally was himself carried up to heaven one night, while he was gazing at the moon; and that this event had been foretold by Merlin:—it would surely be the height of absurdity to dilate on the truth of the Newtonian theory as "the moral evidence" of the truth of the miracles and prophecy. Yet this is what those do, who adduce the excellence of the precepts and spirituality of the general doctrine of the New Testament, as the "moral evidence" of its miracles and of its fulfilling the Messianic prophecies. But for the ambiguity of the word *doctrine*, probably such confusion of thought would have been impossible. "Doctrines" are either spiritual truths, or are statements of external history. Of the former we may have an inward witness;—that is their proper evidence;—but the latter must depend upon adequate testimony and various kinds of criticism.

How quickly might I have come to my conclusion,—how much weary thought and useless labour might I have spared,— if at an earlier time this simple truth had been pressed upon me, that since the religious faculties of the poor and half-educated cannot investigate Historical and Literary questions, *therefore* these questions cannot constitute an essential part of Religion. —But perhaps I could not have gained this result by any abstract act of thought, from want of freedom to think: and there are advantages also in expanding slowly under great pressure, if one *can* expand, and is not crushed by it.

I felt no convulsion of mind, no emptiness of soul, no inward practical change: but I knew that it would be said, this was only because the force of the old influence was as yet unspent, and that a gradual declension in the vitality of my religion must ensue. More than eight years have since past, and I feel I have now a right to contradict that statement. To any "Evangelical" I have a right to say, that while he has a *single*, I have a *double* experience; and I know, that the spiritual fruits which he values, have no connection whatever with the complicated and elaborate creed, which his school imagines, and I once imagined, to be the roots out of which they are fed. That they depend directly on *the heart's belief in the sympathy of God with individual man*,* I am well assured: but that doctrine does not rest upon the Bible or upon Christianity; for it is a postulate, from which every Christian advocate is forced to start. If it be denied, he cannot take a step forward in his argument. He talks to men about Sin and Judgment to come, and the need of Salvation, and so proceeds to the Saviour. But his very first step,—the idea of Sin,—*assumes* that God concerns himself with our actions, words, thoughts; *assumes* therefore that sympathy of God with every man, which (it seems) can only be known by an infallible Bible.

I know that many Evangelicals will reply, that I never can have had "the true" faith; else I could never have lost it: and as for my not being conscious of spiritual change, they will accept this as confirming their assertion. Undoubtedly I cannot prove that I ever felt as they now feel: perhaps they love their present opinions *more than* truth, and are careless to

---

* I did not calculate that any assailant would be so absurd as to lecture me on the topic, that God has no sympathy *with our sins and follies*. Of course what I mean is, that he has complacency in our moral perfection. See p. 125 above.

examine and verify them; with that I claim no fellowship. But there are Christians, and Evangelical Christians, of another stamp, who love their creed, *only* because they believe it to be true, but love truth, as such, and truthfulness, more than any creed: with these I claim fellowship. Their love to God and man, their allegiance to righteousness and true holiness, will not be in suspense and liable to be overturned by new discoveries in geology and in ancient inscriptions, or by improved criticism of texts and of history, nor have they any imaginable interest in thwarting the advance of scholarship. It is strange indeed to undervalue *that* Faith, which alone is purely moral and spiritual, alone rests on a basis that cannot be shaken, alone lifts the possessor above the conflicts of erudition, and makes it impossible for him to fear the increase of knowledge.

I fully expected that reviewers and opponents from the evangelical school would laboriously insinuate or assert, that I *never was* a Christian and do not understand anything about Christianity spiritually. My expectations have been more than fulfilled; and the course which my assailants have taken leads me to add some topics to the last paragraph. I say then, that if I had been slain at the age of twenty-seven, when I was chased* by a mob of infuriated Mussulmans for selling New Testaments, they would have trumpeted me as an eminent saint and martyr. I add, that many circumstances within easy possibility might have led to my being engaged as an official teacher of a congregation at the usual age, which would in all probability have arrested my intellectual development, and have stereotyped my creed for many a long year; and then also they would have acknowledged me as a Christian. A little more stupidity, a little more worldliness, a little more mental dishonesty in me, or perhaps a little more kindness and management in others, would have kept me in my old state, which was acknowledged and would still be acknowledged as Christian. To try to disown me now, is an impotent superciliousness.

At the same time, I confess to several moral changes, as the result of this change in my creed, the principal of which are the following.

---

* This was at Aintab, in the north of Syria. One of my companions was caught by the mob and beaten (as they probably thought) to death. But he recovered very similarly to Paul, in Acts xiv. 20, after long lying senseless.

1. I have found that my old belief narrowed my affections.

It taught me to bestow peculiar love on "the people of God," and it assigned an intellectual creed as one essential mark of this people. That creed may be made more or less stringent; but when driven to its minimum, it includes a recognition of the historical proposition, that "the Jewish teacher Jesus fulfilled the conditions requisite to constitute him the Messiah of the ancient Hebrew prophets." This proposition has been rejected by very many thoughtful and sincere men in England, and by tens of thousands in France, Germany, Italy, Spain. To judge rightly about it, is necessarily a problem of literary criticism; which has both to interpret the Old Scriptures and to establish how much of the biography of Jesus in the New is credible. To judge wrongly about it, may prove one to be a bad critic, but not a less good and less pious man. Yet my old creed enacted an affirmative result of this historical inquiry, as a test of one's spiritual state, and ordered me to think harshly of men like Marcus Aurelius and Lessing, because they did not adopt the conclusion which the professedly uncritical have established. It possessed me with a general gloom concerning Mohammedans and Pagans, and involved the whole course of history and prospects of futurity in a painful darkness from which I am relieved.

2. Its theory was one of selfishness. That is, it inculcated that my first business must be, to save my soul from future punishment, and to attain future happiness; and it bade me to chide myself, when I thought of nothing but about doing present duty and blessing God for present enjoyment.

In point of fact, I never did look much to futurity, nor even in prospect of death could attain to any vivid anticipations or desires, much less was troubled with fears. The evil which I suffered from my theory, was not (I believe) that it really made me selfish—other influences of it were too powerful:—but it taught me to blame myself for unbelief, because I was not sufficiently absorbed in the contemplation of my vast personal expectations. I certainly here feel myself delivered from the danger of factitious sin.

The selfish and self-righteous texts come principally from the three first gospels, and are greatly counteracted by the deeper spirituality of the apostolic epistles. I therefore by no means charge this tendency indiscriminately on the New Testament.

3. It laid down that "the time is short; THE LORD IS AT HAND: the things of this world pass away, and deserve not our affections: the only thing worth spending one's energies on, is, the forwarding of men's salvation." It bade me "watch perpetually, not knowing whether my Lord would return at cockcrowing or at midday."

While I believed this, (which, however disagreeable to modern Christians, is the clear doctrine of the New Testament,) I acted an eccentric and unprofitable part. From it I was saved against my will, and forced into a course in which the doctrine, having been laid to sleep, awoke only now and then to reproach and harass me for my unfaithfulness to it. This doctrine it is, which makes so many spiritual persons lend active or passive aid to uphold abuses and perpetuate mischief in every department of human life. Those who stick closest to the Scripture do not shrink from saying, that "it is not worth while trying to mend the world," and stigmatize as "political and worldly" such as pursue an opposite course. Undoubtedly, if we are to expect our Master at cockcrowing, we shall not study the permanent improvement of this transitory scene. To teach the certain speedy destruction of earthly things, *as the New Testament does,* is to cut the sinews of all earthly progress; to declare war against Intellect and Imagination, against Industrial and Social advancement.

There was a time when I was distressed at being unable to avoid exultation in the worldly greatness of England. My heart would, in spite of me, swell with something of pride, when a Turk or Arab asked what was my country: I then used to confess to God this pride as a sin. I still see that that was a legitimate deduction from the Scripture. "The glory of this world passeth away," and I had professed to be "dead with Christ" to it. The difference is this. I am now as "dead" as then to all of it which my conscience discerns to be sinful, but I have not to torment myself in a (fundamentally ascetic) struggle against innocent and healthy impulses. I now, with deliberate approval, "love the world and the things of the world." I can feel patriotism, and take the deepest interest in the future prospects of nations, and no longer reproach myself. Yet this is quite consistent with feeling the spiritual interests of men to be of all incomparably the highest.

Modern religionists profess to be disciples of Christ, and talk high of the perfect morality of the New Testament, when they certainly do not submit their understanding to it, and are no more like to the first disciples than bishops are like the pennyless apostles. One critic tells me that *I know* that the above is *not* the true interpretation of the apostolic doctrine. Assuredly I am aware that we may rebuke "the world" and "worldliness," in a legitimate and modified sense, as being the system of *selfishness:* true,—and I have avowed this in another work; but it does not follow that Jesus and the apostles did not go farther: and manifestly they did. The true disciple, who would be perfect as his Master, was indeed ordered to sell all, give to the poor and follow him; and when that severity was relaxed by good sense, it was still taught that things which lasted to the other side of the grave alone deserved our affection or our exertion. If any person thinks me ignorant of the Scriptures for being of this judgment, let him so think; but to deny that I am sincere in my avowal, is a very needless insolence.

4. I am sensible how heavy a clog on the exercise of my judgment has been taken off from me, since I unlearned that Bibliolatry, which I am disposed to call the greatest religious evil of England.

Authority has a place in religious teaching, as in education, but it is provisional and transitory. Its chief use is to guide *action*, and assist the formation of habits, before the judgment is ripe. As applied to mere *opinion*, its sole function is to guide inquiry. So long as an opinion is received on authority only, it works no inward process upon us: yet the promulgation of it by authority, is not therefore always useless, since the prominence thus given to it may be a most important stimulus to thought. While the mind is inactive or weak, it will not wish to throw off the yoke of authority: but as soon as it begins to discern error in the standard proposed to it, we have the mark of incipient original thought, which is the thing so valuable and so difficult to elicit; and which authority is apt to crush. An intelligent pupil seldom or never gives *too little* weight to the opinion of his teacher: a wise teacher will never repress the free action of his pupils' minds, even when they begin to question his results. "Forbidding to think" is a still more fatal tyranny than "forbidding to marry:" it paralyzes all the moral powers.

In former days, if any moral question came before me, I was always apt to turn it into the mere lawyerlike exercise of searching and interpreting my written code. Thus, in reading how Henry the Eighth treated his first queen, I thought over Scripture texts in order to judge whether he was right, and if I could so get a solution, I left my own moral powers unexercised. All Protestants see, how mischievous it is to a Romanist lady to have a directing priest, whom she every day consults about everything; so as to lay her own judgment to sleep. We readily understand, that in the extreme case such women may gradually lose all perception of right and wrong, and become a mere machine in the hands of her director. But the Protestant principle of accepting the Bible as the absolute law, acts towards the same end; and only fails of doing the same amount of mischief, because a book can never so completely answer all the questions asked of it, as a living priest can. The Protestantism which pities those as "without chart and compass" who acknowledge no infallible written code, can mean nothing else, than that "the less occasion we have to trust our moral powers, the better;" that is, it represents it as of all things most desirable to be able to benumb conscience by disuse, under the guidance of a mind from without. Those who teach this, need not marvel to see their pupils become Romanists.

But Bibliolatry not only paralyzes the moral sense; it also corrupts the intellect, and introduces a crooked logic, by setting men to the duty of extracting absolute harmony out of discordant materials. All are familiar with the subtlety of lawyers, whose task it is to elicit a single sense out of a heap of contradictory statutes. In their case such subtlety may indeed excite in us impatience or contempt; but we forbear to condemn them, when it is pleaded that practical convenience, not truth, is their avowed end. In the case of theological ingenuity, where truth is the professed and sacred object, a graver judgment is called for. When the Biblical interpreter struggles to reconcile contradictions, or to prove that wrong is right, merely because he is bound to maintain the perfection of the Bible; when to this end he condescends to sophistry and pettifogging evasions; it is difficult to avoid feeling disgust as well as grief. Some good people are secretly conscious that the Bible is not an infallible book; but they dread the consequences of proclaiming this " to the vulgar." Alas! and have they measured the evils which the fostering of this lie is producing in the minds, not of the educated only, but emphatically of the ministers of religion?

Many who call themselves Christian preachers busily undermine moral sentiment, by telling their hearers, that if they do not believe the Bible (or the Church), they can have no firm religion or morality, and will have no reason to give against following brutal appetite. This doctrine it is, that so often makes men atheists in Spain, and profligates in England, as soon as they unlearn the national creed: and the school which have done the mischief, moralize over the wickedness of human nature when it comes to pass, instead of blaming the falsehood which they have themselves inculcated.

CHAPTER VII.

ON THE MORAL PERFECTION OF JESUS.

LET no reader peruse this chapter, who is not willing to enter into a discussion, as free and unshrinking, concerning the personal excellencies and conduct of Jesus, as that of Mr. Grote concerning Socrates. I have hitherto met with most absurd rebuffs for my scrupulosity. One critic names me as a principal leader in a school which extols and glorifies the character of Jesus; after which he proceeds to reproach me with inconsistency, and to insinuate dishonesty. Another expresses himself as deeply wounded that, in renouncing the belief that Jesus is more than man, I suggest to compare him to a clergyman whom I mentioned as eminently holy and perfect in the picture of a partial biographer; such a comparison is resented with vivid indignation, as a blurting out of something "unspeakably painful." Many have murmured that I do *not* come forward to extol the excellencies of Jesus, but appear to prefer Paul. More than one taunt me with an inability to justify my insinuations that Jesus, after all, was not really perfect; one is "extremely disappointed" that I have not attacked him; in short, it is manifest that many would much rather have me say out my whole heart, than withhold anything. I therefore give fair warning to all, not to read any further, or else to blame themselves if I inflict on them "unspeakable pain," by differing from their judgment of a historical or unhistorical character. As for those who confound my tenderness with hypocrisy and conscious weakness, if they trust themselves to read to the end, I think they will abandon that fancy.

But how am I brought into this topic? It is because, after my mind had reached the stage narrated in the last chapter, I fell in with a new doctrine among the Unitarians,—that the evidence of Christianity is essentially popular and spiritual, consisting in *the Life of Christ*, who is a perfect man and the absolute moral image of God,—therefore fitly called "God manifest in the flesh," and, as such, Moral Head of the human race. Since this view was held in conjunction with those at which I had arrived myself concerning miracles, prophecy, the untrustworthiness of Scripture as to details, and the essential unreasonableness of imposing dogmatic propositions as a creed, I had to consider why I could not adopt such a modification, or (as it appeared to me) reconstruction, of Christianity; and I gave reasons in the first edition of this book, which, avoiding direct treatment of the character of Jesus, seemed to me adequate on the opposite side.

My argument was reviewed by a friend, who presently published the review with his name, replying to my remarks on this scheme. I thus find myself in public and avowed controversy with one who is endowed with talents, accomplishments, and genius, to which I have no pretensions. The challenge has certainly come from myself. Trusting to the goodness of my cause, I have ventured it into an unequal combat; and from a consciousness of my admired friend's high superiority, I do feel a little abashed at being brought face to face against him. But possibly the less said to the public on these personal matters, the better.

I have to give reasons why I cannot adopt that modified scheme of Christianity which is defended and adorned by James Martineau; according to which it is maintained that though the Gospel Narratives are not to be trusted in detail, there can yet be no reasonable doubt *what* Jesus *was;* for this is elicited by a "higher moral criticism," which (it is remarked) I neglect. In this theory, Jesus is avowed to be a man born like other men; to be liable to error, and (at least in some important respects) mistaken. Perhaps no general proposition is to be accepted *merely* on the word of Jesus; in particular, he misinterpreted the Hebrew prophecies. "He was not *less* than the Hebrew Messiah, but *more*." No moral charge is established against him, until it is shown, that in applying the old prophecies to himself, he was *conscious* that they did not fit. His error was one of mere fallibility in matters of intellectual and literary estimate. On the other hand, Jesus had an infallible moral perception, which reveals itself to the true-hearted reader, and is testified by the common consciousness of Christendom. It has pleased the Creator to give us one sun in the heavens, and one Divine soul in history, in order to correct the aberrations of our individuality, and unite all mankind into one family of God. Jesus is to be presumed to be perfect until he is shown to be imperfect. Faith in Jesus, is not reception of propositions, but reverence for a person; yet this is *not* the condition of salvation or essential to the Divine favour.

Such is the scheme, abridged from the ample discussion of my eloquent friend. In reasoning against it, my arguments will, to a certain extent, be those of an orthodox Trinitarian;* since we might both maintain that the belief in the absolute divine morality of Jesus is not tenable, when the belief in *every other* divine and superhuman quality is denied. Should I have any "orthodox" reader, my arguments may shock his feelings less, if he keeps this in view. In fact, the same action or word in Jesus may be consistent or inconsistent with moral perfection, according to the previous assumptions concerning his person.

I. My friend has attributed to me a "prosaic and embittered view of human nature," apparently because I have a very intense belief of Man's essential imperfection. To me, I confess, it is almost a first principle of thought, that as all sorts of perfection coexist in God, so is no sort of perfection possible to man. I do not know how for a moment to imagine an Omniscient Being who is not Almighty, or an Almighty who is not All-Righteous. So neither do I know how to conceive of Perfect Holiness anywhere but in the Blessed and only Potentate.

Man is finite and crippled on all sides; and frailty in one kind causes frailty in another. Deficient power causes deficient knowledge, deficient knowledge betrays him into false opinion, and entangles him into false positions. It may be a defect of my imagination, but I do not feel that it implies any bitterness, that even in the case of one who abides in primitive lowliness, to attain even negatively an absolutely pure good-

---

* I have by accident just taken up the "British Quarterly," and alighted upon the following sentence concerning Madame Roland:—"*To say that she was without fault, would be to say that she was not human.*" This so entirely expresses and concludes all that I have to say, that I feel surprize at my needing at all to write such a chapter as the present.

ness seems to me impossible; and much more, to exhaust all goodness, and become a single Model-Man, unparalleled, incomparable, a standard for all other moral excellence. Especially I cannot conceive of any human person rising out of obscurity, and influencing the history of the world, unless there be in him forces of great intensity, the harmonizing of which is a vast and painful problem. Every man has to subdue himself first, before he preaches to his fellows; and he encounters many a fall and many a wound in winning his own victory. And as talents are various, so do moral natures vary, each having its own weak and strong side; and that one man should grasp into his single self the highest perfection of every moral kind, is to me at least as incredible as that one should preoccupy and exhaust all intellectual greatness. I feel the prodigy to be so peculiar, that I must necessarily wait until it is overwhelmingly proved, before I admit it. No one can without unreason urge me to believe, on any but the most irrefutable arguments, that a man, finite in every other respect, is infinite in moral perfection.

My friend is "at a loss to conceive in what way a superhuman physical nature could tend in the least degree to render moral perfection more credible." But I think he will see, that it would entirely obviate the argument just stated, which, from the known frailty of human nature in general, deduced the indubitable imperfection of an individual. The reply is then obvious and decisive: "This individual is *not* a mere man; his origin is wholly exceptional; therefore his moral perfection may be exceptional; your experience of *man's* weakness goes for nothing in his case." If I were already convinced that this person was a great Unique, separated from all other men by an impassable chasm in regard to his physical origin, I (for one) should be much readier to believe that he was Unique and Unapproachable in other respects: for all God's works have an internal harmony. It could not be for nothing that this exceptional personage was sent into the world. That he was intended as head of the human race, in one or more senses, would be a plausible opinion; nor should I feel any incredulous repugnance against believing his morality to be, if not divinely perfect, yet separated from that of common men so far, that he might be a God to us, just as every parent is to a young child.

This view seems to my friend a weakness; be it so. I need not press it. What I do press, is,—whatever *might* or might *not* be conceded concerning one in human form, but of superhuman origin,—at any rate, one who is conceded to be, out and out, of the same nature as ourselves, is to be judged of by our experience of that nature, and is therefore to be *assumed* to be variously imperfect, however eminent and admirable in some respects. And no one is to be called an imaginer of deformity, because he takes for granted that one who is Man has imperfections which were not known to those who compiled memorials of him. To impute to a person, without specific evidence, some definite frailty or fault, barely because he is human, would be a want of good sense; but not so, to have a firm belief that every human being is finite in moral as well as in intellectual greatness.

We have a very imperfect history of the apostle James; and I do not know that I could adduce any fact specifically recorded concerning him in disproof of his absolute moral perfection, if any of his Jerusalem disciples had chosen to set up this as a dogma of religion. Yet no one would blame me, as morose, or indisposed to acknowledge genius and greatness, if I insisted on believing James to be frail and imperfect, while admitting that I knew almost nothing about him. And why? —Singly and surely, because we know him to be *a man:* that suffices. To set up James or John or Daniel as my Model, and my Lord; to be swallowed up in him and press him upon others for a Universal Standard, would be despised as a self-degrading idolatry and resented as an obtrusive favouritism. Now why does not the same equally apply, if the name Jesus is substituted for these? Why, in defect of all other knowledge than the bare fact of his manhood, are we not unhesitatingly to take for granted that he does *not* exhaust all perfection, and is at best only one among many brethren and equals?

II. My friend, I gather, will reply, " because so many thousands of minds in all Christendom attest the infinite and unapproachable goodness of Jesus." It therefore follows to consider, what is the weight of this attestation. Manifestly it depends, first of all, on the independence of the witnesses: secondly, on the grounds of their belief. If all those, who confess the moral perfection of Jesus, confess it as the result of unbiassed examination of his character; and if, of those acquainted with the narrative, none espouse the opposite side; this would be a striking testimony, not to be despised. But in fact, few indeed of the "witnesses" add any weight at all to the argument. No Trinitarian can doubt that Jesus is morally perfect, without doubting fundamentally every part of his religion. He believes it, *because* the entire system demands it, and *because* various texts of Scripture avow it: and this very fact makes it morally impossible for him to enter upon an unbiassed inquiry, whether that character which is drawn for Jesus in the four gospels, is, or is not, one of absolute perfection, deserving to be made an exclusive model for all times and countries. My friend never was a Trinitarian, and seems not to know how this operates; but I can testify, that when I believed in the immaculateness of Christ's character, it was not from an unbiassed criticism, but from the pressure of authority, (the authority of *texts*,) and from the necessity of the doctrine to the scheme of Redemption. Not merely strict Trinitarians, but all who believe in the Atonement, however modified,—all who believe that Jesus will be the future Judge,—*must* believe in his absolute perfection: hence the fact of their belief is no indication whatever that they believe on the ground which my friend assumes,—viz. an intelligent and unbiassed study of the character itself, as exhibited in the four narratives.

I think we may go farther. We have no reason for thinking that *this* was the sort of evidence which convinced the apostles themselves, and first teachers of the gospel;—if indeed in the very first years the doctrine was at all conceived of. It cannot be shown that any one believed in the moral perfection of Jesus, who had not already adopted the belief that he was Messiah, and *therefore* Judge of the human race. My friend makes the pure immaculateness of Jesus (discernible by him in the gospels) his foundation, and deduces *from* this the quasi-Messiahship: but the opposite order of deduction appears to have been the only one possible in the first age. Take Paul as a specimen. He believed the doctrine in question; but not from reading the four gospels,— for they did not exist. Did he then believe it by hearing Ananias (Acts ix. 17) enter into details concerning the deeds and words of Jesus? I cannot imagine that any wise or thoughtful person would so judge, which after all would be a gratuitous invention. The Acts of the Apostles give us many speeches which set forth the grounds of accepting Jesus as Messiah; but they never press his absolute moral perfection as a fact and a fundamental fact. "He went about doing good, and healing all that were oppressed of the devil," is the utmost that is advanced on this side: prophecy is urged, and his resurrection is asserted, and the inference is drawn that "Jesus is the Christ." Out of this flowed the farther inferences that he was Supreme Judge,—and moreover, was Paschal Lamb, and Sacrifice, and High Priest, and Mediator; and since every one of these characters demanded a belief in his moral perfections, that doctrine also necessarily followed, and was received before our present gospels existed. My friend therefore cannot abash me by the *argumentum ad verecundiam;* (which to me seems highly out of place in this connexion;) for the opinion, which is, as to this single point, held by him in common with the first Christians, was held by them on transcendental reasons which he totally discards; and all after generations have been confirmed in the doctrine by Authority, *i. e.* by the weight of texts or church decisions: both of which he also discards. If I could receive the doctrine, merely because I dared not to differ from the whole Christian world, I might aid to swell odium against rejectors, but I should not strengthen the cause at the bar of reason. I feel therefore that my friend must not claim Catholicity as on his side. Trinitarians and Arians are alike useless to his argument: nay, nor can he claim more than a small fraction of Unitarians; for as many of them as believe that Jesus is to be the Judge of living and dead (as the late Dr. Lant Carpenter did) must as *necessarily* believe his immaculate perfection as if they were Trinitarians.

The New Testament does not distinctly explain on what grounds this doctrine was believed; but we may observe that in 1 Peter i. 19 and 2 Cor. v. 21, it is coupled with the Atonement, and in 1 Peter ii. 21, Romans xv. 3, it seems to be inferred from prophecy. But let us turn to the original Eleven, who were eye and ear witnesses of Jesus, and consider on what grounds they can have believed (if we assume that they did all believe) the absolute moral perfection of Jesus. It is too ridiculous to imagine them studying the writings of Matthew in order to obtain conviction,—if any of that school, whom alone I now address, could admit that written documents were thought of before the Church outstept the limits of Judea. If the Eleven believed the doctrine for some transcendental reason,—as by a Supernatural Revelation, or on account of Prophecy, and to complete the Messiah's character, —then their attestation is useless to my friend's argument: will it then gain anything, if we suppose that they *believed* Jesus to be perfect, because they *saw* him to be perfect? To me this would seem no attestation worth having, but rather a piece of impertinent ignorance. If I attest that a person whom I have known was an eminently good man, I command a certain amount of respect to my opinion, and I do him honour. If I celebrate his good deeds and report his wise words, I extend his honour still farther. But if I proceed to assure people, *on the evidence of my personal observation of him*, that he was immaculate and absolutely perfect, was the pure Moral Image of God, that he deserves to be made the Exclusive Model of imitation, and is the standard by which every other man's morality is to be corrected,—I make myself ridiculous; my panegyrics lose all weight, and I produce far less conviction than when I praised within human limitations. I do not know how my friend will look on this point, (for his judgment on the whole question perplexes me, and the views which I call *sober* he names *prosaic*,) but I cannot resist the conviction that universal common-sense would have rejected the teaching of the Eleven with contempt, if they had presented, as the basis of the gospel, their *personal testimony* to the godlike and unapproachable moral absolutism of Jesus. But even if such a basis was possible to the Eleven, it was impossible to Paul and Silvanus and Timothy and Barnabas and Apollos, and the other successful preachers to the Gentiles. High moral goodness, within human limitations, was undoubtedly announced as a fact of the life of Jesus; but upon this followed the supernatural claims, and the argument of prophecy; *without* which my friend desires to build up his view.—I have thus developed why I think he has no right to claim Catholicity for his judgment. I have risked to be tedious, because I find that when I speak concisely, I am enormously misapprehended. I close this topic by observing, that the great animosity with which my very mild intimations against the popular view have been met from numerous quarters, show me that Christians do not allow this subject to be calmly debated, and have not come to their own conclusion as the result of a calm debate. And this is amply corroborated by my own consciousness of the past. I never dared, nor could have dared, to criticize coolly and simply the pretensions of Jesus to be an absolute model of morality, until I had been delivered from the weight of authority and miracle, oppressing my critical powers.

III. I have been asserting, that he who believes Jesus to be a mere man, ought at once to believe his moral excellence finite and comparable to that of other men; and, that our judgment to this effect cannot be reasonably overborne by the "universal consent" of Christendom.—Thus far we are dealing *à priori*, which here fully satisfies me: in such an argument I need no *à posteriori* evidence to arrive at my own conclusion. Nevertheless, I am met by taunts and clamour, which are not meant to be indecent, but which to my feeling are such. My critics point triumphantly to the four gospels, and demand that I will make a personal attack on a character which they revere, even when they know that I cannot do so without giving great offence. Now if any one were to call my old schoolmaster, or my old parish priest, a perfect and universal Model, and were to claim that I would entitle him Lord, and think of him as the only true revelation of God; should I not be at liberty to say, without disrespect, that "I most emphatically deprecate such extravagant claims for him"? Would this justify an outcry, that I will publicly avow *what* I judge to be his defects of character, and will *prove* to all his admirers that he was a sinner like other men? Such a demand would be thought, I believe, highly unbecoming and extremely unreasonable. May not my modesty, or my regard for his memory, or my unwillingness to pain his family, be accepted as sufficient reasons for silence? or would any one scoffingly attribute my reluctance to attack him, to my conscious inability to make good my case against his being "God manifest in the flesh"? Now what, if one of his admirers had written panegyrical memorials of him; and his character, therein described, was so faultless, that a stranger to him was not able to descry any moral defect whatever in it? Is such a stranger bound to believe him to be the Divine Standard of morals, unless he can put his finger on certain passages of the book which imply weaknesses and faults? And is it insulting a man, to refuse to worship him? I utterly protest against every such pretence. As I have an infinitely stronger conviction that Shakespeare was not in *intellect* Divinely and Unapproachably perfect, than that I can certainly point out in him some definite intellectual defect; as, moreover, I am vastly more sure that Socrates was *morally* imperfect, than that I am able to censure him rightly; so also, a disputant who concedes to me that Jesus is a mere man, has no right to claim that I will point out some moral flaw in him, or else acknowledge him to be a Unique Unparalleled Divine Soul. It is true, I do see defects, and very serious ones, in the character of Jesus, as drawn by his disciples; but I cannot admit that my right to disown the pretensions made for him turns on my ability to define his frailties. As long as (in common with my friend) I regard Jesus as a man, so long I hold with *dogmatic* and *intense conviction* the inference that he was morally imperfect, and ought not to be held up as unapproachable in goodness; but I have, in comparison, only *a modest* belief that I am able to show his points of weakness.

While therefore in obedience to this call, which has risen from many quarters, I think it right not to refuse the odious task pressed upon me,—I yet protest that my conclusion does not depend upon it. I might censure Socrates unjustly, or at least without convincing my readers, if I attempted that task; but my failure would not throw a feather's weight into the argument that Socrates was a Divine Unique and universal Model. If I write now what is painful to readers, I beg them to remember that I write with much reluctance, and that it is their own fault if they read.

In approaching this subject, the first difficulty is, to know how much of the four gospels to accept as *fact*. If we could believe the whole, it would be easier to argue; but my friend Martineau (with me) rejects belief of many parts: for instance, he has but a very feeble conviction that Jesus ever spoke the discourses attributed to him in John's gospel. If therefore I were to found upon these some imputation of moral weakness, he would reply, that we are agreed in setting these aside, as untrustworthy. Yet he perseveres in asserting that it is beyond all reasonable question *what* Jesus *was;* as though proven inaccuracies in all the narratives did not make the results uncertain. He says that even the poor and uneducated are fully impressed with "the majesty and sanctity" of Christ's mind; as if *this* were what I am fundamentally denying; and not, only so far as would transcend the known limits of human nature: surely "majesty and sanctity" are not inconsistent with many weaknesses. But our judgment concerning a man's motives, his temper, and his full conquest over self, vanity and impulsive passion, depends on the accurate knowledge of a vast variety of minor points; even the curl of the lip, or the discord of eye and mouth, may change our moral judgment of a man; while, alike to my friend and me it is certain that much of what is stated is untrue. Much moreover of what he holds to be untrue does not seem so to any but to the highly educated. In spite therefore of his able reply, I abide in my opinion that he is unreasonably endeavouring to erect what is essentially a piece of doubtful biography and difficult literary criticism into first-rate religious importance.

I shall however try to pick up a few details which seem, as much as any, to deserve credit, concerning the pretensions, doctrine and conduct of Jesus.

First, I believe that he habitually spoke of himself by the title *Son of Man*,—a fact which pervades all the accounts, and was likely to rivet itself on his hearers. Nobody but he himself ever calls him Son of Man.

Secondly, I believe that in assuming this title he tacitly alluded to the viith chapter of Daniel, and claimed for himself the throne of judgment over all mankind.—I know no reason to doubt that he actually delivered (in substance) the discourse in Matth. xxv. "When the Son of Man shall come in his glory, ... before him shall be gathered all nations, ... and he shall separate them, &c. &c.": and I believe that by *the Son of Man* and *the King* he meant himself. Compare Luke xii. 40, ix. 56.

Thirdly, I believe that he habitually assumed the authoritative dogmatic tone of one who was a universal Teacher in moral and spiritual matters, and enunciated as a primary duty of men to learn submissively of his wisdom and acknowledge his supremacy. This element in his character, *the preaching of himself*, is enormously expanded in the fourth gospel, but it distinctly exists in Matthew. Thus in Matth. xxiii 8: "Be not ye called Rabbi [*teacher*], for one is your Teacher, even Christ; and all ye are brethren." . . . . Matth. x. 32: "Whosoever shall confess ME before men, him will I confess before my Father which is in heaven. . . . . He that loveth father or mother more than ME is not *worthy of* ME, &c." . . . . Matth. xi. 27: "All things are delivered unto ME of my Father; and *no man knoweth the Son but the Father;* neither knoweth any man the Father, save the Son; and he to whomsoever *the Son will reveal him*. Come unto ME, all ye that labour, ... and *I* will give you rest. Take MY yoke upon you, &c."

My friend, I find, rejects Jesus as an authoritative teacher, distinctly denies that the acceptance of Jesus in this character is any condition of salvation and of the divine favour, and treats of my "demand of an oracular Christ," as inconsistent with my own principles. But this is mere misconception of what I have said. I find *Jesus himself* to set up oracular claims. I find an assumption of pre-eminence and unapproachable moral wisdom to pervade every discourse from end to end of the gospels. If I may not believe that Jesus assumed an oracular manner, I do not know what moral peculiarity in him I am permitted to believe. I do not *demand* (as my friend seems to think) that *he shall be* oracular, but in common with all Christendom, I open my eyes and see that *he is;* and until I had read my friend's review of my book, I never understood (I suppose through my own prepossessions) that he holds Jesus *not* to have assumed the oracular style.

If I cut out from the four gospels this peculiarity, I must cut out, not only the claim of Messiahship, which my friend admits to have been made, but nearly every moral discourse and every controversy: and *why?* except in order to make good a predetermined belief that Jesus was morally perfect. What reason can be given me for not believing that Jesus declared: "If any one deny ME before men, *him will I deny* before my Father and his angels?" or any of the other texts which couple the favour of God with a submission to such pretensions of Jesus? I can find no reason whatever for doubting that he preached HIMSELF to his disciples, though in the three first gospels he is rather timid of doing this to the Pharisees and to the nation at large. I find him uniformly to claim, sometimes in tone, sometimes in distinct words, that we will sit at his feet as little children and learn of him. I find him ready to answer off-hand, all difficult questions, critical and lawyer-like, as well as moral. True, it is no tenet of mine that intellectual and literary attainment is essential in an individual person to high spiritual eminence. True, in another book I have elaborately maintained the contrary. Yet in that book I have described men's spiritual progress as often arrested at a certain stage by a want of intellectual development; which surely would indicate that I believed even Intellectual blunders and an infinitely perfect exhaustive morality to be incompatible. But our question here (or at least *my* question) is not, whether Jesus might misinterpret prophecy, and yet be morally perfect; but whether, *after assuming to be an oracular teacher*, he can teach some fanatical precepts, and advance dogmatically weak and foolish arguments, without impairing our sense of his absolute moral perfection.

I do not think it useless here to repeat (though not for my

friend) concise reasons which I gave in my first edition against admitting dictatorial claims for Jesus. *First*, it is an unplausible opinion that God would deviate from his ordinary course, in order to give us anything so undesirable as an authoritative Oracle would be;—which would paralyze our moral powers, exactly as an infallible church does, in the very proportion in which we succeeded in eliciting responses from it. It is not needful here to repeat what has been said to that effect in p. 138. *Secondly*, there is no imaginable criterion, by which we can establish that the wisdom of a teacher *is* absolute and illimitable. All that we can possibly discover, is the relative fact, that another is *wiser than we;* and even this is liable to be overturned on special points, as soon as differences of judgment arise. *Thirdly*, while it is by no means clear what are the new truths, for which we are to lean upon the decisions of Jesus, it is certain that we have no genuine and trustworthy account of his teaching. If God had intended us to receive the authoritative *dicta* of Jesus, he would have furnished us with an unblemished record of those dicta. To allow that we have not this, and that we must disentangle for ourselves (by a most difficult and uncertain process) the "true" sayings of Jesus, is surely self-refuting. *Fourthly*, if I *must* sit in judgment on the claims of Jesus to be the true Messiah and Son of God, how can I concentrate all my free thought into that one act, and thenceforth abandon free thought? This appears a moral suicide, whether Messiah or the Pope is the object whom we *first* criticize, in order to instal him over us, and *then*, for ever after, refuse to criticize. In short, *we cannot build up a system of Oracles on a basis of Free Criticism.* If we are to submit our judgment to the dictation of some other,—whether a church or an individual,—we must be first subjected to that other by some event from without, as by birth; and not by a process of that very judgment which is henceforth to be sacrificed. But from this I proceed to consider more in detail, some points in the teaching and conduct of Jesus, which do not appear to me consistent with absolute perfection.

The argument of Jesus concerning the tribute to Cæsar is so dramatic, as to strike the imagination and rest on the memory; and I know no reason for doubting that it has been correctly reported. The book of Deuteronomy (xvii. 15) distinctly forbids Israel to set over himself as king any who is not a native Israelite; which appeared to be a religious condemnation of submission to Cæsar. Accordingly, since Jesus assumed the tone of unlimited wisdom, some of Herod's party asked him, whether it was lawful to pay tribute to Cæsar. Jesus replied: "Why tempt ye me, hypocrites? Show me the tribute money." When one of the coins was handed to him, he asked: "Whose image and superscription is this?" When they replied: "Cæsar's," he gave his authoritative decision: "Render *therefore* to Cæsar *the things that are Cæsar's.*"

In this reply not only the poor and uneducated, but many likewise of the rich and educated, recognize "majesty and sanctity:" yet I find it hard to think that my strong-minded friend will defend the justness, wisdom and honesty of it. To imagine that because a coin bears Cæsar's head, *therefore* it is Cæsar's property, and that he may demand to have as many of such coins as he chooses paid over to him, is puerile, and notoriously false. The circulation of foreign coin of every kind was as common in the Mediterranean then as now; and everybody knew that the coin was the property of the *holder*, not of him whose head it bore. Thus the reply of Jesus, which pretended to be a moral decision, was unsound and absurd: yet it is uttered in a tone of dictatorial wisdom, and ushered in by a grave rebuke, "Why tempt ye me, hypocrites?" He is generally understood to mean, "Why do you try to implicate me in a political charge?" and it is supposed that he prudently *evaded* the question. I have indeed heard this interpretation from high Trinitarians; which indicates to me how dead is their moral sense in everything which concerns the conduct of Jesus. No reason appears why he should not have replied, that Moses forbade Israel *voluntarily* to place himself under a foreign king, but did not inculcate fanatical and useless rebellion against overwhelming power. But such a reply, which would have satisfied a more commonplace mind, has in it nothing brilliant and striking. I cannot but think that Jesus shows a vain conceit in the cleverness of his answer: I do not think it so likely to have been a conscious evasion. But neither does his rebuke of the questioners at all commend itself to me. How can any man assume to be an authoritative teacher, and then claim that men shall not put his wisdom to the proof? Was it not their *duty* to do so? And when, in result, the trial has proved the defect of his wisdom, did they not perform a useful public service? In truth, I cannot see the Model Man in his rebuke.—Let not my friend say that the error was merely intellectual: blundering self-sufficiency is a moral weakness.

I might go into detail concerning other discourses, where error and arrogance appear to me combined. But, not to be tedious,—in general I must complain that Jesus purposely adopted an enigmatical and pretentious style of teaching, unintelligible to his hearers, and needing explanation in private. That this was his systematic procedure, I believe, because, in spite of the great contrast of the fourth gospel to the others, it has this peculiarity in common with them. Christian divines are used to tell us that this mode was *peculiarly instructive* to the vulgar of Judæa; and they insist on the great wisdom displayed in his choice of the lucid parabolical style. But in Matth. xiii. 10-15, Jesus is made confidentially to avow precisely the opposite reason, viz. that he desires the vulgar *not* to understand him, but only the select few to whom he gives private explanations. I confess I believe the Evangelist rather than the modern Divine. I cannot conceive how so strange a notion could ever have possessed the companions of Jesus, if it had not been true. If really this parabolical method had been peculiarly intelligible, what could make them imagine the contrary? Unless they found it very obscure themselves, whence came the idea that it was obscure to the multitude? As a fact, it *is* very obscure, to this day. There is much that I most imperfectly understand, owing to unexplained metaphor: as: "Agree with thine adversary quickly, &c. &c.:" "Whoso calls his brother* a fool, is in danger of hell fire:" "Every one must be salted with fire, and every sacrifice salted with salt. Have salt in yourselves, and be at peace with one another." Now every man of original and singular genius has his own forms of thought; in so far as they are natural, we must not complain, if to us they are obscure. But the moment *affectation* comes in, they no longer are reconcilable with the perfect character: they indicate vanity, and incipient sacerdotalism. The distinct notice that Jesus avoided to expound his parables to the multitude, and made this a boon to the privileged few; and that without a parable he spake not to the multitude; and the pious explanation, that this was a fulfilment of Prophecy, " I will open my mouth in parables, I will utter dark sayings on the harp,"

---

* I am acquainted with the interpretation, that the word Môrè is not here Greek, *i.e., fool*, but is Hebrew, and means *rebel*, which is stronger than Raca, *silly fellow*. This gives partial, but only partial relief.

L

persuade me that the impression of the disciples was a deep reality. And it is in entire keeping with the general narrative, which shows in him so much of mystical assumption. Strip the parables of the imagery, and you find that sometimes one thought has been dished up four or five times, and generally, that an idea is dressed into sacred grandeur. This mystical method made a little wisdom go a great way with the multitude; and to such a mode of economizing resources the instinct of the uneducated man betakes itself, when he is claiming to act a part for which he is imperfectly prepared.

It is common with orthodox Christians to take for granted, that unbelief of Jesus was a sin, and belief a merit, at a time when no rational grounds of belief were as yet public. Certainly, whoever asks questions with a view to *prove* Jesus, is spoken of vituperatingly in the gospels; and it does appear to me that the prevalent Christian belief is a true echo of Jesus's own feeling. He disliked being put to the proof. Instead of rejoicing in it, as a true and upright man ought,—instead of blaming those who accept his pretensions on too slight grounds,—instead of encouraging full inquiry and giving frank explanations, he resents doubt, shuns everything that will test him, is very obscure as to his own pretensions, (so as to need probing and positive questions, whether he *does* or *does not* profess to be Messiah,) and yet is delighted at all easy belief. When asked for miracles, he sighs and groans at the unreasonableness of it; yet does not honestly and plainly renounce pretension to miracle, as Mr. Martineau would, but leaves room for credit to himself for as many miracles as the credulous are willing to impute to him. It is possible that here the narrative is unjust to his memory. So far from being the picture of perfection, it sometimes seems to me the picture of a conscious and wilful impostor. His general character is too high for *this;* and I therefore make deductions from the account. Still, I do not see how the present narrative could have grown up, if he had been really simple and straightforward, and not perverted by his essentially false position. Enigma and mist seem to be his element; and when I find his high satisfaction at all personal recognition and bowing before his individuality, I almost doubt whether, if one wished to draw the character of a vain and vacillating pretender, it would be possible to draw anything more to the purpose than this. His general rule (before a certain date) is, to be cautious in public, but bold in private to the favoured few. I cannot think that such a character, appearing now, would seem to my friend a perfect model of a man.

No precept bears on its face clearer marks of coming from the genuine Jesus, than that of *selling all and following him*. This was his original call to his disciples. It was enunciated authoritatively on various occasions. It is incorporated with precepts of perpetual obligation, in such a way, that we cannot without the greatest violence pretend that he did not intend it as a precept* to *all* his disciples. In Luke xii. 22-40, he addresses the disciples collectively against Avarice; and a part of the discourse is: " Fear not, little flock; for it is your Father's good pleasure to give you the kingdom. *Sell that ye have, and give alms:* provide yourselves bags that wax not old; a treasure in the heavens that faileth not, &c. .... Let your loins be girded about, and your lights burning," &c. To say that he was not intending to teach a universal morality,† is to admit that his precepts are a trap; for they then mix up and confound mere contingent duties with universal sacred obligations, enunciating all in the same breath, and with the same solemnity. I cannot think that Jesus intended any separation. In fact, when a rich young man asked of him what he should do, that he might inherit eternal life, and pleaded that he had kept the ten commandments, but felt that to be insufficient, Jesus said unto him : "*If thou wilt be perfect*, go and sell that thou hast, and give to the poor, and thou shalt have treasure in heaven:" so that the duty was not contingent upon the peculiarity of a man possessing apostolic gifts, but was with Jesus the normal path for all who desired perfection. When the young man went away sorrowing, Jesus moralized on it, saying: " How hardly shall a rich man enter into the kingdom of heaven :" which again shows, that

---

* Indeed we have in Luke vi. 20-24, a version of the Beatitudes so much in harmony with this lower doctrine, as to make it an open question, whether the version in Matth. v. is not an improvement upon Jesus, introduced by the purer sense of the collective church. In Luke, he does not bless the poor *in spirit*, and those who hunger *after righteousness*, but absolutely the "poor" and the "hungry," and all who honour *Him* ; and in contrast, curses *the rich* and those who are full.

† At the close, is the parable about the absent master of a house; and Peter asks, "Lord! (Sir!) speakest thou this parable unto *us*, or also unto *all?*" Who would not have hoped an ingenuous reply, "To you only," or, "To everybody"? Instead of which, so inveterate is his tendency to muffle up the simplest things in mystery, he replies, "Who then is that faithful and wise steward," &c., &c., and entirely evades reply to the very natural question.

an abrupt renunciation of wealth was to be the general and ordinary method of entering the kingdom. Hereupon, when the disciples asked: " Lo! we *have* forsaken all, and followed thee: what shall we have *therefore?*" Jesus, instead of rebuking their self-righteousness, promised them as a reward, that they should sit upon twelve* thrones, judging the twelve tribes of Israel. A precept thus systematically enforced, is illustrated by the practice, not only of the twelve, but apparently of the seventy, and what is stronger still, by the practice of the five thousand disciples after the celebrated days of the first Pentecost. There was no longer a Jesus on earth to itinerate with, yet the disciples in the fervour of first love obeyed his precept: the rich sold their possessions, and laid the price at the apostles' feet.

The mischiefs inherent in such a precept rapidly showed themselves, and good sense corrected the error. But this very fact proves most emphatically that the precept was preapostolic, and came from the genuine Jesus; otherwise it could never have found its way into the gospels. It is undeniable, that the first disciples, by whose tradition alone we have any record of what Jesus taught, understood him to deliver this precept to *all* who desired to enter into the kingdom of heaven,—all who desired to be perfect: why then are we to refuse belief, and remould the precepts of Jesus till they please our own morality? This is not the way to learn historical fact.

That to inculcate religious beggary as the *only* form and mode of spiritual perfection, is fanatical and mischievous, even the church of Rome will admit. Protestants universally reject it as a deplorable absurdity;—not merely wealthy bishops, squires and merchants, but the poorest curate also. A man could not preach such doctrine in a Protestant pulpit without incurring deep reprobation and contempt; but when preached by Jesus, it is extolled as divine wisdom,—and disobeyed.

Now I cannot look on this as a pure intellectual error, consistent with moral perfection. A deep mistake as to the nature of such perfection seems to me inherent in the precept itself; a mistake which indicates a moral unsoundness. The conduct of Jesus to the rich young man appears to me a melancholy exhibition of perverse doctrine, under an ostentation of superior wisdom. The young man asked for bread,

* This implied that Judas, as one of the twelve, had earned the heavenly throne by the price of earthly goods.

and Jesus gave him a stone. Justly he went away sorrowful, at receiving a reply which his conscience rejected as false and foolish. But this is not all. Jesus was necessarily on trial, when any one, however sincere, came to ask questions so deeply probing the quality of his wisdom as this: "How may I be perfect?" and to be on trial was always disagreeable to him. He first gave the reply, "Keep the commandments;" and if the young man had been satisfied, and had gone away, it appears that Jesus would have been glad to be rid of him: for his tone is magisterial, decisive and final. This, I confess, suggests to me, that the aim of Jesus was not so much to *enlighten* the young man, as to stop his mouth, and keep up his own ostentation of omniscience. Had he desired to enlighten him, surely no mere dry dogmatic command was needed, but an intelligent guidance of a willing and trusting soul. I do not pretend to certain knowledge in these matters. Even when we hear the tones of voice and watch the features, we often mistake. We have no such means here of checking the narrative. But the best general result which I can draw from the imperfect materials, is what I have said.

After the merit of "selling all and following Jesus," a second merit, not small, was, to receive those whom he sent. In Matt. x., we read that he sends out his twelve disciples, (also seventy in Luke,) men at that time in a very low state of religious development, — men who did not themselves know what the Kingdom of Heaven meant,—to deliver in every village and town a mere formula of words: "Repent ye: for the Kingdom of Heaven is at hand." They were ordered to go without money, scrip or cloak, but to live on religious alms; and it is added,—that if any house or city does not receive them, *it shall be more tolerable for Sodom and Gomorrha in the day of judgment* than for it. He adds, v. 40: "He that receiveth *you*, receiveth *me*, and he that receiveth *me*, receiveth Him that sent me."—I quite admit, that in all probability it was (on the whole) the more pious part of Israel which was likely to receive these ignorant missionaries; but inasmuch as they had no claims whatever, intrinsic or extrinsic, to reverence, it appears to me a very extravagant and fanatical sentiment thus emphatically to couple the favour or wrath of God with their reception or rejection.

A third, yet greater merit in the eyes of Jesus, was, to acknowledge him as the Messiah predicted by the prophets, which he was not, according to my friend. According to Matthew (xvi. 13), Jesus put leading questions to the disciples in order to elicit a confession of his Messiahship, and emphatically blessed Simon for making the avowal which he desired; but instantly forbade them to tell the great secret to any one. Unless this is to be discarded as fiction, Jesus, although to his disciples in secret he confidently assumed Messianic pretensions, had a just inward misgiving, which accounts both for his elation at Simon's avowal, and for his prohibition to publish it.

In admitting that Jesus was not the Messiah of the prophets, my friend says, that if Jesus were *less* than Messiah, we can reverence him no longer; but that he was *more* than Messiah. This is to me unintelligible. The Messiah whom he claimed to be, was not only the son of David, celebrated in the prophets, but emphatically the Son of Man of Daniel vii., who shall come in the clouds of heaven, to take dominion, glory and kingdom, that all people, nations and languages shall serve him,—an everlasting kingdom which shall not pass away. How Jesus himself interprets his supremacy, as Son of Man, in Matt. x., xi., xxiii., xxv., and elsewhere, I have already observed. To claim such a character, seems to me like plunging from a pinnacle of the temple. If miraculous power holds him up and makes good his daring, he is more than man; but if otherwise, to have failed will break all his bones. I can no longer give the same human reverence as before to one who has been seduced into vanity so egregious; and I feel assured *à priori* that such presumption *must have* entangled him into evasions and insincerities, which *naturally* end in crookedness of conscience and real imposture, however noble a man's commencement, and however unshrinking his sacrifices of goods and ease and life.

The time arrived at last, when Jesus felt that he must publicly assert Messiahship; and this was certain to bring things to an issue. I suppose him to have hoped that he was Messiah, until hope and the encouragement given him by Peter and others grew into a persuasion strong enough to act upon, but not always strong enough to still misgivings. I say, I suppose this; but I build nothing on my supposition. I however see, that when he had resolved to claim Messiahship publicly, one of two results was inevitable, *if* that claim was ill-founded:—viz., either he must have become an impostor, in order to screen his weakness; or, he must have retracted his pretensions amid much humiliation, and have retired into privacy to learn sober wisdom. From these alternatives *there was escape only by death*, and upon death Jesus purposely rushed.

All Christendom has always believed that the death of Jesus was *voluntarily* incurred; and unless no man ever became a wilful martyr, I cannot conceive why we are to doubt the fact concerning Jesus. When he resolved to go up to Jerusalem, he was warned by his disciples of the danger; but so far was he from being blind to it, that he distinctly announced to them that he knew he should suffer in Jerusalem the shameful death of a malefactor. On his arrival in the suburbs, his first act was, ostentatiously to ride into the city on an ass's colt in the midst of the acclamations of the multitude, in order to exhibit himself as having a just right to the throne of David. Thus he gave a handle to imputations of intended treason.—He next entered the temple courts, where doves and lambs were sold for sacrifice, and—(I must say it to my friend's amusement, and in defiance of his kind but keen ridicule,) committed a breach of the peace by flogging with a whip those who trafficked in the area. By such conduct he undoubtedly made himself liable to legal punishment, and probably might have been publicly scourged for it, had the rulers chosen to moderate their vengeance. But he "meant to be prosecuted for treason, not for felony," to use the words of a modern offender. He therefore commenced the most exasperating attacks on all the powerful, calling them hypocrites and whited sepulchres and vipers' brood; and denouncing upon them the "condemnation of hell." He was successful. He had both enraged the rulers up to the point of thirsting for his life, and given colour to the charge of political rebellion. He resolved to die; and he died. Had his enemies contemptuously let him live, he would have been forced to act the part of Jewish Messiah, or renounce Messiahship.

If any one holds Jesus to be not amenable to the laws of human morality, I am not now reasoning with such a one. But if any one claims for him a human perfection, then I say that his conduct on this occasion was neither laudable nor justifiable; far otherwise. There are cases in which life may be thrown away for a great cause; as when a leader in battle rushes upon certain death, in order to animate his own men; but the case before us has no similarity to that. If our accounts are not wholly false, Jesus knowingly and purposely exasperated the rulers into a great crime,—the crime of taking his life from personal resentment. His inflammatory addresses to the multitude have been defended as follows:

"The prophetic Spirit is sometimes oblivious of the rules of the drawing-room; and inspired Conscience, like the inspiring God, seeing a hypocrite, will take the liberty to say so, and act accordingly. Are the superficial amenities, the soothing fictions, the smotherings of the burning heart, ... really paramount in this world, and never to give way? and when a soul of *power, unable to refrain,* rubs off, though it be with rasping words, all the varnish from rottenness and lies, is he to be tried in our courts of compliment for a misdemeanor? Is there never a higher duty than that of either pitying or converting guilty men,—the duty of publicly exposing them? of awakening the popular conscience, and sweeping away the conventional timidities, for a severe return to truth and reality? No rule of morals can be recognized as just, which prohibits conformity of human speech to fact, and insists on terms of civility being kept with all manner of iniquity."

I certainly have not appealed to any conventional morality of drawing-room compliment, but to the highest and purest principles which I know; and I lament to find my judgment so extremely in opposition. To me it seems that *inability to refrain* shows weakness, not *power,* of soul, and that nothing is easier than to give vent to violent invective against bad rulers. The last sentence quoted, seems to say, that the speaking of Truth is never to be condemned: but I cannot agree to this. When Truth will only exasperate, and cannot do good, silence is imperative. A man who reproaches an armed tyrant in words too plain, does but excite him to murder; and the shocking thing is, that this seems to have been the express object of Jesus. No good result could be reasonably expected. Publicly to call men in authority by names of intense insult, the writer of the above distinctly sees will never convert them; but he thinks it was adapted to awaken the popular conscience. Alas! it needs no divine prophet to inflame a multitude against the avarice, hypocrisy, and oppression of rulers, nor any deep inspiration of conscience in the multitude to be wide awake on that point themselves. A Publius Clodius or a Cleon will do that work as efficiently as a Jesus; nor does it appear that the poor are made better by hearing invectives against the rich and powerful. If Jesus had been aiming, in a good cause, to excite rebellion, the mode of address which he assumed seems highly appropriate; and in such a calamitous necessity, to risk exciting murderous enmity would be the act of a hero: but as the account stands, it seems to me the deed of a fanatic. And it is to me manifest that he overdid his attack, and failed to commend it to the conscience of his hearers For up to this point the multitude was in his favour. He was notoriously so acceptable to the many, as to alarm the rulers; indeed the belief of his popularity had shielded him from prosecution. But after this fierce address he has no more popular support. At his public trial the vast majority judge him to deserve punishment, and prefer to ask free forgiveness for Barabbas, a bandit who was in prison for murder. We moderns, nursed in an arbitrary belief concerning these events, drink in with our first milk the assumption that Jesus alone was guiltless, and all the other actors in this sad affair inexcusably guilty. Let no one imagine that I defend for a moment the cruel punishment which raw resentment inflicted on him. But though the rulers felt the rage of Vengeance, the people, who had suffered no personal wrong, were moved only by ill-measured Indignation. The multitude love to hear the powerful exposed and reproached, up to a certain limit; but if reproach go clearly beyond all that they feel to be deserved, a violent sentiment reacts on the head of the reviler: and though popular indignation (even when free from the element of selfishness) ill fixes the due *measure* of Punishment, I have a strong belief that it is righteous, when it pronounces the verdict Guilty.

Does my friend deny that the death of Jesus was wilfully incurred? The "orthodox" not merely admit, but maintain it. Their creed justifies it by the doctrine, that his death was a "sacrifice" so pleasing to God, as to expiate the sins of the world. This honestly meets the objections to self-destruction; for how better could life be used, than by laying it down for such a prize? But besides all other difficulties in the very idea of atonement, the orthodox creed startles us by the incredible conception, that a voluntary sacrifice of life should be unacceptable to God, unless offered by ferocious and impious hands. If Jesus had "authority from the Father to lay down his life," was he unable to stab himself in the desert, or on the sacred altar of the Temple, without involving guilt to any human being? Did He, who is at once "High Priest" and

Victim, when "offering up himself" and "presenting his own blood unto God," need any justification for using the sacrificial knife? The orthodox view more clearly and unshrinkingly avows, that Jesus deliberately goaded the wicked rulers into the deeper wickedness of murdering him; but on my friend's view, that Jesus was *no* sacrifice, but only a Model man, his death is an unrelieved calamity. Nothing but a long and complete life could possibly test the fact of his perfection; and the longer he lived, the better for the world.

In entire consistency with his previous determination to die, Jesus, when arraigned, refused to rebut accusation, and behaved as one pleading Guilty. He was accused of saying that if they destroyed the temple, he would rebuild it in three days; but how this was to the purpose, the evangelists who name it do not make clear. The fourth however (without intending so to do) explains it; and I therefore am disposed to believe his statement, though I put no faith in his long discourses. It appears (John ii. 18—20) that Jesus after scourging the people out of the temple-court, was asked for a sign to justify his assuming so very unusual authority: on which he replied: "Destroy this temple, and in three days I will raise it up." Such a reply was regarded as a manifest evasion; since he was sure that they would not pull the temple down in order to try whether he could raise it up miraculously. Now if Jesus really meant what the fourth gospel says he meant;—if he "spoke of *the temple of his body;*"—how was any one to guess that? It cannot be denied, that such a reply, *primâ facie*, suggested, that he was a wilful impostor: was it not then his obvious duty, when this accusation was brought against him, to explain that his words had been mystical and had been misunderstood? The form of the imputation in Mark xiv. 58, would make it possible to imagine,—if the *three days* were left out, and if his words were *not* said in reply to the demand of a sign,—that Jesus had merely avowed that though the outward Jewish temple were to be destroyed, he would erect a church of worshippers as a spiritual temple. If so, "John" has grossly misrepresented him, and then obtruded a very far-fetched explanation. But whatever was the meaning of Jesus, if it was honest, I think he was bound to explain it; and not leave a suspicion of imposture to rankle in men's minds.* Finally, if the whole were

---

* If the account in John is not wholly false, I think the reply in every case discreditable. If literal, it all but indicates wilful imposture. If

fiction, and he never uttered such words, then it was his duty to deny them, and not remain dumb like a sheep before its shearers.

After he had confirmed by his silence the belief that he had used a dishonest evasion indicative of consciousness that he was no real Messiah, he suddenly burst out with a full reply to the High Priest's question; and avowed that he *was* the Messiah, the Son of God; and that they should hereafter see him sitting on the right-hand of power, and coming in the clouds of heaven,—of course to enter into judgment on them all. I am the less surprized that this precipitated his condemnation, since he himself seems to have designed precisely that result. The exasperation which he had succeeded in kindling led to his cruel death; and when men's minds had cooled, natural horror possessed them for such a retribution on such a man. His *words* had been met with *deeds:* the provocation he had given was unfelt to those beyond the limits of Jerusalem; and to the Jews who assembled from distant parts at the feast of Pentecost he was nothing but the image of a sainted martyr.

I have given more than enough indications of points in which the conduct of Jesus does not seem to me to have been that of a perfect man: how any one can think him a Universal Model, is to me still less intelligible. I might say much more on this subject. But I will merely add, that when my friend gives the weight of his noble testimony to the Perfection of Jesus, I think it is due to himself and to us that he should make clear what he means by this word "Jesus." He ought to publish—(I say it in deep seriousness, not sarcastically)— an expurgated gospel; for in truth I do not know how much of what I have now adduced from the gospel as *fact*, he will admit to be fact. I neglect, he tells me, "a higher moral criticism," which, if I rightly understand, would explode, as evidently unworthy of Jesus, many of the representations pervading the gospels: as, that Jesus claimed to be an oracular teacher, and attached spiritual life or death to belief or disbelief in this claim. My friend says, it is beyond all serious question *what* Jesus *was:* but his disbelief of the narrative

mystical. it is disingenuously evasive; and it tended, not to instruct, but to irritate, and to move suspicion and contempt. Is this the course for a religious teacher?—to speak darkly, so as to mislead and prejudice; and this, when he represents it as a matter of spiritual life and death to accept his teaching and his supremacy?

seems to be so much wider than mine, as to leave me more uncertain than ever about it. If he will strike out of the gospels all that he disbelieves, and so enable me to understand *what* is the Jesus whom he reveres, I have so deep a sense of his moral and critical powers, that I am fully prepared to expect that he may remove many of my prejudices and relieve my objections: but I cannot honestly say that I see the least probability of his altering my conviction, that in *consistency* of goodness Jesus fell far below vast numbers of his unhonoured disciples.

CHAPTER VIII.

ON BIGOTRY AND PROGRESS.

IF any Christian reader has been patient enough to follow me thus far, I now claim that he will judge my argument and me, as before the bar of God, and not by the conventional standards of the Christian churches.

Morality and Truth are principles in human nature both older and more widespread than Christianity or the Bible: and neither Jesus nor James nor John nor Paul could have addressed or did address men in any other tone, than that of claiming to be themselves judged by some pre-existing standard of moral truth, and by the inward powers of the hearer. Does the reader deny this? or, admitting it, does he think it impious to accept their challenge? Does he say that we are to love and embrace Christianity, without trying to ascertain whether it be true or false? If he say, Yes,—such a man has no love or care for Truth, and is but by accident a Christian. He would have remained a faithful heathen, had he been born in heathenism, though Moses, Elijah and Christ preached a higher truth to him. Such a man is condemned by his own confession, and I here address him no longer.

But if Faith is a spiritual and personal thing, if Belief given at random to mere high pretensions is an immorality, if Truth is not to be quite trampled down, nor Conscience to be wholly palsied in us,—then what, I ask, was I to do, when I saw that the genealogy in the first chapter of Matthew is an erroneous copy of that in the Old Testament? and that the writer has not only copied wrong, but also counted wrong, so as to mistake eighteen for fourteen? Can any man, who glories in the name of Christian, lay his hand on his heart, and say, it was my duty to blind my eyes to the fact, and think of it no further? Many, alas, I know, would have whispered this to me; but if any one were to proclaim it, the universal conscience of mankind would call him impudent.

If however this first step was right, was a second step wrong? When I further discerned that the two genealogies in Matthew and Luke were at variance, utterly irreconcilable, —and both moreover nugatory, because they are genealogies of Joseph, who is denied to be the father of Jesus,—on what ground of righteousness, which I could approve to God and my conscience, could I shut my eyes to this second fact?

When forced, against all my prepossessions, to admit that the two first chapters of Matthew and the two first chapters of Luke are mutually destructive,* would it have been faithfulness to the God of Truth, or a self-willed love of my own prejudices, if I had said, "I will not inquire further, for fear it should unsettle my faith?" The reader's conscience will witness to me, that, on the contrary, I was bound to say, what I did say: "I *must* inquire farther, in order that I may plant the foundations of my faith more deeply on the rock of Truth."

Having discovered, that not all that is within the canon of the Scripture is infallibly correct, and that the human understanding is competent to arraign and convict at least some kinds of error therein contained;—where was I to stop? and if I am guilty, where did my guilt begin? The further I inquired, the more errors crowded upon me, in History, in Chronology, in Geography, in Physiology, in Geology.† Did it *then* at last become a duty to close my eyes to the painful light? and if I had done so, ought I to have flattered myself that I was one of those, who being of the truth, come to the light, that their deeds may be reproved?

---

* See Strauss on the Infancy of Jesus.

† My "Eclectic" reviewer (who is among the least orthodox and the least uncandid) hence deduces, that I have confounded the two questions, "Does the Bible contain errors in human science?" and, "Is its purely spiritual teaching true?" It is quite wonderful to me, how educated men can so totally overlook what I have so plainly and so often written. This very passage might show the contrary, if he had but quoted the whole paragraph, instead of the middle sentence only. See also pp. 67, 74, 75, 86, 87, 125.

Moreover, when I had clearly perceived, that since all evidence for Christianity must involve *moral* considerations, to undervalue the moral faculties of mankind is to make Christian evidence an impossibility and to propagate universal scepticism;—was I then so to distrust the common conscience, as to believe that the Spirit of God pronounced Jael blessed, for perfidiously murdering her husband's trusting friend? Does any Protestant reader feel disgust and horror, at the sophistical defences set up for the massacre of St. Bartholomew and other atrocities of the wicked Church of Rome? Let him stop his mouth, and hide his face, if he dares to justify the foul crime of Jael.

Or when I was thus forced to admit, that the Old Testament praised immorality, as well as enunciated error; and found nevertheless in the writers of the New Testament no indication that they were aware of either; but that, on the contrary, "the Scripture" (as the book was vaguely called) is habitually identified with the infallible "word of God;"—was it wrong in me to suspect that the writers of the New Testament were themselves open to mistake?

When I farther found, that Luke not only claims no infallibility and no inspiration, but distinctly assigns human sources as his means of knowledge;—when the same Luke had already been discovered to be in irreconcilable variance with Matthew concerning the infancy of Jesus;—was I sinful in feeling that I had no longer any guarantee against *other* possible error in these writers? or ought I to have persisted in obtruding on the two evangelists an infallibility of which Luke shows himself unconscious, which Matthew nowhere claims, and which I had demonstrative proof that they did not both possess? A thorough-going Bibliolater will have to impeach me as a sinner on this count.

After Luke and Matthew stood before me as human writers, liable to and convicted of human error, was there any reason why I should look on Mark as more sacred? And having perceived all three to participate in the common superstition, derived from Babylon and the East, traceable in history to its human source, existing still in Turkey and Abyssinia,—the superstition which mistakes mania, epilepsy, and other forms of disease, for possession by devils;—should I have shown love of truth, or obstinacy in error, had I refused to judge freely of these three writers, as of any others who tell similar marvels? or was it my duty to resolve, at any rate and against evidence, to acquit them of the charge of superstition and misrepresentation?

I will not trouble the reader with any further queries. If he has justified me in his conscience thus far, he will justify my proceeding to abandon myself to the results of inquiry. He will feel, that the Will cannot, may not, dare not dictate, whereto the inquiries of the Understanding shall lead; and that to allege that it *ought*, is to plant the root of Insincerity, Falsehood, Bigotry, Cruelty, and universal Rottenness of Soul.

The vice of Bigotry has been so indiscriminately imputed to the religious, that they seem apt to forget that it is a real sin;—a sin which in Christendom has been and is of all sins most fruitful, most poisonous: nay, grief of griefs! it infects many of the purest and most lovely hearts, which want strength of understanding, or are entangled by a sham theology, with its false facts and fraudulent canons. But upon all who mourn for the miseries which Bigotry has perpetrated from the day when Christians first learned to curse; upon all who groan over the persecutions and wars stirred up by Romanism; upon all who blush at the overbearing conduct of Protestants in their successive moments of brief authority,— a sacred duty rests in this nineteenth century of protesting against Bigotry, not from a love of ease, but from a spirit of earnest justice.

Like the first Christians, they must become *confessors* of the Truth; not obtrusively, boastfully, dogmatically, or harshly; but, "speaking the truth in love," not be ashamed to avow, if they do not believe all that others profess, and that they abhor the unrighteous principle of judging men by an authoritative creed. The evil of Bigotry which has been most observed, is its untameable injustice, which converted the law of love into licensed murder or gratuitous hatred. But I believe a worse evil still has been, the intense reaction of the human mind against Religion for Bigotry's sake. To the millions of Europe, bigotry has been a confutation of all pious feeling. So unlovely has religion been made by it,

Horribili super aspectu mortalibus instans,

that now, as 2000 years ago, men are lapsing into Atheism or Pantheism; and a totally new "dispensation" is wanted to retrieve the lost reputation of Piety.

Two opposite errors are committed by those who discern that the pretensions of the national religious systems are overstrained and unjustifiable. One class of persons inveighs warmly, bitterly, rudely against the bigotry of Christians; and know not how deep and holy affections and principles, in spite of narrowness, are cherished in the bosom of the Christian society. Hence their invective is harsh and unsympathizing; and appears so essentially unjust and so ignorant, as to exasperate and increase the very bigotry which it attacks. An opposite class know well, and value highly, the moral influences of Christianity, and from an intense dread of harming or losing these, do not dare plainly and publicly to avow their own convictions. Great numbers of English laymen are entirely assured, that the Old Testament abounds with error, and that the New is not always unimpeachable: yet they only whisper this; and in the hearing of a clergyman, who is bound by Articles and whom it is indecent to refute, keep a respectful silence. As for ministers of religion, these, being called perpetually into a practical application of the received doctrine of their church, are of all men least able to inquire into any fundamental errors in that doctrine. Eminent persons among them will nevertheless aim after and attain a purer truth than that which they find established: but such a case must always be rare and exceptive. Only by disusing ministerial service can any one give fair play to doubts concerning the wisdom and truth of that which he is solemnly ministering: hence that friend of Arnold's was wise in this world, who advised him to take a curacy in order to settle his doubts concerning the Trinity.—Nowhere from any body of priests, clergy, or ministers, as an Order, is religious progress to be anticipated, until intellectual creeds are destroyed. A greater responsibility therefore is laid upon laymen, to be faithful and bold in avowing their convictions.

Yet it is not from the practical ministers of religion, that the great opposition to religious reform proceeds. The "secular clergy" (as the Romanists oddly call them) were seldom so bigoted as the "regulars." So with us, those who minister to men in their moral trials have for the most part a deeper moral spirit, and are less apt to place religion in systems of propositions. The *robur legionum* of bigotry, I believe, is found,—first, in non-parochial clergy, and next, in the anonymous writers for religious journals and "conserva-

"tive" newspapers; who too generally* adopt a style of which they would be ashamed, if the names of the writers were attached; who often seem desirous to make it clear that it is their trade to carp, insult, or slander; who assume a tone of omniscience, at the very moment when they show narrowness of heart and judgment. To such writing those who desire to promote earnest Thought and tranquil Progress ought anxiously to testify their deep repugnance. A large part of this slander and insult is prompted by a base pandering to the (real or imagined) taste of the public, and will abate when it visibly ceases to be gainful.

The law of God's moral universe, as known to us, is that of Progress. We trace it from old barbarism to the methodized Egyptian idolatry; to the more flexible Polytheism of Syria and Greece; the poetical Pantheism of philosophers, and the moral monotheism of a few sages. So in Palestine and in the Bible itself we see, first of all, the image-worship of Jacob's family, then the incipient elevation of Jehovah above all other Gods by Moses, the practical establishment of the worship of Jehovah alone by Samuel, the rise of spiritual sentiment under David and the Psalmists, the more magnificent views of Hezekiah's prophets, finally in the Babylonish captivity the new tenderness assumed by that second Isaiah and the later Psalmists. But ceremonialism more and more encrusted the restored nation; and Jesus was needed to spur and stab the conscience of his contemporaries, and recal them to more spiritual perceptions; to proclaim a coming "kingdom of heaven," in which should be gathered all the children of God that were scattered abroad; where the law of love should reign, and no one should dictate to another. Alas! that this great movement had its admixture of human imperfection. After this, Steven the protomartyr, and Paul once his persecutor, had to expose the emptiness of all external sanctifications, and free the world from the law of Moses. *Up* to this point all Christians approve of progress; but *at* this point they want to arrest it.

The arguments of those who resist Progress are always the

* Any orthodox periodical which dares to write charitably, is at once subjected to fierce attack as *unorthodox*.

same, whether it be Pagans against Hebrews, Jews against Christians, Romanists against Protestants, or modern Christians against the advocates of a higher spiritualism. Each established system assures its votaries, that now at length they have attained a final perfection: that their foundations are irremovable: progress *up* to that position was a duty, *beyond* it is a sin. Each displaces its predecessor by superior goodness, but then each fights against his successor by odium, contempt, exclusions and (when possible) by violences. Each advances mankind one step, and forbids them to take a second. Yet if it be admitted that in the earlier movement the party of progress was always right, confidence that the case is now reversed is not easy to justify.

Every persecuting church has numbered among its members thousands of pious people, so grateful for its services, or so attached to its truth, as to think those impious who desire something purer and more perfect. Herein we may discern, that every nation and class is liable to the peculiar illusion of overesteeming the sanctity of its ancestral creed. It is as much our duty to beware of this illusion, as of any other. All know how easily our patriotism may degenerate into an unjust repugnance to foreigners, and that the more intense it is, the greater the need of antagonistic principles. So also, the real excellencies of our religion may only so much the more rivet us in a wrong aversion to those who do not acknowledge its authority or perfection.

It is probable that Jesus desired a state of things in which all who worship God spiritually should have an acknowledged and conscious union. It is clear that Paul longed above all things to overthrow the "wall of partition" which separated two families of sincere worshippers. Yet we now see stronger and higher walls of partition than ever, between the children of the same God,—with a new law of the letter, more entangling to the conscience, and more depressing to the mental energies, than any outward service of the Levitical law. The cause of all this is to be found in *the claim of Messiahship for Jesus*. This gave a premium to crooked logic, in order to prove that the prophecies meant what they did not mean and could not mean. This perverted men's notions of right and wrong, by imparting factitious value to a literary and historical proposition, "Jesus is the Messiah," as though that were or could be religion. This gave merit to credulity, and led pious men to extol it as a brave and noble deed, when any one overpowered the scruples of good sense, and scolded them down as the wisdom of this world, which is hostile to God. This put the Christian church into an essentially false position, by excluding from it in the first century all the men of most powerful and cultivated understanding among the Greeks and Romans. This taught Christians to boast of the hostility of the wise and prudent, and in every controversy ensured that the party which had the merit of mortifying reason most signally should be victorious. Hence, the downward career of the Church into base superstition was determined and inevitable from her very birth; nor was any improvement possible, until a reconciliation should be effected between Christianity and the cultivated reason which it had slighted and insulted.

Such reconciliation commenced, I believe, from the tenth century, when the Latin moralists began to be studied as a part of a theological course. It was continued with still greater results when Greek literature became accessible to churchmen. Afterwards, the physics of Galileo and of Newton began not only to undermine numerous superstitions, but to give to men a confidence in the reality of abstract truth, and in our power to attain it in other domains than that of geometrical demonstration. This, together with the philosophy of Locke, was taken up into Christian thought, and Political Toleration was the first fruit. Beyond that point, English religion has hardly gone. For in spite of all that has since been done in Germany for the true and accurate *exposition* of the Bible, and for the scientific establishment of the history of its component books, we still remain deplorably ignorant here of these subjects. In consequence, English Christians do not know that they are unjust and utterly unreasonable, in expecting thoughtful men to abide by the creed of their ancestors. Nor, indeed, is there any more stereotyped and approved calumny, than the declaration so often emphatically enunciated from the pulpit, that *unbelief in the Christian miracles is the fruit of a wicked heart and of a soul enslaved to sin.* Thus do estimable and well-meaning men, deceived and deceiving one another, utter base slander in open church, where it is indecorous to reply to them,—and think that they are bravely delivering a religious testimony.

No difficulty is encountered, so long as the *inward* and the *outward* rule of religion agree,—by whatever names men call them,—the Spirit and the Word.—or Reason and the Church,

—or Conscience and Authority. None need settle which of the two rules is the greater, so long as the results coincide: in fact, there is no controversy, no struggle, and also probably no progress. A child cannot guess whether father or mother has the higher authority, until discordant commands are given; but then commences the painful necessity of disobeying one in order to obey the other. So, also, the great and fundamental controversies of religion arise, only when a discrepancy is detected between the inward and the outward rule: and then, there are only two possible solutions. If the Spirit within us and the Bible (or Church) without us are at variance, *we must either follow the inward and disregard the outward law; else we must renounce the inward law and obey the outward.* The Romanist bids us to obey the Church and crush our inward judgment: the Spiritualist, on the contrary, follows his inward law, and, when necessary, defies Church, Bible, or any other authority. The orthodox Protestant is better and truer than the Romanist, because the Protestant is not, like the latter, consistent in error, but often goes right: still he *is* inconsistent as to this point. Against the Spiritualist he uses Romanist principles, telling him that he ought to submit his "proud reason" and accept the "Word of God" as infallible, even though it appear to him to contain errors. But against the Romanist the same disputant avows Spiritualist principles, declaring that since "the Church" appears to him to be erroneous, he dares not to accept it as infallible. What with the Romanist he before called "proud reason," he now designates as Conscience, Understanding, and perhaps the Holy Spirit. He refused to allow the right of the Spiritualist to urge, that *the Bible* contains contradictions and immoralities, and therefore cannot be received; but he claims a full right to urge that *the Church* has justified contradictions and immoralities, and therefore is not to be submitted to. The perception that this position is inconsistent, and, to him who discerns the inconsistency, dishonest, is every year driving Protestants to Rome. And *in principle* there are only two possible religions: the Personal and the Corporate; the Spiritual and the External. I do not mean to say that in Romanism there is nothing but what is Corporate and External; for that is impossible to human nature: but that this is what the theory of their argument demands; and their doctrine of Implicit* (or Virtual) Faith

---

*. *Explicit* Faith in a doctrine, means, that we understand what the propositions are, and accept them. But if through blunder we accept a

entirely supersedes intellectual perception as well as intellectual conviction. The theory of each church is the force which determines to what centre the whole shall gravitate. However men may talk of spirituality, yet let them once enact that the freedom of individuals shall be absorbed in a corporate conscience, and you find that the narrowest heart and meanest intellect sets the rule of conduct for the whole body.

It has been often observed how the controversies of the Trinity and Incarnation depended on the niceties of the Greek tongue. I do not know whether it has ever been inquired, what confusion of thought was shed over Gentile Christianity, from its very origin, by the imperfection of the New Testament Greek. The single Greek* word πίστις needs probably three translations into our far more accurate tongue,—viz., Belief, Trust, Faith; but especially Belief and Faith have important contrasts. Belief is purely intellectual; Faith is properly spiritual. Hence the endless controversy about Justification by πίστις, which has so vexed Christians; hence the slander cast on *unbelievers* or *misbelievers* (when they can no longer be burned or exiled), as though they were *faithless* and *infidels*.

But nothing of this ought to be allowed to blind us to the truly spiritual and holy developments of historical Christianity, —much less, make us revert to the old Paganism or Pantheism which it supplanted.—The great doctrine on which all practical religion depends,—the doctrine which nursed the infancy and youth of human nature,—is, "the sympathy of God with the perfection of individual man." Among Pagans this was so marred by the imperfect characters ascribed to the Gods, and the dishonourable fables told concerning them, that the philosophers who undertook to prune religion too generally cut away the root, by alleging† that

wrong set of propositions, so as to believe a false doctrine, we nevertheless have *Implicit* (or Virtual) Faith in the true one, if only we say from the heart: "Whatever the Church believes, I believe." Thus a person, who, through blundering, believes in Sabellianism or Arianism, which the Church has condemned, is regarded to have *virtual faith* in Trinitarianism, and all the "merit" of that faith, because of his good will to submit to the Church; which is the really saving virtue.

* Δικαιοσύνη (righteousness), Διαθήκη (covenant, testament), Χάρις (grace), are all terms pregnant with fallacy.

† Horace and Cicero speak the mind of their educated contemporaries, in saying that "we ought to pray to God *only* for external blessings, but trust to our own efforts for a pure and tranquil soul,"—a singular reversing of spiritual religion!

God was mere Intellect and wholly destitute of Affections. But happily among the Hebrews the purity of God's character was vindicated; and with the growth of conscience in the highest minds of the nation the ideal image of God shone brighter and brighter. The doctrine of his Sympathy was never lost, and from the Jews it passed into the Christian church. This doctrine, applied to that part of man which is divine, is the wellspring of Repentance and Humility, of Thankfulness, Love, and Joy. It reproves and it comforts; it stimulates and animates. This it is which led the Psalmist to cry, "Whom have I in heaven but Thee? there is none upon earth that I desire beside Thee." This has satisfied prophets, apostles, and martyrs with God as their Portion. This has been passed from heart to heart for full three thousand years, and has produced bands of countless saints. Let us not cut off our sympathies from those, who have learnt to sympathize with God; nor be blind to that spiritual good which they have; even if it be, more or less sensibly, tinged with intellectual error. In fact, none but God knows, how many Christian hearts are really pure from bigotry. I cannot refuse to add my testimony, such as it is, to the effect, that *the majority is always truehearted*. As one tyrant, with a small band of unscrupulous tools, manages to use the energies of a whole nation of kind and well-meaning people for cruel purposes, so the bigoted few, who work out an evil theory with consistency, often succeed in using the masses of simpleminded Christians as their tools for oppression. Let us not think more harshly than is necessary of the anathematizing churches. Those who curse us with their lips, often love us in their hearts. A very deep fountain of tenderness can mingle with their bigotry itself: and with tens of thousands, the evil belief is a dead form, the spiritual love is a living reality. Whether Christians like it or not, we must needs look to Historians, to Linguists, to Physiologists, to Philosophers, and generally, to men of cultivated understanding, to gain help in all those subjects which are preposterously called *Theology:* but for devotional aids, for pious meditations, for inspiring hymns, for purifying and glowing thoughts, we have still to wait upon that succession of kindling souls, among whom may be named with special honour David and Isaiah, Jesus and Paul, Augustine, A Kempis, Fenelon, Leighton, Baxter, Doddridge, Watts, the two Wesleys, and Channing.

Religion was created by the inward instincts of the soul: it had afterwards to be pruned and chastened by the sceptical understanding. For its perfection, the co-operation of these two parts of man is essential. While religious persons dread critical and searching thought, and critics despise instinctive religion, each side remains imperfect and curtailed.

It is a complaint often made by religious historians, that no church can sustain its spirituality unimpaired through two generations, and that in the third a total irreligion is apt to supervene. Sometimes indeed the transitions are abrupt, from an age of piety to an age of dissoluteness. The liability to such lamentable revulsions is plainly due to some insufficiency in the religion to meet all the wants of human nature. To scold at that nature is puerile, and implies an ignorance of the task which religion undertakes. To lay the fault on the sovereign will of God, who has "withheld his grace" from the grandchildren of the pious, might be called blasphemy, if we were disposed to speak harshly. The fault lies undoubtedly in the fact, that Practical Devoutness and Free Thought stand apart in unnatural schism. But surely the age is ripe for something better;—for a religion which shall combine the tenderness, humility, and disinterestedness, that are the glory of the purest Christianity, with that activity of intellect, untiring pursuit of truth, and strict adherence to impartial principle, which the schools of modern science embody. When a spiritual church has its senses exercised to discern good and evil, judges of right and wrong by an inward power, proves all things and holds fast that which is good, fears no truth, but rejoices in being corrected, intellectually as well as morally,—it will not be liable to be "carried to and fro" by shifting winds of doctrine. It will indeed have movement, namely, a steady *onward* one, as the schools of science have had, since they left off to dogmatize, and approached God's world as learners; but it will lay aside disputes of words, eternal vacillations, mutual illwill and dread of new light, and will be able without hypocrisy to proclaim "peace on earth and goodwill towards men," even towards those who reject its beliefs and sentiments concerning "God and his glory."

NOTE ON PAGE 168.

THE author of the "Eclipse of Faith," in his Defence (p. 168), referring to my reply in p. 101 above, says:—" In this very paragraph Mr. Newman shows that I have *not* misrepresented him, nor is it true that I overlooked his novel hypothesis. He says that 'Gibbon is exhibiting and developing the deep-seated causes of the *spread* of Christianity before Constantine,'—which Mr. Newman says had *not* spread. On the contrary, he assumes that the Christians were 'a small fraction,' and thus *does* dismiss in two sentences, I might have said three words, what Gibbon had strained every nerve in his celebrated chapter to account for."

Observe his phrase, "On the contrary." It is impossible to say more plainly, that Gibbon represents the spread of Christianity before Constantine to have been very great, and then laboured in vain to account for that spread; and that I, *arbitrarily setting aside Gibbon's fact as to the magnitude of the " spread,"* cut the knot which he could not untie.

But the fact, as between Gibbon and me, is flatly the reverse. I advance nothing novel as to the numbers of the Christians, no hypothesis of my own, no assumption. I have merely adopted Gibbon's own historical estimate, that (judging, as he does judge, by the examples of Rome and Antioch), the Christians before the rise of Constantine were but a small fraction of the population. Indeed, he says, not above *one-twentieth* part; on which I laid no stress.

It may be that Gibbon is here in error. I shall willingly withdraw any historical argument, if shown that I have unawares rested on a false basis. In balancing counter statements and reasons from diverse sources, different minds come to different statistical conclusions. Dean Milman ("Hist. of Christianity," vol. ii. p. 341) when deliberately weighing opposite opinions, says cautiously, that "Gibbon is perhaps inclined to underrate" the number of the Christians. He adds: "M. Beugnot agrees much with Gibbon, and I should conceive, with regard to the West, is clearly right."

I beg the reader to observe, that I have *not* represented the numerical strength of the Christians in Constantine's army to be great. Why my opponent should ridicule my use of the phrase *Christian regiments*, I am too dull to understand. ("Who would not think," says he, "that it was one of Constantine's *aide-de-camps* that was speaking?") It may be that I am wrong in using the plural noun, and that there was only *one* such regiment,—that which carried the Labarum, or standard of the cross (Gibbon, ch. 20), to which so much efficacy was attributed in the war against Licinius. I have no time at present, nor any need, for further inquiries on such matters. It is to the devotion and organization of the Christians, not to their proportionate numbers, that I attributed weight. If (as Milman says) Gibbon and Beugnot are "clearly right" as regards *the West*—i. e., as regards all that vast district which became the area of modern European Christendom, I see nothing in my argument which requires modification.

But why did Christianity, while opposed by the ruling powers, spread "*in the East?*" In the very chapter from which I have quoted, Dean Milman justifies me in saying, that to this question I may simply reply, "I do not know," without impairing my present argument. (I myself find no difficulty in it whatever; but I protest against the assumption, that I am bound to believe a religion preternatural, unless I can account for its origin and diffusion to the satisfaction of its adherents.) Dean Milman, vol. ii. pp. 322–340, gives a full account of the Manichæan religion, and its rapid and great spread in spite of violent persecution. MANI, the founder, represented himself as "a man invested with a divine mission." His doctrines are described by Milman as wild and mystical metaphysics, combining elements of thought from Magianism, Judaism, Christianity, and Buddhism. "His worship was simple, without altar, temple, images, or any imposing ceremonial. Pure and simple prayer was their only form of adoration." They talked much of "Christ" as a heavenly principle, but "did not believe in his birth or death. Prayers and Hymns addressed to the source of light, exhortations to subdue the dark and sensuous element within, and the study of the marvellous book of Mani, constituted their devotion. Their manners were austere and ascetic; they tolerated, but only tolerated, marriage, and that only among the inferior orders. The theatre, the banquet, and even the bath, they severely proscribed. Their diet was of fruits and herbs; they shrank with abhorrence from animal food." Mani met with fierce hostility from West and East alike; and at last was entrapped by the Persian king Baharam, and "was flayed alive. His skin, stuffed with straw, was placed over the gate of the city of Shahpoor."

Such a death was as cruel and as ignominious as that of crucifixion; yet his doctrines " expired not with their author. In the East and in the West they spread with the utmost rapidity. . . . . The extent of its success may be calculated by the implacable hostility of other religions to the doctrines of Mani ; *the causes of that success are more difficult to conjecture.*"

Every reason, which, as far as I know, has ever been given, why it should be hard for early Christianity to spread, avail equally as reasons against the spread of Manichæism. The state of the East, which admitted the latter without miracle, admitted the former also. It nevertheless is pertinent to add, that the recent history of Mormonism, compared with that of Christianity and of Manichæism, may suggest that the martyr-death of the founder of a religion is a positive aid to its after-success.

CHAPTER IX.

REPLY TO THE DEFENCE OF THE "ECLIPSE OF FAITH."

THIS small treatise was reviewed, unfavourably of course, in most of the religious periodicals, and among them in the " Prospective Review," by my friend James Martineau. I had been about the same time attacked in a book called the " Eclipse of Faith," written (chiefly against my treatise on the Soul) in the form of a Platonic Dialogue ; in which a sceptic, a certain Harrington, is made to indulge in a great deal of loose and bantering argumentation, with the view of ridiculing my religion, and doing so by ways of which some specimen will be given.

I made an indignant protest in a new edition of this book, and added also various matter in reply to Mr. Martineau, which will still be found here. He in consequence in a second article* of the " Prospective" reviewed me afresh ; but,

* The "Eclipse" had previously been noticed in the same review, on the whole favourably, by a writer of evidently a different religious school, and before I had exposed the evil arts of my assailant.

in the opening, he first pronounced his sentence in words of deep disapproval against the "Eclipse of Faith."

"The method of the work," says he, "its plan of appealing from what seems shocking in the Bible to something more shocking in the world, simply doubles every difficulty without relieving any; and tends to enthrone a devil everywhere, and leave a God nowhere..... The whole force of the writer's thought,—his power of exposition, of argument, of sarcasm, is thrown, in spite of himself, into the irreligious scale..... If the work be really written* in good faith, and be not rather a covert attack on all religion, it curiously shows how the temple of the author's worship stands on the same foundation with the *officina* of Atheism, and in such close vicinity that the passer-by cannot tell from which of the two the voices stray into the street."

The author of the "Eclipse," buoyed up by a large sale of his work to a credulous public, put forth a "Defence," in which he naturally declined to submit to the judgment of this reviewer. But my readers will remark, that Mr. Martineau, writing against me, and seeking to rebut my replies to him— (nay, I fear I must say my *attack* on him; for I have confessed, almost with compunction, that it was I who first stirred the controversy)—was very favourably situated for maintaining a calmly judicial impartiality. He thought us both wrong, and he administered to us each the medicine which seemed to him needed. He passed his strictures on what he judged to be my errors, and he rebuked my assailant for profane recklessness.

I had complained, not of this merely, but of monstrous indefensible garbling and misrepresentation, pervading the whole work. The dialogue is so managed, as often to suggest what is false concerning me, yet without asserting it; so as to enable him to disown the slander, while producing its full effect against me. Of the directly false statements and garblings I gave several striking exhibitions. His reply to all this in the first edition of his "Defence" was reviewed in a *third* article of the "Prospective Review." Its ability and reach of thought are attested by the fact that it has been mistaken for the writing of Mr. Martineau; but (as clearly as reviews ever speak on such subjects) it is intimated in the opening that this new article is from a new hand, "at the

* The authorship is since acknowledged by Mr. Henry Rogers, in the title to his article on Bishop Butler in the "Encyclopædia Britannica."

risk of revealing *division of persons and opinions* within the limits of the mystic critical *We*." Who is the author, I do not know; nor can I make a likely guess at any one who was in more than distant intercourse with me.

This third reviewer did not bestow one page, as Mr. Martineau had done, on the "Eclipse;" did not summarily pronounce a broad sentence without details, but dedicated thirty-four pages to the examination and proof. He opens with noticing the parallel which the author of the "Eclipse" has instituted between his use of ridicule and that of Pascal; and replies that he signally violates Pascal's two rules, *first*, to speak with truth against one's opponents and not with calumny; *secondly*, not to wound them needlessly. "Neglect of the first rule (says he) has given to these books [the "Eclipse" and its "Defence"] their apparent controversial success; disregard of the second their literary point." He adds, "We shall show that their author misstates and misrepresents doctrines; garbles quotations, interpolating words which give the passage he cites reference to subjects quite foreign from those to which in the original they apply, while retaining the inverted commas, which are the proper sign of faithful transcription; that similarly, he allows himself the licence of omission of the very words on which the controversy hangs, while in appearance citing *verbatim;* . . . . and that he habitually employs a sophistry too artful (we fear) to be undesigned. May he not himself have been deceived, some indulgent reader perhaps asks, by the fallacies which have been so successful with others? It would be as reasonable to suppose that the grapes which deluded the birds must have deluded Zeuxis who painted them."

So grave an accusation against my assailant's truthfulness, coming not from me, but from a third party, and that, evidently a man who knew well what he was saying and why,—could not be passed over unnoticed, although that religious world, which reads one side only, continued to buy the "Eclipse" and its "Defence" greedily, and not one in a thousand of them was likely to see the "Prospective Review." In the second edition of the "Defence" the writer undertakes to defend himself against my advocate, in an Appendix of 19 closely printed pages, the "Defence" itself being 218. The "Eclipse," in its 9th edition of small print, is 393 pages. And how does he set about his reply? By trying to identify the third writer with the second (who was notoriously

Mr. Martineau), and to impute to him ill temper, chagrin, irritation, and wounded self-love, as the explanation of this third article! He says (p. 221) :—

"The third writer—if, as I have said, he be not the second—sets out on a new voyage of discovery ... and still humbly following in the wake of Mr. Newman's great critical discoveries,* repeats that gentleman's charges of falsifying passages, garbling and misrepresentation. In doing so, he employs language, and *manifests a temper*, which I should have thought that respect for himself, if not for his opponent, would have induced him to suppress. It is enough to say, that he quite rivals Mr. Newman in sagacity, and if possible, has more successfully denuded himself of charity. . . . If he be the same as the second writer, I am afraid that the little Section XV." [*i. e.*, the reply to Mr. Martineau in 1st edition of the "Defence"] "must have offended the *amour propre* more deeply than it ought to have done, considering the wanton and outrageous assault to which it was a very lenient reply; and that the critic affords another illustration of the old maxim, that there are none so implacable as those who have done a wrong.

"As the spectacle of the reeling Helot taught the Spartans sobriety, so his *bitterness* shall teach me moderation. I know enough of human nature to understand that it is very possible for an *angry* man—and *chagrin and irritation are too legibly written on every page of this article*—to be betrayed into gross injustice."

The reader will see from this the difficulty of *my* position in this controversy. Mr. Martineau, while defending himself, deprecated the profanity of my other opponent, and the atheistic nature of his arguments. He spoke as a bystander, and with the advantage of a judicial position, and it is called "wanton and outrageous." A second writer goes into detail, and exposes some of the garbling arts which have been used against me; it is imputed† to ill temper, and is insinuated to be from a spirit of personal revenge. How much less can *I* defend myself, and that, against untruthfulness, without incurring such imputation! My opponent speaks to a public

---

* That is, my "discovery" that the writer of the "Eclipse of Faith" grossly misquotes and misinterprets me.

† Page 225, he says, that such criticism "is quite worthy of Mr. Newman's *friend*, defender and admirer;" assuming a fact, in order to lower my defender's credit with his readers.

who will not read my replies. He picks out what he pleases of my words, and takes care to divest them of their justification. I have (as was to be expected) met with much treatment from the religious press which I know cannot be justified; but all is slight, compared to that ot which I complain from this writer. I will presently give a few detailed instances to illustrate this. While my charge against my assailant is essentially moral, and I cannot make any parade of charity, he can speak patronizingly of me now and then, and makes his main attacks on my *logic* and *metaphysics*. He says, that in writing his first book, he knew no characteristics of me, except that I was "a gentleman, a scholar, and *a very indifferent metaphysician.*" At the risk of encountering yet more of banter and insult, I shall here quote what the third "Prospective Reviewer" says on this topic. (Vol. x. p. 208) :—

"Our readers will be able to judge how well qualified the author is to sneer at Mr. Newman's metaphysics, which are far more accurate than his own, or to ridicule his logic. The tone of contempt which he habitually assumes preposterously reverses the relative intellectual *status*, so far as sound systematic thought is concerned, of the two men."

I do not quote this as testimony to myself, but as testimony that others, as well as I, feel the *contemptuous tone* assumed by my adversary in precisely that subject on which modesty is called for. On metaphysics there is hitherto an unreconciled diversity among men who have spent their lives in the study; and a large part of the endless religious disputes turns on this very fact. However, the being told, in a multitude of ingenious forms, that I am a wretched logician, is not likely to ruffle my tranquillity. What does necessarily wound me, is his misrepresenting my thoughts to the thoughtful, whose respect I honour; and poisoning the atmosphere between me and a thousand religious hearts. That these do not despise me, however much contempt he may vent, I know only too well through their cruel fears of me.

I have just now learned incidentally, that in the last number (a supplementary number) of the "Prospective Review," there was a short reply to the second edition of Mr. Rogers's "Defence," in which the Editors officially *deny* that the third writer against Mr. Rogers is the same as the second; which, I gather from their statement, the "British Quarterly" had taken on itself to *affirm*.

I proceed to show what liberties my critic takes with my arguments, and what he justifies.

I. In the closing chapter of my third edition of the "Phases," I had complained of his bad faith in regard to my arguments concerning the Authoritative imposition of moral truth from without. I showed that, after telling his reader that I offered no proof of my assertions, he dislocated my sentences, altered their order, omitted an adverb of inference, and isolated three sentences out of a paragraph of forty-six lines: that his omission of the inferential adverb showed his deliberate intention to destroy the reader's clue to the fact, that I had given proof where he suppresses it and says that I have given none; that the sentences quoted as 1, 2, 3, by him, with me have the order 3, 2, 1; while what he places first, is with me an immediate and necessary deduction from what has preceded. Now how does he reply? He does not deny my facts, but he justifies his process. I must set his words before the reader. (*Defence*, 2nd ed., p. 85.)

"The strangest thing is to see the way in which, after parading this supposed 'artful dodge,'* which, I assure you, gentle reader, was all a perfect novelty to my consciousness,— Mr. Newman goes on to say, that the author of the 'Eclipse' has altered the order of his sentences to suit a purpose. He says: 'The sentences quoted as 1, 2, 3, by him, with me have the order 3, 2, 1.' I answer, that Harrington was simply anxious to set forth at the head of his argument, in the clearest and briefest form, the *conclusions*† he believed Mr. Newman to hold, and which he was going to confute. He had no idea of any relation of subordination or dependence in the above sophisms, as I have just proved them to be, whether arranged as 3, 2, 1, or 1, 2, 3, or 2, 3, 1, or in any other order in which the possible permutations of three things, taken 3 and 3 together, can exhibit them; *ex nihilo, nil fit*; and three nonentities can yield just as little. Jangle as many changes as you will on these three cracked bells, no logical harmony can ever issue out of them."

Thus, because he does not see the validity of my argument,

---

* As he puts "artful dodge" into quotation marks, his readers will almost inevitably believe that this vulgar language is mine. In the same spirit he speaks of me as "making merry" with a Book Revelation; as if I had the slightest sympathy or share in the style and tone which pervades the "Eclipse." But there is no end of such things to be denounced.

† Italics in the original.

he is to pretend that I have offered none: he is not to allow his readers to judge for themselves as to the validity, but they have to take his word that I am a very "queer" sort of logician, ready "for any feats of logical legerdemain."

I have now to ask, what is garbling, if the above is not? He admits the facts, but justifies them as having been convenient from his point of view; and then finds my charity to be "very grotesque," when I do not know how, without hypocrisy, to avoid calling a spade a spade.

I shall here reprint the pith of my argument, somewhat shortened:—

"No heaven-sent Bible can guarantee the veracity of God to a man who doubts that veracity. Unless we have independent means of knowing that God is truthful and good, his word (if we be ever so certain that it is really his word) has no authority to us: *hence* no book revelation can, without sapping its own pedestal, deny the validity of our *a priori* conviction that God has the virtues of goodness and veracity, and requires like virtues in us. *And in fact*, all Christian apostles and missionaries, like the Hebrew prophets, have always confuted Paganism by direct attacks on its immoral and unspiritual doctrines, and have appealed to the consciences of heathens, as competent to decide in the controversy. Christianity itself has *thus* practically confessed what is theoretically clear, that an authoritative external revelation of moral and spiritual truth is essentially impossible to man. What God reveals to us, he reveals within, through the medium of our moral and spiritual senses. External teaching may be a training of those senses, but affords no foundation for certitude."

This passage deserved the enmity of my critic. He quoted bits of it, very sparingly, never setting before his readers my continuous thought, but giving his own free versions and deductions. His fullest quotation stood thus, given only in an after-chapter:—

"What God reveals to us, he reveals *within*, through the medium of our moral and spiritual senses." "Christianity itself has practically confessed what is theoretically clear, (*you must take Mr. Newman's word for both*,)* that an authoritative external revelation of moral and spiritual truth is essentially

---

* In the ninth edition, p. 104, I find that to cover the formal falsehood of these words, he adds: "what he calls his arguments are assertions only," still withholding that which would confute him.

impossible to man." "No book-revelation can, without sapping its own pedestal, &c., &c."

These three sentences are what Mr. Rogers calls the three cracked bells, and thinks by raising a laugh, to hide his fraud. I have carefully looked through the whole of his dialogue concerning Book Revelation in his 9th edition of the "Eclipse" (pp. 63–83 of close print). He still excludes from it every part of my argument, only stating in the opening (p. 63) as my conclusions, that a book-revelation is impossible, and that God reveals himself from within, not from without. In his *Defence* (which circulates far less than the "Eclipse," to judge by the number of editions) he displays his bravery by at length printing my argument; but in the "Eclipse" he continues to suppress it, at least as far as I can discover by turning to the places where it ought to be found.

In p. 77 (9th ed.) of the "Eclipse," he *implies*, without absolutely asserting, that I hold the Bible to be an impertinence. He repeats this in p. 85 of the "Defence." Such is his mode. I wrote: "*Without this* a priori *belief*, the Bible is an impertinence," but I say, man *has* this *a priori* belief, on which account the Bible is *not* an impertinence. My last sentence in the very passage before us, expressly asserts the value of (good) external teaching. This my critic laboriously disguises.

He carefully avoids allowing his readers to see that I am contending fundamentally for that which the ablest Christian divines have conceded and maintained; that which the common sense of every missionary knows, and every one who is not profoundly ignorant of the Bible and of history ought to know. Mr. Rogers is quite aware, that no apostle ever carried a Bible in his hand and said to the heathen, "Believe that there is a good and just God, *because* it is written in this book;" but they appealed to the hearts and consciences of the hearers as competent witnesses. He does not even give his reader enough of my paragraph to make intelligible what I *meant* by saying "Christianity has practically confessed;" and yet insists that I am both unreasonable and uncharitable in my complaints of him.

I here reprint the summary of my belief concerning our knowledge of morality as fundamental, and not to be tampered with under pretence of religion. "If an angel from heaven bade me to lie, and to steal, and to commit adultery, and to murder, and to scoff at good men, and usurp dominion over my equals, and do unto others everything that I wish *not* to have done to me; I ought to reply, BE THOU ANATHEMA! This, I believe, was Paul's doctrine; this is mine."

It may be worth while to add how in the "Defence" Mr. Rogers pounces on my phrase "*a priori* view of the Divine character," as an excuse for burying his readers in metaphysics, in which he thinks he has a natural right to dogmatize against and over me. He must certainly be aware of the current logical (not metaphysical) use of the phrase *a priori:* as when we say, that Le Verrier and Adams demonstrated *a priori* that a planet *must* exist exterior to Uranus, before any astronomer communicated information that it *does* exist. Or again: the French Commissioners proved by actual measurement that the earth is an oblate spheroid, of which Newton had convinced himself *a priori*.

I always avoid a needless argument of metaphysics. Writing to the general public, I cannot presume that they are good judges of anything but a practical and moral argument. The *a priori* views of God, of which I here speak, involve no subtle questions; they are simply those views which are attained *independently of the alleged authoritative information*, and, of course, are founded upon considerations *earlier* than it.

But it would take too much of space and time, and be far too tedious to my readers, if I were to go in detail through Mr. Rogers's objections and misrepresentations. I have the sad task of attacking *his good faith*, to which I further proceed.

II. In the preface to my second edition of the "Hebrew Monarchy," I found reason to explain briefly in what sense I use the word inspiration. I said, I found it to be current in three senses; "first, as an extraordinary influence peculiar to a few persons, as to prophets and apostles; secondly, *as an ordinary influence of the Divine Spirit on the hearts of men, which quickens and strengthens their moral and spiritual powers*, and is accessible to them all (in a certain stage of development) *in some proportion to their own faithfulness.* The third view teaches that genius and inspiration are two names for one thing. . . . . *Christians for the most part hold the two first conceptions*, though they generally call the second *spiritual influence*, not inspiration; the third, seems to be common in the Old Testament. It so happens that the *second is the only inspiration which I hold.*" [I here superadd the italics.] On this passage Mr. Rogers commented as follows ("Defence" p. 156):—

"The latest utterance of Mr. Newman on the subject [of inspiration] that I have read, occurs in his preface to the second edition of his "Hebrew Monarchy," where he tells us, that he believes it is an influence accessible to all men, *in a certain stage of development!* [Italics.] Surely it will be time to consider his theory of inspiration, when he has told us a little more about it. To my mind, if the very genius of mystery had framed the definition, it could not have uttered anything more indefinite."

Upon this passage the "Prospective" reviewer said his say as follows (vol. x. p. 217) :—

"The writer will very considerately defer criticism on Mr. Newman's indefinite definition, worthy of the genius of mystery, till its author has told us a little more about it. Will anyone believe that he himself deliberately omits the substance of the definition, and gives in its stead a parenthetical qualification, which might be left out of the original, without injury either to the grammatical structure, or to the general meaning of the sentence in which it occurs?" He proceeds to state what I did say, and adds : "Mr. Newman, in the very page in which this statement occurs, expressly identifies his doctrine with the ordinary Christian belief of Divine influence. His words are exactly coincident in sense with those employed by the author of the "Eclipse," where he acknowledges the reality of 'the ordinary, though mysterious action, by which God aids those who sincerely seek him in every good word and work.' The moral faithfulness of which Mr. Newman speaks, is the equivalent of the sincere search of God in good word and work, which his opponent talks of."

I must quote the *entire* reply given to this in the "Defence," second edition, p. 224 :—

"And now for a few examples of my opponent's criticisms. 1. I said in the "Defence" that I did not understand Mr. Newman's notions of inspiration, and that, as to his very latest utterance—namely, that it was an influence *accessible to all men in a certain stage of development* [italics], it was utterly unintelligible to me. 'Will any one believe (says my critic) that he deliberately omits the substance of the definition, and gives in its stead a parenthetical qualification, which might be left out of the original without injury either to the grammatical structure or to the general meaning of the sentence in which it occurs?' Was anything ever more amusing ? A parenthetical clause which might be left out of the original without injury to the grammatical structure or to the general meaning ! *Might* be left out? Ay, to be sure it might, and not only 'without injury,' but with benefit; just as the dead fly which makes the ointment of the apothecary to stink might be left out of *that* without injury. But it was *not* left out; and it is precisely because it was there, and diffused so remarkable an odour over the whole, that I characterized the definition as I did—and most justly. Accessible to all men in a certain stage of development! When and how *accessible?* What *species* of development, I beseech you, is meant? And what is the *stage* of it? The very thing, which, as I say, and as everybody of common sense must see, renders the definition utterly vague, is the very clause in question."

Such is his *entire* notice of the topic. From any other writer I should indeed have been amazed at such treatment. I had made the very inoffensive profession of agreeing with the current doctrine of Christians concerning spiritual influence. As I was not starting any new theory, but accepting what is notorious, nothing more than an indication was needed. I gave, what I should not call definition, but description of it. My critic conceals that I have avowed agreement with Christians; refers to it as a theory of my own; complains that it is obscure; pretends to quote my definition, and leaves out all the cardinal words of it, which I have above printed in italics. My defender, in the "Prospective Review," exposes these mal-practices; points out that my opponent is omitting the main words, while complaining of deficiency; that I profess to agree with Christians in general; and *that I evidently agree with my critic in particular.* The critic undertakes to reply to this, and the reader has before him the whole defence. The man who, as it were, puts his hand on his heart to avow that he anxiously sets before his readers, if not what I *mean*, yet certainly what I have *expressed*,—still persists in hiding from them the facts of the case; avoids to quote from the reviewer so much as to let out that I profess to agree* with what is prevalent among Christians and have no peculiar theory;—still withholds the

---

* I will here add, that this "stinking fly"—the parenthesis ("in a certain stage of development")—was added merely to avoid dogmatizing on the question, how early in human history or in human life this mysterious action of the divine spirit is recognizable as commencing.

cardinal points of what he calls my definition; while he tries to lull his reader into inattention by affecting to be highly amused, and by bantering and bullying in his usual style, while perverting the plainest words in the world.

I have no religious press to take my part. I am isolated, as my assailant justly remarks. For a wonder, a stray review here and there has run to my aid, while there is a legion on the other side—newspapers, magazines, and reviews. Now if any orthodox man, any friend of my assailant, by some chance reads these pages, I beg him to compare my quotations, thus fully given, with the originals; and if he find anything false in them, then let him placard me as a LIAR in the whole of the religious press. But if he finds that I am right, then let him learn in what sort of man he is trusting—what sort of champion of *truth* this religious press has cheered on.

· III. I had complained that Mr. Rogers falsely represented me to make a fanatical "divorce" between the intellectual and the spiritual, from which he concluded that I ought to be indifferent as to the worship of Jehovah or of the image which fell down from Jupiter. He has pretended that my religion, according to me, has received nothing by traditional and historical agencies; that it owes nothing to men who went before me; that I believe I have (in my single unassisted bosom) "a spiritual faculty so bright as to anticipate all essential* spiritual verities;" that had it not been for traditional religion, "we should everywhere have heard the invariable utterance of spiritual religion in the one dialect of the heart,"—that "this divinely implanted faculty of spiritual discernment anticipates all external truth," &c. &c. I then adduced passages to show that his statement was emphatically and utterly contrary to fact. In his "Defence," he thus replies, p. 75:—

"I say with an unfaltering conscience, that no controvertist ever more honestly and sincerely sought to give his opponent's views, than I did Mr. Newman's, after the most diligent study of his rather obscure books; and that whether I have succeeded or not in giving what he *thought*, I have certainly given what he *expressed*. It is quite true that I supposed Mr. Newman intended to "divorce" faith and intellect; and

* If the word *essential* is explained away, *this* sentence may be attenuated to a truism.

what else on earth could I suppose, in common even with those who were most leniently disposed towards him, from such sentiments as these? ALL THE GROUNDS OF BELIEF PROPOSED TO THE MERE UNDERSTANDING HAVE NOTHING TO DO WITH FAITH AT ALL. THE PROCESSES OF THOUGHT HAVE NOTHING TO QUICKEN THE CONSCIENCE OR AFFECT THE SOUL. *How then can the state of the soul be tested by the conclusion to which the intellect is led?* I was *compelled*, I say, to take these passages as everybody else took them, to *mean* what they obviously *express*."

Here he so isolates three assertions of mine from their context, as to suggest for each of them a false meaning, and make it difficult for the reader who has not my book at hand to discover the delusion. The first is taken from a discussion of the arguments concerning the soul's immortality ("Soul," p. 223, 2nd edition), on which I wrote thus, p. 219:— that to judge of the accuracy of a metaphysical argument concerning mind and matter, requires not a pure conscience and a loving soul, but a clear and calm head; that if the doctrine of immortality be of high religious importance, we cannot believe it to rest on such a basis, that those in whom the religious faculties are most developed may be more liable to err concerning it than those who have no religious faculty in action at all. On the contrary, concerning truths which are really spiritual it is an obvious axiom,* that "he who is spiritual judgeth all things, and he himself is judged of no man." After this I proceeded to allude to the history of the doctrine among the Hebrews, and quoted some texts of the Psalms, the *argument* of which, I urged, is utterly inappreciable to the pure logician, "because it is spiritually discerned." I continued as follows:—

"This is as it should be. Can a mathematician understand physiology, or a physiologist questions of law? A true love of God in the soul itself, an insight into Him depending on that love, and a hope rising out of that insight, are prerequisite for contemplating this spiritual doctrine, which is a spontaneous impression of the gazing soul, powerful (perhaps) in proportion to its faith; whereas all the grounds of belief proposed to the mere understanding have nothing to do with faith at all."

I am expounding the doctrine of the great Paul of Tarsus,

* Paul to the Corinthians, 1st Ep. II.

who indeed applies it to this very topic,—the future bliss which God has prepared for them that love him. Does Mr. Rogers attack Paul as making a fanatical divorce between faith and intellect, and say that he is *compelled* so to understand him, when he avows that "the natural man understandeth not the things of God; for they are foolishness unto him." "When the world by wisdom knew not God, it pleased God by the foolishness of preaching to save them that believe." Here is a pretended champion of Evangelical truth seeking to explode as absurdities the sentiments and judgments which have ever been at the heart of Christianity, its pride and its glory!

But I justify my argument as free from fanaticism—and free from obscurity when the whole sentence is read—to a Jew or Mohammedan, quite as much as to a Christian.

My opponent innocently asks, *how much* I desire him to quote of me? But is innocence the right word, when he has quoted but two lines and a half, out of a sentence of seven and a half, and has not even given the clause complete? By omitting, in his usual way, the connecting particle *whereas*, he hides from the reader that he has given but half my thought; and this is done, after my complaint of this very proceeding. A reader who sees the whole sentence, discerns at once that I oppose "the *mere* understanding," to the whole soul; in short, that by the man who has *mere* understanding, I mean him whom Paul calls "the natural man." Such a man may have metaphysical talents and acquirements, he may be a physiologist or a great lawyer; nay, I will add, (to shock my opponent's tender nerves), *even if he be an Atheist*, he may be highly amiable and deserving of respect and love; but if he has no spiritual development, he cannot have insight into spiritual truth. Hence such arguments for immortality as *can* be appreciated by him, and *cannot* be appreciated by religious men as such, "have nothing to do with faith at all."

The two other passages are found thus, in p. 245 of the "Soul," 2nd edition. After naming local history, criticism of texts, history of philosophy, logic, physiology, demonology, and other important but very difficult studies, I ask :—

"Is it not extravagant to call inquiries of this sort *spiritual* or to expect any spiritual* results from them? When the

---

* This clause is too strong. "Expect *direct* spiritual results," might have been better.

spiritual man (as such) cannot judge, the question is removed into a totally different court from that of the soul, the court of the critical understanding. . . . . How then can the state of the soul be tested by the conclusion to which the intellect is led ? What means the anathematizing of those who remain unconvinced ? And how can it be imagined that the Lord of the soul cares more about a historical than about a geological, metaphysical, or mathematical argument ? The processes of thought have nothing to quicken the conscience or affect the soul."

From my defender in the "Prospective Review" I learn that in the first edition of the "Defence" the word *thought* in the last sentence above was placed in italics. He not only protested against this and other italics as misleading, but clearly explained my sense, which, as I think, needs no other interpreter than the context. In the new edition the italics are removed, but the unjust isolation of the sentences remains. "*The* processes of thought," of which I spoke, are not "*all* processes," but the processes *involved in the abstruse inquiries to which I had referred.* To say that *no* processes of thought quicken the conscience, or affect the soul, would be a gross absurdity. This, or nothing else, is what he imputes to me; and even after the protest made by the "Prospective" reviewer, my assailant not only continues to hide that I speak of *certain* processes of thought, not *all* processes, but even has the hardihood to say that he takes the passages as *everybody else* does, and that he is *compelled* so to do.

In my own original reply I appealed to places where I had fully expressed my estimate of intellectual progress, and its ultimate beneficial action. All that I gain by this, is new garblings and taunts for inconsistency. "Mr. Newman," says he, "is the last man in the world to whom I would deny the benefit of having contradicted himself." But I must confine myself to the garbling. "Defence," p. 95 :—

"Mr. Newman affirms that my representations of his views on this subject are the most direct and intense reverse of all that he has most elaborately and carefully written !" He still says, "*what* God reveals, he reveals within and not without," and " he *did* say (though, it seems, he says no longer), that ' of God we know everything from within, nothing from without;' yet he says I have grossly misrepresented him."

This pretended quotation is itself garbled. I wrote,

("Phases," 1st edition, p. 152)—" Of *our moral and spiritual* God we know nothing without, everything within." By omitting the adjectives, the critic produces a statement opposed to my judgment and to my writings; and then goes on to say. " Well, if Mr. Newman will engage to prove contradictions, ... I think it is no wonder that his readers do not understand him."

I believe it is a received judgment, which I will not positively assert to be true, but I do not think I have anywhere denied, that God is discerned by us in the universe as a designer, creator, and mechanical ruler, through a mere study of the world and its animals and all their adaptations, *even without* an absolute necessity of meditating consciously on the intelligence of man and turning the eyes within. Thus a creative God may be said to be discerned "from without." But in my conviction, that God is not *so* discerned to be *moral* or *spiritual* or to be *our* God ; but by moral intellect and moral experience acting "inwardly." If Mr. Rogers chooses to deny the justness of my view, let him deny it; but by omitting the emphatic adjectives he has falsified my sentence, and then has founded upon it a charge of inconsistency. In a previous passage (p. 79) he gave this quotation in full, in order to reproach me for silently withdrawing it in my second edition of the " Phases." He says :—

" The two sentences in small capitals are not found in the new edition of the ' Phases.' *They are struck out.* It is no doubt the right of an author to erase in a new edition any expressions he pleases; but when he is about to charge another with having grossly garbled and stealthily misrepresented him, it is as well to let the world know *what* he has erased and *why*. He says that my representation of his sentiments is the most direct and intense reverse of all that he has most elaborately and carefully written. It certainly is not the intense reverse of all that he has most elaborately and carefully *scratched out*."

I exhibit here the writer's own italics.

By this attack on my good faith, and by pretending that my withdrawal of the passage is of serious importance, he distracts the reader's attention from the argument there in hand (p. 79), which is, *not* what are my sentiments and judgments, but whether he had a right to dissolve and distort my chain of reasoning (see I. above) while affecting to quote me, and pretending that I gave nothing but assertion. As regards my "elaborately and carefully *scratching out,*" this was done; 1. Because the passage seemed to me superfluous; 2. Because I had pressed the topic elsewhere; 3. Because I was going to enlarge on it in my reply to him, p. 199 of my second edition.* When the real place comes where my critic is to deal with the substance of the passage (p. 94 of "Defence"), the reader has seen how he mutilates it.

The other passage of mine which he has adduced, employs the word *reveals,* in a sense analogous to that of *revelation,* in avowed relation to *things moral and spiritual,* which would have been seen, had not my critic reversed the order of my sentences; which he does again in p. 78 of the "Defence," after my protest against his doing so in the "Eclipse." I wrote: (Soul, p. 59) "Christianity itself has thus practically confessed, what is theoretically clear, that an authoritative *external* revelation of moral and spiritual truth is essentially impossible to man. What God reveals to us, he reveals *within,* through the medium of our moral and spiritual senses." The words, "What God reveals," seen in the light of the preceding sentence, means: "That portion of *moral and spiritual truth* which God reveals." This cannot be discovered in the isolated quotation; and as, both in p. 78 and in p. 95, he chooses to quote my word *What* in italics, his reader is led on to interpret me as saying "*every thing whatsoever* which we know of God, we learn from within;" a statement which is not mine.

Besides this, the misrepresentation of which I complained is not confined to the rather metaphysical words of *within* and *without,* as to which the most candid friends may differ, and may misunderstand one another;—as to which also I may be truly open to correction;—but he assumes the right to tell his readers that my doctrine undervalues Truth, and Intellect, and Traditional teaching, and External suggestion, and Historical influences, and counts the Bible an imperti-

---

* The substance of what I wrote was this. Socrates and Cicero ask, *where did we pick up our intelligence?* It did not come from nothing; it must reside in the mind of him from whom we and this world came; God must be more intelligent than man, his creature.—But this argument may be applied with equal truth, not to intelligence only, but to all the essential high qualities of man, everything noble and venerable. Whence came the principle of love, which is the noblest of all? It must reside in God more truly and gloriously than in man. He who made loving hearts must himself be loving. Thus the intelligence and love of God are known through our consciousness of intelligence and love *within.*

nence. When he fancies he can elicit this and that, by his own logic, out of sentences and clauses torn from their context, he has no right to disguise what I have said to the contrary, and claim to justify his fraud by accusing me of self-contradiction. Against all my protests, and all that I said to the very opposite previous to any controversy, he coolly alludes to it (p. 40 of the "Defence") as though it were my avowed doctrine, that: "*Each* man, looking exclusively within, can *at once* rise to the conception of God's infinite perfections."

IV. When I agree with Paul or David (or think I do), I have a right to quote their words reverentially; but when I do so, Mr. Rogers deliberately justifies himself in ridiculing them, pretending that he only ridicules *me*. He thus answers my indignant denunciation in the early part of his "Defence," p. 5:—

"Mr. Newman warns me with much solemnity against thinking that 'questions pertaining to God are advanced by boisterous glee.' I do not think that the 'Eclipse' is characterised by boisterous glee; and certainly I was not at all aware, that the things which *alone** I have ridiculed— some of them advanced by him, and some by others—deserved to be treated with solemnity. For example, that an authoritative external revelation,† which most persons have thought possible enough, is *im*possible,—that man is most likely born for a dog's life, and 'there an end'—that there are great defects in the morality of the New Testament, and much imperfection in the character of its founder,—that the miracles of Christ might be real, because Christ was a *clairvoyant* and mesmerist,—that God was not a Person, but a Personality;—I say, I was not aware that these things, and such as these, which alone I ridiculed, were questions 'pertaining to God,' in any other sense than the wildest hypotheses in some sense pertain to science, and the grossest heresies to religion."

Now first, is his statement true ?

Are these the *only* things which he ridiculed ?

---

* He puts *alone* in italics. A little below he repeats, "which alone I ridiculed."

† He should add: "external *authoritative* revelation *of moral and spiritual truth*." No communication from heaven could have moral weight, to a heart previously destitute of moral sentiment, or unbelieving in the morality of God.—What is there in this that deserves ridicule ?

I quoted in my reply to him enough to show what was the class of "things pertaining to God" to which I referred. He forces me to requote some of the passages. "Eclipse," p. 82 [1st ed.] "You shall be permitted to say (what I will not contradict), that though *Mr. Newman may be inspired* for aught I know . . . . inspired as much as (say) *the inventor of Lucifer matches*—yet that his book is not divine,—that it is purely human."

Again: p. 126 [1st ed.] "Mr. Newman says to those who say they are unconscious of these facts of spiritual pathology, that *the consciousness of the spiritual man is not the less true, that* [though?] *the unspiritual man is not privy to it;* and this most devout gentleman quotes with unction the words: *For the spiritual man judgeth all things, but himself is judged of no man.*"

P. 41, [1st ed.], "I have rejected creeds, and I have found what the Scripture calls, *that peace which passeth all understanding.*" "I am sure it passes mine, (says Harrington) if you have really found it, and I should be much obliged to you, if you would let me participate in the discovery." "Yes, says Fellowes: . . . . ' *I have escaped from the bondage of the letter and have been introduced into the liberty of the Spirit* . . . . *The letter killeth, but the spirit giveth life. The fruit of the Spirit is joy, peace, not*——.'" "Upon my word (said Harrington, laughing), I shall presently begin to fancy that Douce Davie Deans has turned infidel."

I have quoted enough to show the nature of my complaints. I charge the satirist with profanity, for ridiculing sentiments which *he himself* avows to be holy, ridiculing them for no other reason but that with *me also* they are holy and revered. He justifies himself in p. 5 of his "Defence," as above, by denying my facts. He afterwards, in Section XII. p. 147, admits and defends them; to which I shall return.

I beg my reader to observe how cleverly Mr. Rogers slanders me in the quotation already made, from p. 5, by insinuating, first, that it is my doctrine, "that man is *most likely* born for *a dog's life*, and there an end;" next, that I have taken under my patronage the propositions, that "the miracles of Christ might be real, because Christ was a *clairvoyant* and mesmerist, and that God is not a Person but a Personality." I cannot but be reminded of what the "Prospective" reviewer says of Zeuxis and the grapes, when I observe the delicate skill of touch by which the critic puts on just enough colour to affect the reader's mind, but not so much as to draw him to closer examination. I am at a loss to believe that he supposes me to think that a theory of mesmeric wonders (as the complement of an atheistic creed?) is "a question pertaining to God," or that my rebuke bore the slightest reference to such a matter. As to Person and Personality, it is a subtle distinction which I have often met from Trinitarians; who, when they are pressed with the argument that three divine Persons are nothing but three Gods, reply that Person is not the correct translation of the mystical *Hypostasis* of the Greeks, and Personality is perhaps a truer rendering. If I were to answer with the jocosity in which my critic indulges, I certainly doubt whether he would justify me. So too, when a Pantheist objects (erringly, as I hold) that a Person is necessarily something finite, so that God cannot be a Person; if, against this, a Theist contend that God is at once a Person and a Principle, and invent a use of the word Personality to overlap both ideas; we may reject his nomenclature as too arbitrary, but what rightful place ridicule has here, I do not see. Nevertheless, it had wholly escaped my notice that the satirist had ridiculed it, as I now infer that he did.

He tells me he *was not aware* that the holding that *there are great defects in the morality of the New Testament, and much imperfection in the character of its Founder, was a question pertaining to God.* Nor indeed was *I* aware of it.

I regard questions concerning a book and a human being to be purely secular, and desire to discuss them, not indeed with ridicule but with freedom. When *I* discuss them, he treats my act as intolerably offensive, as though the subject were sacred; yet he now pretends that *I* think such topics "pertain to God," and he was not aware of it until I told him so! Thus he turns away the eyes of his readers from my true charge of profanity, and fixes them upon a fictitious charge so as to win a temporary victory. At the same time, since Christians believe the morality of the *Old* Testament to have great defects, and that there was much imperfection in the character of its eminent saints, prophets, and sages; I cannot understand how my holding the very same opinion concerning the *New* Testament should be a peculiarly appropriate ground of banter and merriment; nor make me more justly offensive to Christians, than the Pauline doctrine is to Jews.

In more than one place of this "Defence" he misrepresents what I have written on Immortality, in words similar to those here used, though here he does *not** expressly add my name. In p. 59, he says, that "according to Mr. Newman's theology, it is most *probable* [in italics] that the successive generations of men, with perfect indifference to their relative moral conditions, their crimes or wrongs, are all knocked on the head together; and that future adjustment and retribution is a dream." (So p. 72.) In a note to the next page, he informs his readers that if I say that I have left the question of immortality *doubtful*, it does not affect the argument; for I have admitted "the probability" of there being no future life.

This topic was specially discussed by me in a short chapter of my treatise on the "Soul," to which alone it is possible for my critic to refer. In that chapter assuredly I do *not* say what he pretends; what I *do* say is, (after rejecting, as unsatisfactory to me, the popular arguments from metaphysics, and from the supposed need of a future state to *redress the inequalities of this life;*) p. 232: "But do I then deny a future life, or seek to undermine a belief of it? *Most assuredly not;* but I would put the belief (whether it is to be weaker or firmer) on a *spiritual* basis, and on none other."

I am ashamed to quote further from that chapter in this place; the ground on which I there tread is too sacred for controversy. But that a Christian advocate should rise from reading it to tell people that he has a right to *ridicule* me for holding that "man is *most likely born for a dog's life*, and there an end;" absorbs my other feelings in melancholy. I am sure that any candid person, reading that chapter, must see that I was hovering between doubt, hope, and faith, on this subject, and that if any one could show me that a Moral Theism and a Future Life were essentially combined, I should joyfully embrace the second, as a fit complement to the first. This writer takes the opposite for granted; that if he can convince me that the doctrine of a Future Life is essential to Moral Theism, he will—not *add* to—but *refute* my Theism! Strange as this at first appears, it is explained by his method.

---

* He puts it between two other statements which avowedly refer to me.

He draws a hideous picture of what God's world has been in the past, and indeed is in the present; with words so reeking of disgust and cruelty, that I cannot bear to quote them; and ample quotation would be needful. Then he infers, that since I must admit all this, I virtually believe in an immoral Deity. I suppose his instinct rightly tells him, that I shall not be likely to reason, "Because God can be so very cruel or careless to-day, he is sure to be very merciful and vigilant hereafter." Accepting his facts as a *complete* enumeration of the phenomena of the present world, I suppose it is better inductive logic to say: "He who can be himself so cruel, and endure such monsters of brutality for six or more thousand years, must (by the laws of external induction) be the same, and leave men the same, for all eternity; and is clearly reckless of moral considerations." If I adopt this alternative, I become a Pagan or an Atheist, one or other of which Mr. Rogers seems anxious to make me. If he would urge, that to look at the dark and terrible side of human life is onesided and delusive, and that the God who is known to us in Nature has so tempered the world to man and man to the world as to manifest his moral intentions;—(arguments, which I think, my critic must have heard from Socrates or Plato, without pouring out on them scalding words, such as I feel and avow to be blasphemous;)—then he might perhaps help my faith where it is weakest, and give me (more or less) aid to maintain a future life dogmatically, instead of hopefully and doubtfully. But now, to use my friend Martineau's words: "His method doubles every difficulty without relieving any, and tends to enthrone a Devil everywhere, and leave a God nowhere."

Since he wrote his second edition of the "Defence," I have brought out my work called "Theism," in which (without withdrawing my objections to the popular idea of future *Retribution*) I have tried to reason out a doctrine of Future Life from spiritual considerations. I have no doubt that my critic would find them highly absurd, and perhaps would pronounce them ineffably ludicrous, and preposterous feats of logic. If I could hide their existence from him, I certainly would, lest he misquote and misinterpret them. But as I cannot keep the book from him, I here refer to it to say, that if I am to maintain this most profound and mysterious doctrine with any practical intensity, my convictions in the power of the human mind to follow such high inquiries, need to be greatly *strengthened*, not to be undermined by such arguments and such detestable pictures of this world, as Mr. Rogers holds up to me.

He throws at me the imputation of holding, that "man is *most likely* born for a *dog's life*, and there an end." And is then the life of a saint for seventy years, or for seven years, no better than a dog's life? What else but a *long* dog's life does this make heaven to be? Such an undervaluing of a short but noble life, is consistent with the scheme which blasphemes earth in order to ennoble heaven, and then claims to be preeminently logical. According to the clear evidence of the Bible, the old saints in general were at least as uncertain as I have ever been concerning future life; nay, according to the writer to the Hebrews, "through fear of death they were all their lifetime subject to bondage." If I had called *that* a dog's life, how eloquently would Mr. Rogers have rebuked me!

V. But I must recur to his defence of the profanity with which he treats sacred sentiments and subjects. After pretending, in p. 5, that he had ridiculed nothing but the things quoted above, he at length, in pp. 147-156, makes formal admission of my charge and *justifies himself*. The pith of his general reply is in the following, p. 152:—

"'Now (says Mr. Newman) I will not here farther insist on the monstrosity of bringing forward St. Paul's words in order to pour contempt upon them; a monstrosity which no sophistry of Mr. Harrington can justify!' I think the *real* monstrosity is, that men should so coolly employ St. Paul's words,—for it is a quotation from the treatise on the "Soul,"—to mean something totally different from anything he intended to convey by them, and employ the dialect of the Apostles to contradict their doctrines; that is the monstrosity . . . . It is very hard to conceive that Mr. Newman did not see this. . . . . But had he gone on only a few lines, the reader would have seen Harrington saying: 'These words you have just quoted were well in St. Paul's mouth, and had a meaning. In yours, I suspect, they would have none, or a very different one.'"

According to this doctrine of Mr. Rogers, it would not have been profane in an unbelieving Jew to *make game* of Moses, David, and the Prophets, whenever they were quoted by Paul. The Jew most profoundly believed that Paul quoted the old Scriptures in a false, as well as in a new meaning. One Christian divine does not feel free to ridicule the words of Paul when quoted erroneously (as he thinks) by another Christian divine? Why then, when quoted by me? I hold it to be a great insolence to deny my right to quote Paul or David, as much as Plato or Homer, and adopt their language whenever I find it to express my sentiment. Mr. Rogers's claim to deride highly spiritual truth, barely because I revere it, is a union of inhumanity and impiety. He has nowhere shown that Paul meant something "totally different" from the sense which I put on his words. I know that he cannot. I do not pretend always to bind myself to the definite sense of my predecessors; nor did the writers of the New Testament. They often adopt and apply *in an avowedly new sense* the words of the Old Testament; so does Dr. Watts with the Hebrew Psalms. Such adaptation, in the way of development and enlargement, when done with sincerely pious intention, has never been reproved or forbidden by Christians. Whether I am wise or unwise in my interpretations, the *subject* is a sacred one, and I treat it solemnly; and no errors in my " logic" can justify Mr. Rogers in putting on the mask of a profane sceptic, who scoffs (not once or twice, but through a long book) at the most sacred and tender matters, such as one always dreads to bring before a promiscuous public, lest one cast pearls before swine. And yet unless devotional books be written, especially by those who have as yet no church, how are we to aid one another in the uphill struggle to maintain some elements of a heavenly life? Can anything be more heartless, or more like the sneering devil they talk of, than Mr. Harrington? And here one who professes himself a religious man, and who deliberately, after protest, calls *me* an INFIDEL, is not satisfied with having scoffed in an hour of folly—(in such an hour, I can well believe, that melancholy record the "Eclipse of Faith," was first penned)—but he persists in justifying his claim to jeer and snarl and mutilate, and palm upon me senses which he knows are deliberately disavowed by me, all the while pretending that it is my bad logic which justifies him! We know that very many religious men *are* bad logicians: if I am as puzzle-headed a fool as Mr. Rogers would make people think me, how does that justify his mocking at my religion? He justifies himself on the ground that I criticize the New Testament as freely as I should Cicero (p. 147). Well, then let him criticize me, as freely (and with as little of suppression) as I criticize it. But I do not *laugh* at it; God forbid! The reader will see how little reason Mr. Rogers had to imagine that I had not read so far as to see Harrington's defence; which defence is, either an insolent assumption, or at any rate not to the purpose.

I will here add, that I have received letters from numerous Christians to thank me for my book on the "Soul," in such terms as put the conduct of Mr. Rogers into the most painful contrast: painful, as showing that there are other Christians who know, and *he does not know*, what is the true heart and strength of Christianity. He trusts in logic and ridicules the Spirit of God.

That leads me to his defence of his suggestion that I might be possibly as much inspired as the inventor of lucifer matches. He says, p. 154:—

"Mr. Newman tells me, that I have clearly a profound unbelief in the Christian doctrine of divine influence, or I could not thus grossly insult it. I answer . . . . that which Harrington ridiculed, as the context would have shown Mr. Newman, if he had had the patience to read on, and the calmness to judge, is the chaotic view of inspiration, *formally* held by Mr. Parker, who is *expressly* referred to, "Eclipse," p. 81." In 9th edition, p. 71.

The passage concerning Mr. Parker is in the *preceding* page: I had read it, and I do not see how it at all relieves the disgust which every right-minded man must feel at this passage. My disgust is not personal: though I might surely ask,—If Parker has made a mistake, how does that justify insulting *me*? As I protested, I have made no peculiar claim to inspiration. I have simply claimed "that which all* pious Jews and Christians since David have always claimed." Yet he pertinaciously defends this rude and wanton passage, adding, p. 155: "As to the inventor of lucifer matches, I am thoroughly convinced that he has shed more light upon the world and been abundantly more useful to it, than many a cloudy expositor of modern spiritualism." Where to look for the "many" expositors of spiritualism, I do not know. Would they were more numerous.

Mr. Parker differs from me as to the use of the phrase "Spirit of God." I see practical reasons, which I have not here space to insist on, for adhering to the *Christian*, as distinguished from the *Jewish* use of this phrase. Theodore Parker follows the phraseology of the Old Testament, accord-

---

* Mr. Rogers asks on this: "Does Mr. Newman mean that he claims as much as the *apostles* claimed, *whether they did so rightfully or not!*" See how acutely a logician can pervert the word *all!*

ing to which Bezaleel and others received the spirit of God to aid them in mere mechanical arts, building and tailoring. To ridicule Theodore Parker for this, would seem to me neither witty nor decent in an *un*believer; but when one does so, who professes to believe the whole Old Testament to be sacred, and stoops to lucifer matches and the Eureka shirt, as if this were a refutation, I need a far severer epithet. Mr. Rogers implies that the light of a lucifer match is comparable to the light of Theodore Parker; what will be the judgment of mankind a century hence, if the wide dissemination of the "Eclipse of Faith" lead to inscribing the name of Henry Rogers permanently in biographical dictionaries? Something of this sort may appear:—

"THEODORE PARKER, the most eminent moral theologian whom the first half of the nineteenth century produced in the United States. When the churches were so besotted, as to uphold the curse of slavery because they found it justified in the Bible; when the Statesmen, the Press, the Lawyers, and the Trading Community threw their weight to the same fatal side; Parker stood up to preach the higher law of God against false religion, false statesmanship, crooked law and cruel avarice. He enforced three great fundamental truths, God, Holiness, and Immortality. He often risked life and fortune to rescue the fugitive slave. After a short and very active life, full of good works, he died in blessed peace, prematurely worn out by his perpetual struggle for the true, the right, and the good. His preaching is the crisis which marked the turn of the tide in America from the material to the moral, which began to enforce the eternal laws of God on trade, on law, on administration, and on the professors of religion itself."

And what will be then said of him, who now despises the noble Parker? I hope something more than the following:—

"HENRY ROGERS, an accomplished gentleman and scholar, author of many books, of which by far the most popular was a smart satirical dialogue, disfigured by unjustifiable garbling and profane language, the aim of which was to sneer down Theodore Parker and others who were trying to save spiritual doctrine out of the wreck of historical Christianity."

Jocose scoffing, and dialogue writing is the easiest of tasks; and if Mr. Rogers's co-religionists do not take the alarm, and come in strength upon Messrs. Longman, imploring them to suppress these books of Mr. Rogers, persons who despise *all* religion (with whom Mr. Rogers pertinaciously confounds me under the term infidel), may one of these days imitate his sprightly example against his creed and church. He himself seems to me at present incurable. I do not appeal to *him*, I appeal to his co-religionists, how they would like the publication of a dialogue, in which his free and easy sceptic "Mr. Harrington" might reason on the *opposite* side to that pliable and candid man of straw "Mr. Fellowes?" I here subjoin for their consideration, an imaginary extract of the sort which, by their eager patronage of the "Eclipse of Faith," they are inviting against themselves.

Extract.

I say, Fellowes! (said Harrington), what was that, that Parker and Rogers said about the Spirit of God?

Excuse me (said Fellowes), Theodore Parker and Henry Rogers hold very different views. Mr. Rogers would be much hurt to hear you class him with Parker.

I know (replied he), but they both hold that God inspires people; and that is a great point in common, as I view it. Does not Mr. Rogers believe the Old Testament inspired and all of it true?

Certainly (said Fellowes): at least he was much shocked with Mr. Newman for trying to discriminate its chaff from its wheat.

Well then, he believes, does not he, that Jehovah filled men *with the spirit of wisdom* to help them make a suit of clothes for Aaron?

Fellowes, after a pause, replied:—That is certainly written in the 28th chapter of Exodus.

Now, my fine fellow! (said Harrington), here is a question to *rile* Mr. Rogers. If Aaron's toggery needed one portion of the spirit of wisdom from Jehovah, how many portions does the Empress Eugenie's best crinoline need?

Really (said Fellowes, somewhat offended), such ridicule seems to me profane.

Forgive me, dear friend (replied Harrington, with a sweet smile). *Your* views I never will ridicule; for I know you have imbibed somewhat of Francis Newman's fancy, that one ought to feel tenderly towards other men's piety. But Henry Rogers is made of stouter stuff; he manfully avows that a religion, if it is true, ought to stand the test of ridicule, and he deliberately approves this weapon of attack.

I cannot deny that (said Fellowes, lifting his eyebrows).

But I was going to ask (continued Harrington), whether Mr. Rogers does not believe that Jehovah filled Bezaleel with the Spirit of God, for the work of jeweller, coppersmith, and mason?

Of course he does (answered Fellowes), the text is perfectly clear, in the 31st of Exodus; Bezaleel and Aholiab were both inspired to become cunning workmen.

By the Goose (said Harrington)—forgive a Socratic oath —I really do not see that Mr. Rogers differs much from Theodore Parker. If a man cannot hack a bit of stone or timber without the Spirit of God, Mr. Rogers will have hard work to convince me, that any one can make a rifled cannon without the Spirit of God.

There is something in that (said Fellowes). In fact, I have sometimes wondered how Mr. Rogers could say that which *looks* so profane, as what he said about the Eureka shirt.

Pray what is that? (said Harrington;) and where?

It is in his celebrated "Defence," 2nd edition, p. 155. "*If* Minos and Praxiteles are inspired in the same sense as Moses and Christ, then the inventor of lucifer matches, as well as the inventor of the Eureka shirts, must be also admitted"—to be inspired.

Do you mean that he is trying to save the credit of Moses, by maintaining that the Spirit of God which guides a sculptor is *not* the same in kind as that which guides a saint?

No (replied Fellowes, with surprise), he is not defending Moses; he is attacking Parker.

Bless me (said Harrington, starting up), what is become of the man's logic! Why, Parker and Moses are in the same boat. Mr. Rogers fires at it, in hope to sink Parker; and does not know that he is sending old Moses to Davy's locker.

Now this is too bad (said Fellowes), I really cannot bear it.

Nah! Nah! good friend (said Harrington, imploringly), be calm; and remember, we have agreed that ridicule—against *Mr. Rogers*, not against *you*—is fair play.

That is true (replied Fellowes with more composure).

Now (said Harrington, with a confidential air), you are my friend, and I will tell you a secret—be sure you tell no one—I think that Henry Rogers, Theodore Parker, and Francis Newman are three ninnies; all wrong; for they all profess to believe in divine inspiration: yet they are not ninnies of the same class. I *admit* to Mr. Rogers that there is a real difference.

How do you mean (said Fellowes, with curiosity aroused)?

Why (said Harrington, pausing and becoming impressive), Newman is a flimsy mystic; he has no foundation, but he builds logically enough—at least as far as I see—on his fancies and other people's fancies. This is to be a simple ninny. But Mr. Rogers fancies he believes a mystical religion, and doesn't; and fancies he is very logical, and isn't. This is to be a doubly distilled ninny.

Really I do not call this ridicule, Mr. Harrington (said Fellowes, rising), I must call it slander. What right have you to say that Mr. Rogers does not believe in the holy truths of the New Testament?

Surely (replied Harrington) I have just *as* much right as Mr. Rogers has to say that Mr. Newman does not believe the holy sentiments of St. Paul, when Mr. Newman says he does. Do you remember how Mr. Rogers told him it was absurd for an infidel like him to think he was in a condition to rebuke any one for being profane, or fancy he had a right to say that he believed this and that mystical text of Paul, which, Mr. Rogers avows, Newman *totally* mistakes and does *not* believe as Paul meant it. Now I may be very wrong; but *I* augur that Newman *does* understand Paul, and Rogers does *not*. For Rogers is of the Paley school, and a wit; and a brilliant chap he is, like Macaulay. Such men cannot be mystics nor Puritans in Pauline fashion; they cannot bear to hear of a religion *from within;* but, as I heard a fellow say the other day, Newman has never worked off the Puritan leaven.

Well (said Fellowes), but why do you call Mr. Rogers illogical?

I think you have seen one instance already, but that is a trifle compared to his fundamental blunder (said Harrington).

What can you mean? how fundamental (asked his friend)?

Why, he says, that *I* (for instance) who have no faith whatever in what he calls revelation, cannot have any just belief or sure knowledge of the moral qualities of God; in fact, am logically bound (equally with Mr. Newman) to regard God as *im*moral, if I judge by my own faculties alone. Does he not say that?

Unquestionably; he has a whole chapter (ch. III.) of his "Defence" to enforce this on Mr. Newman (replied Fellowes).

Well, next, he tells me, that when the Christian message, as from God, is presented to me, I am to believe it on the word of a God whom I suppose to be, or *ought* to suppose to be, immoral. If I suppose A B a rogue, shall I believe the message which the rogue sends me?

Surely, Harrington, you forget that you are speaking of God, not of man: you ought not to reason so (said Fellowes, somewhat agitated).

Surely, Fellowes, it is *you* who forget (retorted Harrington) that syllogism depends on form, not on matter. Whether it be God or Man, makes no difference; the logic must be tried by turning the terms into X Y Z. But I have not said all. Mr. Rogers says, I am bound to throw away the moral principles which I already have, at the bidding of a God whom I am bound to believe to be immoral.

No, you are unfair (said Fellowes), I know he says that revelation would confirm and *improve* your moral principles.

But I am *not* unfair. It is he who argues in a circle. What will be *improvement*, is the very question pending. He says, that if Jehovah called to me from heaven, "O Harrington! O Harrington! take thine innocent son, thine only son, lay him on the altar and kill him," I should be bound to regard obedience to the command an *improvement* of my morality; and this, though, up to the moment when I heard the voice, I had been *bound logically* to believe Jehovah to be an IMMORAL God. What think you of that for logic?

I confess (said Fellowes, with great candour) I must yield up my friend's reputation as a *logician;* and I begin to think he was unwise in talking so contemptuously of Mr. Newman's reasoning faculties. But in truth, I love my friend for the great *spiritual* benefits I have derived from him, and cannot admit to you that he is not a very sincere believer in mystical Christianity.

What benefits, may I ask? (said Harrington).

I have found by his aid the peace which passeth understanding (replied he).

It passes my understanding, if you have (answered Harrington, laughing), and I shall be infinitely obliged by your allowing me to participate in the discovery. In plain truth, I do not trust your mysticism.

But are you in a condition to form an opinion? (said Fellowes, with a serious air). Mr. Rogers has enforced on me St. Paul's maxim: "The natural man discerneth not the things of the Spirit of God."

My most devout gentleman! (replied Harrington), how unctuous you are! Forgive my laughing; but it does *so* remind me of Douce Davie Deans. I will make you professor of spiritual insight, &c., &c., &c.

Now is not this disgusting? Might I not justly call the man a "profane dog" who approved of it? Yet everything that is worst here *is closely copied from the Eclipse of Faith, or justified by the Defence*. How long will it be before English Christians cry out Shame against those two books?

VI. I must devote a few words to define the direction and justification of my argument in one chapter of this treatise. All good arguments are not rightly addressed to all persons. An argument good in itself may be inappreciable to one in a certain mental state, or may be highly exasperating. If a thoughtful Mohammedan, a searcher after truth, were to confide to a Christian a new basis on which he desired to found the Mohammedan religion—viz., the absolute moral perfection of its prophet, and were to urge on the Christian this argument in order to convert him, I cannot think that any one would blame the Christian for demanding what is the evidence of the *fact*. Such an appeal would justify his dissecting the received accounts of Mohammed, pointing out what appeared to be flaws in his moral conduct; nay, if requisite, urging some positive vice, such as his excepting himself from his general law of *four wives only*. But a Christian missionary would surely be blamed (at least I should blame him), if, in preaching to a mixed multitude of Mohammedans against the authority of their prophet, he took as his basis of refutation the prophet's personal sensuality. We are able to foresee that the exasperation produced by such an argument must derange the balance of mind in the hearers, even if the argument is to the purpose; at the same time, it may be really away from the purpose to *them*, if their belief has no closer connexion with the personal virtue of the prophet, than has that of Jews and Christians with the virtue of Balaam or Jonah. I will proceed to imagine, that while a missionary was teaching, talking, and distributing tracts to recommend his own views of religion, a Moolah were to go round and inform everybody that this Christian believed Mohammed to be an unchaste man, and had used the very argument to such and such a person. I feel assured that we should all pronounce this proceeding to be a very cunning act of spiteful bigotry.

My own case, as towards certain Unitarian friends of mine, is quite similar to this. They preach to me the absolute moral perfection of a certain man (or rather, of a certain portrait) as a sufficient basis for my faith. Hereby they challenge me, and as it were force me, to inquire into its perfection. I have tried to confine the argument within a narrow circle. It is addressed by me specifically to them and not to others. I would *not* address it to Trinitarians; partly, because they are not in a mental state to get anything from it but pain, partly because much of it becomes intrinsically bad *as argument* when addressed to them. Many acts and words which would be *right* from an incarnate God, or from an angel, are (in my opinion) highly *unbecoming* from a man; consequently I must largely remould the argument before I could myself approve of it, if so addressed. The principle of the argument is such as Mr. Rogers justifies, when he says that Mr. Martineau *quite takes away all solid reasons for believing in Christ's absolute perfection.* ("Defence," p. 220.) I opened my chapter (chapter VII.) above with a distinct avowal of my wish to confine the perusal of it to a very limited circle. Mr. Rogers (acting, it seems, on the old principle, that whatever one's enemy deprecates, is a good) instantly pounces on the chapter, avows that "if infidelity *could* be ruined, such imprudencies* would go far to ruin it," p. 22; and because he believes that it will be "unspeakably† painful" to the orthodox for whom I do *not* intend it, he prints the greater part of it in an Appendix, and expresses his regret that he cannot publish "every syllable of it," p. 22. Such is his tender regard for the feeling of his co-religionists.

My defender in the "Prospective Review" wound up as follows (x. p. 227):—

"And now we have concluded our painful task, which nothing but a feeling of what justice—literary, and personal—required, would have induced us to undertake. The tone of intellectual disparagement and moral rebuke which certain critics,—deceived by the shallowest sophisms with which an unscrupulous writer could work on their prepossessions and insult their understandings—have adopted towards Mr. New-

---

* There is much meaning in the word *imprudence*, on which I need not comment.

† "Unspeakably painful" is his phrase for something much smaller, ("Eclipse" ninth edition p. 194) which he insists on similarly obtruding, against my will and protest.

man, made exposure necessary. The length to which our remarks have extended requires apology. Evidence to character is necessarily cumulative, and not easily compressible within narrow limits. Enough has been said to show that there is not an art discreditable in controversy, to which recourse is not freely had in the 'Eclipse of Faith' and the Defence of it."

The reader must judge for himself whether this severe and terrible sentence of the reviewer proceeds from ill-temper and personal mortification, as the author of the Eclipse and its Defence gratuitously lays down, or whether it was prompted by a sense of justice, as he himself affirms.

APPENDIX I.

It is an error not at all peculiar to the author of the " Eclipse of Faith," but is shared with him by many others, and by one who has treated me in a very different spirit, that Christians are able to use atheistic arguments against me without wounding Christianity. As I have written a rather ample book, called "Theism," expressly designed to establish against Atheists and Pantheists that moral Theism which Christians, Jews, and Mohammedans have in common, and which underlies every attempt of any of the three religions to establish its peculiar and supernatural claims; I have no need of entering on that argument here. It is not true, that, as a Theist, I evade the objections urged by real atheists or sceptics; on the contrary, I try to search them to the very bottom. It is only in arguing with Christians that I disown the obligation of reply; and that, because they are as much concerned as I to answer; and ought to be able to give me, *on the ground of natural theology,* good replies to every fundamental objection from the sceptic, if I have not got them myself. To declare the objections of our common adversaries valid against those first principles of religion which are older than Jesus or Moses, is certainly to surrender the cause of Christianity.

If this need more elucidation, let it be observed, that no Christian can take a single step in argument with a heathen, much less establish his claim of authority for the Bible, without presuming that the heathen will admit, on hearing them, those doctrines of moral Theism, which, it is pretended, *I* can have no good reason for admitting. If the heathen sincerely retorts against the missionary such Pagan scepticism as is flung at me by Christians, the missionary's words are vain ; nor is any success possible, unless (with me) he can lay a *prior* foundation of moral Theism, independent of any assumption concerning the claims of the Bible. It avails nothing to preach repentance of sin and salvation from judgment to come, to minds which are truly empty of the belief that God has any care for morality. I of course do not say, and have never said, that the doctrine of the divine holiness, goodness, truth, must have been previously an active belief of the heathen hearer. To have stated a question clearly is often half the solution ; and the teacher, who so states a high doctrine, gives a great aid to the learner's mind. But unless, after it has been affirmed that there is a Great Eternal Being pervading the universe, who disapproves of human evil and commands us to pursue the good, the conscience and intellect of the hearer gives assent, no argument of moral religion can have weight with him ; therefore neither can any argument about miracles, nor any appeal to the "Bible" as authoritative. Of course the book has not as yet any influence over him, nor will its miracles, any more than its doctrines, be received on the ground of their being in the book. Thus a direct and independent discernment of the great truths of moral Theism is a postulate, to be proved or conceded *before* the Christian can begin the argument in favour of Biblical preternaturalism. I had thought it would have been avowed and maintained with a generous pride, that eminently in Christian literature we find the noblest, soundest, and fullest advocacy of moral Theism, as having its evidence in the heart of man within and nature without, *independently of any postulates concerning the Bible.* I certainly grew up for thirty years in that belief. Treatises on Natural Theology, which (with whatever success) endeavoured to trace—not only a constructive God in the outer world, but also a good God when that world is viewed in connexion with man; were among the text-books of our clergy and of our universities, and were in many ways crowned with honour. Bampton Lectures, Bridgewater Treatises, Burnet Prize Essays, have (at least till very recently in one case) been all, I rather think, in the same direction. And surely with excellent reason. To avow that the doctrines of Moral Theism have no foundation to one who sees nothing preternatural in the Bible, is in a Christian such a suicidal absurdity, that whenever an atheist advances it, it is met with indignant denial and contempt.

The argumentative strength of this Appendix, as a reply to those who call themselves "orthodox" Christians, is immensely increased by analysing their subsidiary doctrines, which pretend to relieve, while they prodigiously aggravate, the previous difficulties of Moral Theism; I mean the doctrine of the fall of man by the agency of a devil, and the eternal hell. But every man who dares to think will easily work out such thoughts for himself.

APPENDIX II.

I HERE reproduce (merely that it may not be pretended that I silently withdraw it) the substance of an illustration which I offered in my 2nd edition, p. 184.

When I deny that History can be Religion or a part of Religion, I mean it exactly in the same sense, in which we say that history is not mathematics, though mathematics has a history. Religion undoubtedly comes to us by historical transmission: it has had a slow growth; but so is it with mathematics, so is it with all other sciences. (I refer to mathematics, not as peculiarly like to religion, but as peculiarly unlike: it is therefore an *à fortiori* argument. What is true of them as sciences, is true of all science.) No science can flourish, while it is received on authority. Science comes to us *by* external transmission, but is not believed *because* of that transmission. The history of the transmission is generally instructive, but is no proper part of the science itself. All this is true of Religion.

THE END.

Woodfall and Kinder, Printers, Milford Lane, Strand, London, W.C.

WORKS

BY

THE SAME AUTHOR.

THE ODES OF HORACE. Translated into Unrhymed Metres, with Introduction and Notes. Second Edition. Post 8vo, pp. xxi. and 247, cloth. 4s.

THEISM, DOCTRINAL AND PRACTICAL; or, Didactic Religious Utterances. 4to, pp. 184, cloth. 4s. 6d.

HOMERIC TRANSLATION IN THEORY AND PRACTICE, A Reply to Matthew Arnold. Crown 8vo, pp. 104, stiff covers. 2s. 6d.

HIAWATHA: Rendered into Latin. With Abridgment. 12mo, pp. vii. and 110, sewed. 2s. 6d.

A HISTORY OF THE HEBREW MONARCHY from the Administration of Samuel to the Babylonish Captivity. Third Edition. Crown 8vo, pp. x. and 354, cloth. 8s. 6d.

A HANDBOOK OF MODERN ARABIC, consisting of a Practical Grammar, with numerous Examples, Dialogues, and Newspaper Extracts, in European Type. Post 8vo, pp. xx. and 192, cloth. 6s.

TRANSLATIONS OF ENGLISH POETRY INTO LATIN VERSE. Designed as Part of a New Method of Instructing in Latin. Crown 8vo, pp. xiv. and 202, cloth. 6s.

THE SOUL: Her Sorrows and her Aspirations. An Essay towards the Natural History of the Soul, as the True Basis of Theology. Ninth Edition. Post 8vo, pp. xi. and 162, cloth. 3s. 6d.

MISCELLANIES; chiefly Addresses, Academical and Historical. 8vo, pp. iv. and 356, cloth. 7s. 6d.

THE ILIAD OF HOMER, faithfully translated into Unrhymed English Metre. Royal 8vo, pp. xvi. and 384, cloth. 10s. 6d.

A DICTIONARY OF MODERN ARABIC. 1. Anglo-Arabic Dictionary. 2. Anglo-Arabic Vocabulary. 3. Arabo-English Dictionary. In 2 vols. crown 8vo, pp. xvi. and 376-464, cloth. £1. 1s.

HEBREW THEISM. Royal 8vo, pp. viii. and 172. Stiff wrappers. 4s. 6d.

THE MORAL INFLUENCE OF LAW. A Lecture. Crown 8vo, pp. 16, sewed. 3d.

SIN AGAINST GOD. An Anniversary Discourse, preached at Clerkenwell Unitarian Free Church, St. John's Square, London, on Sunday morning, June 6, 1875. Crown 8vo, pp. 11, sewed. 3d.

RELIGION NOT HISTORY. Foolscap, pp. 58, paper wrappers. 1s.

MORNING PRAYERS IN THE HOUSEHOLD OF A BELIEVER IN GOD. Crown 8vo, pp. 80, limp cloth. 1s. 6d.

REORGANIZATION OF ENGLISH INSTITUTIONS. A Lecture. Delivered in the Manchester Athenæum, October 15. Crown 8vo, pp. 28, sewed. 6d.

A REPLY TO THE ECLIPSE OF FAITH: being Chapter IX. of the Second Edition of the "Phases of Faith." Post 8vo, pp. 28, sewed. 6d.

THE RELATIONS OF PROFESSIONAL TO LIBERAL KNOWLEDGE. A Lecture delivered in University College, London, October 12, 1859, introductory to the Session of the Faculty of Arts and Laws, 1859–60. 8vo, pp. 30, sewed. 1s.

A DISCOURSE AGAINST HERO-MAKING IN RELIGION, delivered in South Place, Finsbury. 8vo, pp. 30, sewed. 1s.

CATHOLIC UNION: Essays towards a Church of the Future as the Organization of Philanthropy. Third Edition. Crown 8vo, pp. 113, cloth. 3s. 6d.

THE PERMISSIVE BILL more urgent than any Extension of the Franchise. An Address at Ramsgate, Feb. 17, 1865. 8vo, pp. 12, sewed. 1d.

ON THE PHILOSOPHICAL CLASSIFICATION OF NATIONAL INSTITUTIONS. A Lecture delivered at the Bristol Institution for the Advancement of Science, Literature, and the Arts, March 4, 1867. 8vo, pp. 24, sewed. 6d.

THE TEXT OF THE IGUVINE INSCRIPTIONS. With Interlinear Latin. Translation and Notes. 8vo, pp. 56, sewed. 2s.

ORTHOEPY; or, A Simple Mode of Accenting English for the Advantage of Foreigners and of all Learners. 8vo, pp. 28, sewed. 1s.

EUROPE AND THE NEAR FUTURE. With Three Letters on the Franco-German War. Crown 8vo, pp. 64, cloth. 2s.

THE RELATION OF PHYSIOLOGY TO SEXUAL MORALS. 8vo, pp. 42, sewed. 1s.

WHAT IS CHRISTIANITY WITHOUT CHRIST? 8vo, pp. 28, wrapper. 1s.

LONDON:
TRÜBNER & CO., LUDGATE HILL.

www.ingramcontent.com/pod-product-compliance
Lightning Source LLC
Chambersburg PA
CBHW031815230426
43669CB00009B/1154